SAVANNAH

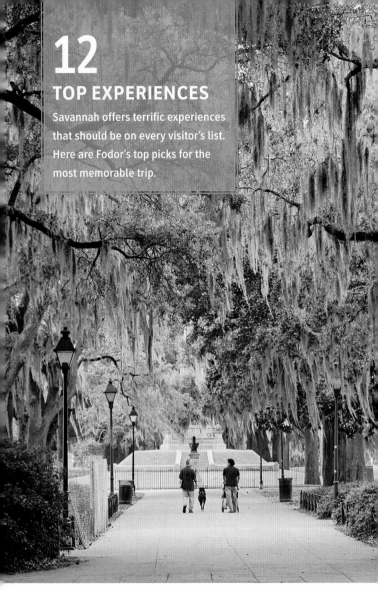

12
TOP EXPERIENCES

Savannah offers terrific experiences that should be on every visitor's list. Here are Fodor's top picks for the most memorable trip.

1 Forsyth Park

Spending time in Forsyth Park is a must for any visitor. People-watching from a bench, seeing a concert at the bandshell, or simply strolling beneath a canopy of Spanish moss–draped branches are wonderful ways to explore. *(Ch. 2)*

2 Tybee Island

Whether you want to relax on the beach, visit the lighthouse, or paddle around in kayaks, there are plenty of ways to enjoy this fun-loving island town. *(Ch. 2)*

3 Antique Shops

In a city this old, there's no shortage of amazing antiques stores. Some of them are more like museums of everyday life. Explore the shops around the Historic District. *(Ch. 7)*

4 Savannah Music Festival

Savannah is in full bloom in late March and early April, providing a magical backdrop for two weeks of performances by some of the world's most talented musicians and vocalists from every genre. *(Ch. 5)*

5 Jepson Center for the Arts

The building's modern architecture might not mesh with the Historic District's stately town homes, but the museum's changing exhibits of contemporary art delight residents and visitors alike. *(Ch. 2)*

6 White Shrimp

Georgia white shrimp are delicious, especially when you taste one fresh from the ocean. Whether served over grits, grilled on a salad, or in any of the myriad other preparations, these crustaceans are a decadent delight. *(Ch. 3)*

7 The Riverfront

Buildings that were once cotton warehouses, shipping offices, and markets have been converted to some of Savannah's liveliest restaurants, bars, and shops. Take a ferry ride across the river to enjoy one of the city's iconic views. *(Ch. 2)*

8 Horse-Drawn Carriage Rides

There is something magical about riding past pristinely restored historic town homes in a horse-drawn carriage. If you're traveling with that special someone, look into deals that include flowers and Champagne. *(Ch. 1)*

9 Bonaventure Cemetery

Situated along the Bull River and shaded by moss-draped live oaks, this cemetery is one of the city's truly memorable sights, full of ornate headstones. It's also the final resting place of local notables like Johnny Mercer. *(Ch. 2)*

10 Mercer Williams House

The former home of Jim Williams—the central figure in John Berendt's *Midnight in the Garden of Good and Evil*—is now a museum. Reading the book makes a visit even better. *(Ch. 2)*

11 Ghost Tours

In "one of the most haunted cities in America," a brush with the paranormal can happen in "haunted buildings" like the Eliza Thompson House. *(Travel Smart)*

12 Fort Pulaski

This 19th-century fortification was considered impenetrable until the Civil War, when weapons technology caught up with it. Walk the ramparts for an incredible view and then follow trails out to the Cockspur Lighthouse. *(Ch. 2)*

CONTENTS

About This Guide 10
**1 EXPERIENCE
SAVANNAH. 11**
What's where 12
Savannah Planner. 14
When to Go 16
Perfect Days in Savannah . . . 17
If You Like 18
Kids and Families 20
**2 EXPLORING
SAVANNAH. 21**
Exploring Savannah. 22
3 WHERE TO EAT 45
Historic District 47
Elsewhere in Savannah. 64
Tybee Island. 68
4 WHERE TO STAY 71
Historic District 73
Elsewhere in Savannah. 85
Tybee Island. 85
**5 NIGHTLIFE AND
PERFORMING ARTS 87**
Nightlife 88
Performing Arts 94
**6 SPORTS AND THE
OUTDOORS. 99**
Sports and Activities 100
7 SHOPPING 109
Shopping Districts. 110
Shopping Reviews 112
**8 HILTON HEAD AND THE
LOWCOUNTRY. 123**
Orientation and Planning . . .124

Hilton Head Island 130
Daufuskie Island 174
**TRAVEL SMART
SAVANNAH. 177**
INDEX 187
ABOUT OUR WRITERS . . 200

MAPS

Savannah Historic District. . 24–25
Greater Savannah. 40
Where to Eat in
Savannah 50–51
Tybee Island. 69
Where to Stay in
Savannah 76–77
Hilton Head and the
Lowcountry 131
Hilton Head Island 133
Where to Eat on
Hilton Head Island 135
Where to Stay on
Hilton Head Island 143
Beaufort 164

ABOUT THIS GUIDE

Fodor's Ratings

Everything in this guide is worth doing—we don't cover what isn't—but exceptional sights, hotels, and restaurants are recognized with additional accolades. **Fodor's**Choice★ indicates our top recommendations. Care to nominate a new place? Visit Fodors.com/contact-us.

Trip Costs

We list prices wherever possible to help you budget well. Hotel and restaurant price categories from **$** to **$$$$** are noted alongside each recommendation. For hotels, we include the lowest cost of a standard double room in high season. For restaurants, we cite the average price of a main course at dinner or, if dinner isn't served, at lunch. For attractions, we always list adult admission fees; discounts are usually available for children, students, and senior citizens.

Hotels

Our local writers vet every hotel to recommend the best overnights in each price category, from budget to expensive. Unless otherwise specified, you can expect private bath, phone, and TV in your room. For expanded hotel reviews, facilities, and deals visit Fodors.com.

Restaurants

Unless we state otherwise, restaurants are open for lunch and dinner daily. We mention dress code only when there's a specific requirement and reservations only when they're essential or not accepted. To make restaurant reservations, visit Fodors.com.

Credit Cards

The hotels and restaurants in this guide typically accept credit cards. If not, we'll say so.

Top Picks

★ **Fodor's**Choice

Listings

⊠ Address
⊠ Branch address
🕮 Mailing address
☎ Telephone
🖷 Fax
⊕ Website
✉ E-mail

🎟 Admission fee
🕓 Open/closed times
Ⓜ Subway
⊹ Directions or Map coordinates

Hotels & Restaurants

🏨 Hotel
🛏 Number of rooms
🍽 Meal plans

✕ Restaurant
🍴 Reservations
🛆 Dress code
🚫 No credit cards
$ Price

Other

⇨ See also
☞ Take note
🏌 Golf facilities

EXPERIENCE
SAVANNAH

WHAT'S WHERE

1 The Historic District. Its strong link to the past is a big part of Savannah's allure. The 2½-square-mile Landmark Historic District is the nation's largest. This area is home to the city's historic squares as well as many of its most desirable accommodations, restaurants, and shopping. The borders of the district are River Street to the north, Gaston Street to the south, and East Broad Street and Martin Luther King Jr. Boulevard to the east and west. The best way to see the Historic District and enjoy its many wonderful squares is on foot or by bicycle. Pedicabs are also available for hire. Parking can be tricky, so if you're staying outside the Historic District, take advantage of the city's reasonably priced parking garages when driving into downtown. It will save time scouring the streets for that elusive parking space.

2 Tybee Island. The barrier island 18 miles east of Savannah, formerly known as Savannah Beach, has been a destination since the 1920s, when a train connected downtown to the beach pavilion where jazz bands played. These days the island is a mix of kitschy shops and interesting restaurants, making for a wonderfully quirky beach town. Whether you're looking to work on your tan, spend a day on a fishing charter, or paddle around in a kayak, this is a must-see during the summer months.

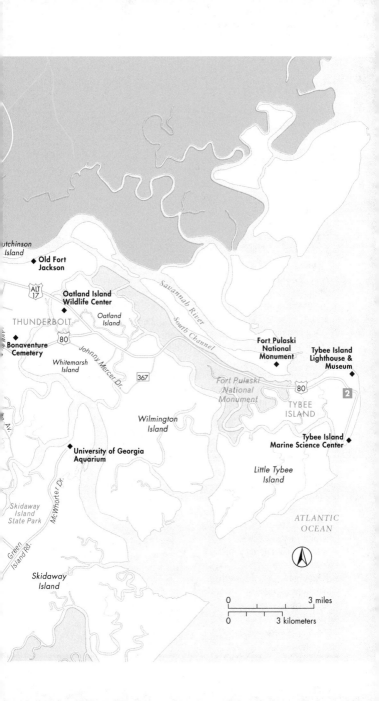

SAVANNAH PLANNER

Visitor Resources

Savannah and Tybee Island each have official resources (⊕ www. savannahvisit.com, ⊕ www.tybeevisit.com) for travelers that include information on tours, dining, attractions, and more.

For information on several prominent local museums, look at the websites of the Coastal Heritage Society (⊕ www.chsgeorgia.org) or the Telfair Museum (⊕ www.telfair.org).

Local restaurant information and a deals card offering savings at member businesses is available from ⊕ www. savannahmenu.com.

You're Welcome Savannah (⊕ www.youre welcomesavannah.com) has the insider's scoop on the city's hottest restaurants, boutiques, and happenings, as well as stunning photography from around town.

The city's Riverfront Association (⊕ www.river streetsavannah.com) has information on events and member businesses along River Street.

Getting Here and Around

You can fly into Savannah and catch a cab into downtown, but you'll probably need a car if you want to explore attractions like Bonaventure Cemetery, Tybee Island, and Fort Pulaski, which are several miles east of downtown.

Getting to Savannah: There are a handful of direct flights into Savannah, but unless you're visiting from New York City, Chicago, or a few other major metropolitan areas, you'll have a connecting flight, most often through Atlanta or Charlotte.

More Flights: Although the airport serves both Savannah and Hilton Head, there is another, considerably smaller airport on Hilton Head Island. If you're looking for additional flight options, it is only about 45 to 60 minutes from Savannah.

On the Ground: Savannah is roughly 10 miles east of Interstate 95, so if you're heading up or down the Eastern seaboard through Georgia, it is an easy stopover. Follow Interstate 16 east until it dead-ends in the Historic District. Interstate 16 traverses west through Georgia to intersect with Interstate 75, the fastest route to or from Atlanta by car.

Other Options: You can reach Savannah by train; there's an Amtrak station several miles west of downtown. Bus travel is also an option. The Greyhound station is located on West Oglethorpe Avenue.

Renting a Car: There are several major car rental companies with offices at the airport, including Avis, Budget, Dollar, Enterprise, Hertz, National/Alamo, and Thrifty.

Planning Your Time

Savannah is not large, but it is atmospheric, so make sure you allow sufficient time to soak in the ambience and see the sights. You'll need at least two or three days to fully appreciate the Historic District and its many sights, not to mention the food, which is an integral part of the Savannah experience. You'll need another day or two to see the sights in the surrounding area, including a jaunt out to Tybee Island for a fishing trip, kayaking tour, or relaxing on the beach. Some travelers head north to Hilton Head or Charleston to round out their Lowcountry experience.

Saving Money

Savannah's low season is around November through the end of January, and there are significantly better deals to be found, generally speaking, to compensate for the chilly weather.

For savings on dining around the city, look into the Savannah Menu Card (⊕ www.savannahmenu.com), which offers special deals such as a free appetizer or discount when presented at member restaurants around the city.

For savings on hotels, Stay in Savannah (⊕ www.stayinsavannah.com) offers discounts at member hotels. The best deals can be found during the off-season. Another way to save on hotels is to book a place south of the Historic District. There are a number of hotels along Abercorn Street, south of De-Renne Avenue, that provide easy access to downtown for less money per night.

Reservations

If you have your heart set on a specific restaurant (particularly one of the city's nicer places), then reservations are essential during the high season (spring and fall). However, it's not unheard of to walk in and get a table, particularly midweek.

Although the city is bustling, there are relatively few instances where reservations are necessary. It's advisable to get tour tickets in advance if you're looking for something like the "haunted hearse" tours or others with relatively limited seating. Walking tours should also be set up in advance, particularly with the smaller tour companies.

WHEN TO GO

Spring and fall are Savannah's peak seasons, when the climate is at its most pleasant and activities are abundant. In March the azaleas bloom and St. Patrick's Day turns the city green. This is hands-down the prettiest, priciest, and most popular time to visit. If you plan on staying in the Historic District in March, it's wise to book at least six months ahead—longer if you plan on snagging a spot along the St. Pat's parade route. April and May are also considered peak, but as humidity and temperatures begin to spike in summer—particularly July and August—Savannah dips into a small lull, a great time for deal-seekers to hunt for hotel offers. Similarly, from December through February, hotel occupancies fall again and you can find the best deals of the year.

Climate

Savannah's climate is mild and comfortable much of the year, and sunny days are abundant. In spring and fall, temperatures typically range from the low 70s to the mid-80s. Locals begin flocking to beaches as early as March and linger long into October. Winter temperatures average in the low 60s and rarely dip below freezing. Summer sees Savannah at its most extreme, particularly in July and August, when highs peak around 100 and humidity soars. This is also hurricane sea-

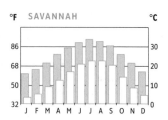

son, and although major storms rarely brush Georgia's coast, you can count on a brief downpour nearly every afternoon, leaving behind steamy conditions.

Festivals

Spring is packed with popular events, like the Savannah Music Festival, the Stopover Music Festival, the Sidewalk Arts Festival, and the annual Tour of Homes and Gardens, which invites visitors into some of the city's best-preserved private residences. But the star of Savannah's festival calendar is St. Patrick's Day, which boasts the second-largest parade of its kind in the world and leaves the city a swirl of leprechaun hats and green beads. On years when March 17 falls on a weekend, attendance can reach a whopping one million. The slightly calmer fall season features the Craft Beer Festival, the Tybee Island Pirate Festival, and the glitzy Savannah Film Festival. And on the first Friday of nearly every month visitors can enjoy live music, art, vendors, and fireworks on River Street.

PERFECT DAYS IN SAVANNAH

Here are a few ideas on how to spend a day in Savannah.

Getting to Know the Historic District

Walk over to the Colonial Park Cemetery at the corner of Oglethorpe and Abercorn. Its dramatic iron gateway is a popular spot to pose for photos, and inside you'll find graves dating back to the Revolutionary War. Walk west along Oglethorpe until you reach Bull Street and then turn north toward Wright Square. There you'll find two impressive 19th-century courthouses overlooking the lovely shaded square. For a sweet treat, drop into the Wright Square Café, where you'll find a selection of artisan chocolates. Continue west on York or State streets until you reach Telfair Square. The Jepson Center for the Arts and the Telfair Museum of Art are here, and each hosts a diverse array of exhibitions. From there, follow Barnard north until you reach the statue of Johnny Mercer in Ellis Square, which is Savannah's most recently restored square. Stroll west through the colorful City Market. From there you can either cross Martin Luther King Jr. Boulevard to visit the beautiful walled gardens at the Ships of the Sea Museum, or turn to the north until you reach River Street, to hit the restaurants and bars.

Beyond the Historic District

To explore farther outside the downtown Historic District, you'll need a car. Start by heading south toward Victory Drive. Stop at Forsyth Park, if you haven't already; there's usually parking along the southern edge. Proceed to Victory Drive and head east. Visit the historic Bonaventure Cemetery, which sits along the banks of the Bull River and is the final resting place of local notables like Johnny Mercer and Conrad Aiken. Afterward, continue east on Victory, which becomes Highway 80, and head to Fort Pulaski, a national park site with a small museum within the walls and trails that wind out into forest and marsh. On your way back into town, stop for some barbecue at Wiley's Championship BBQ on Whitemarsh Island.

Sun and Sand

Tybee Island is only about 18 miles east of downtown Savannah, but it feels like a different world. This quaint and quirky beach town is definitely worth a visit, especially if you're looking to get some sun on your trip. Arrange to take a guided kayak tour, or rent boats and explore on your own in the morning. Grab lunch on the island, and then slather on some sunscreen and head out to the beach to swim, relax, or build a sandcastle in the afternoon.

IF YOU LIKE

Eating Locally

Foodies have plenty of reasons to love dining in Savannah. An influx of young, talented chefs and entrepreneurs have helped put the focus back on locally grown food here.

Green Truck Pub. Don't be fooled by the burger-and-fries-centric menu, because this place is a must-try. The Green Truck only uses only grass-fed beef for its burgers, and everything else is made in-house, including the veggie burgers, salad dressings, and even the ketchup.

Leoci's. Chef Roberto Leoci brings the flavors of his Italian upbringing to each table. These lovingly prepared pastas, flatbreads, and other dishes are made from mostly local ingredients. The back patio presents Savannah outdoor dining at its finest.

The Olde Pink House. The chef at the Pink House, one of Savannah's most iconic restaurants, isn't afraid to update local traditions, such as its "Southern Sushi," which wraps smoked shrimp and grits in coconut-crusted nori.

The Savannah Bee Company. Its Broughton Street flagship store carries more honey-based products than you'd think possible. Its honey varietals are some of the most delicious you'll find. There are also treats like honey lattes at the barista counter.

Strolling the Squares

With more than 20 to choose from, you never walk far in the Historic District before coming across a square, each with its own personality. Here are a few notable squares to look for as you stroll around downtown.

Chippewa Square. Travelers know this swath of green as the location for the bus-stop scenes in *Forrest Gump*. You won't find the bench anymore, but you will see the historic Savannah Theatre, several lovely B&Bs, and a great coffee shop.

Ellis Square. Situated at the west end of City Market, the square had been a parking garage for decades until a massive public project restored the public space, which now includes an interactive fountain, a visitor information kiosk, and public restrooms.

Lafayette Square. Here you'll find historic charm and plenty of trees. Flanked by two notable house museums—the Andrew Low House and the Flannery O'Connor Childhood Home—as well as St. John the Baptist Cathedral, Lafayette is like a trip back in time.

Monterey Square. For a look at some of the city's finest historic homes, including the famous Mercer House, which was the center of the action in *Midnight in the Garden of Good and Evil,* head to Monterey Square.

Telfair Square. Bounded by the Telfair Museum, the Jepson Center, and the Trinity United Methodist Church, this park is a popular meet-up spot.

Shopping

If you believe that shopping is the great American pastime, you'll find the scene in Savannah's Historic District incredibly patriotic. The Historic District hosts an eclectic selection of locally owned boutiques and national brands.

Antiques. There are plenty of amazing spots to find everything from 18th-century desks to mid-century modern baubles, but Jere's, Raskin's, Habersham Antiques, or 37th@Abercorn Antiques are good places to start your hunt.

Broughton Street. Home to a variety of shops, you can find national retailers like Marc Jacobs, J. Crew, Urban Outfitters, and Banana Republic, along with local favorites like the Savannah Bee Company, Paris Market, or 24e.

City Market. A four-block stretch of galleries, boutiques, sidewalk cafés, and artists' studios, this market is a stroller's delight.

The Design District. This stretch of Whitaker Street from Gaston north to Charlton has emerged in recent years as one of the city's most stylish hidden gems, with local shops offering fashion, home goods, and more.

River Street. Although this stretch of Savannah has a reputation as a tourist trap, River Street Sweets sells incredible pralines and other treats. And if you need souvenirs like shot glasses or T-shirts, this is the spot.

KIDS AND FAMILIES

Savannah's Historic District offers a number of wonderful family activities, and not all of them are historic home tours. The surrounding areas, particularly the islands to the east of downtown, provide plenty of other options for family fun.

In the Historic District

One good bet for the kids is the Tricentennial Park, which includes the **Savannah Children's Museum,** the **Savannah History Museum,** and the **Georgia State Railroad Museum,** where you can catch a ride on an antique steam engine during warmer months. Another spot where families flock is the ArtZeum section of the **Jepson Center for the Arts,** which includes interactive exhibits designed to entertain the younger crowd. When it starts to get hot outside, hit the fountain at **Ellis Square,** a popular destination for kids of all ages who want to run through the jets of water shooting up from the ground. **Forsyth Park** is another great spot to spend some quality time. There's a large playground, as well as open fields perfect for tossing a Frisbee or football. The restored historic fort across from the Mansion on Forsyth offers public restrooms, a café, and a visitor information kiosk. For older kids who want their own scene, the **Sentient Bean** coffee shop on the south end of Forsyth

Park is one of the city's few all-ages venues and features a variety of live music, films, and other programs during the evening.

Elsewhere in Savannah

Among the most popular destinations for families in the area is **Tybee Island**. Whether it's a day relaxing on the beach, or something more adventurous, like renting bicycles, kayaks, or other equipment. The **Crab Shack** capitalizes on family traffic with a large display of baby alligators that allows for up-close viewing of the indigenous reptiles. The **Oatland Island Wildlife Center** is a few miles east of downtown Savannah, and features a zoo, among other exhibits related to local history, flora, and fauna.

EXPLORING
SAVANNAH

Updated
by
Summer
Teal
Simpson

SAVANNAH, GEORGIA'S OLDEST CITY, began its modern history on February 12, 1733, when General James Oglethorpe and 120 colonists arrived at Yamacraw Bluff on the Savannah River to form what would be the last British colony in the New World. For a century and a half, the city flourished as a bustling port, serving as a hub of import and export that connected Georgia to the rest of the world.

The past plays an important role in Savannah. Standing in a tranquil square surrounded by historic homes, it's easy to feel as if you have stumbled through a portal into the past. Don't be fooled though, as the city offers much more than antebellum nostalgia for moonlight and magnolias. Savannah is home to several colleges and universities, including the prestigious Savannah College of Art and Design. In the last decade the city has seen a surge of creative energy that has helped infuse a youthful vibe into the traditions of the Hostess City.

When Oglethorpe founded Savannah, one of the original rules forbade strong drink. Temperance didn't last long, and these days Savannah is one of only a few places in the country without an open container law, meaning that you can walk around downtown with a beer or cocktail so long as it's in a plastic cup—known locally as a "to-go cup." Residents joke that in Atlanta they ask what you do for a living, in Macon they ask where you go to church, and in Savannah they ask what you drink.

Maybe it's the heat, but things move a little more slowly in Savannah. If you're visiting from out of town, take a deep breath, relax, and enjoy the languid pace of "Slow-vannah."

EXPLORING SAVANNAH

With an eclectic array of shops, restaurants, museums, and monuments spread across the Historic District, the best way to explore downtown Savannah is on foot. Whether you plan a route ahead of time or just wander aimlessly, a leisurely stroll will always result in unique discoveries. If your feet start to ache, flag down a pedicab driver—these people-powered vehicles are a great way to get around, and the drivers usually tell a good story or two. Or hop on one of the many meandering trolleys, a great way to see the city.

THE HISTORIC DISTRICT

General James Oglethorpe, founder of Georgia, plotted Savannah on a grid in a city plan that has won countless awards in the centuries since. The Historic District is neatly hemmed in by the Savannah River, Gaston Street, East Broad Street, and Martin Luther King Jr. Boulevard. Streets are arrow-straight, and public squares are tucked into the grid at precise intervals. Bull Street, anchored on the north by City Hall and the south by Forsyth Park, charges down the center of the grid and maneuvers around the five public squares that stand in its way. The squares all have some historical significance; many have elaborate fountains, monuments to war heroes, and shaded resting areas with park benches. Beautiful homes and mansions speak lovingly of another era.

TOP ATTRACTIONS

Andrew Low House. Built on the site of the city jail, this residence was constructed in 1848 for Andrew Low, a native of Scotland and one of Savannah's merchant princes. Designed by architect John S. Norris, the residence later belonged to Low's son, William, who inherited his father's wealth and married his longtime sweetheart, Juliette Gordon. The couple moved to England and several years after her husband's death, Juliette returned to this house and founded the Girl Scouts here on March 12, 1912. The house has 19th-century antiques, stunning silver, and some of the finest ornamental ironwork in Savannah, but it is the story and history of the family—even a bedroom named after the family friend and visitor General Robert E. Lee— that is fascinating and well told by the tour guides. ⊠ *329 Abercorn St., Historic District* ☎ *912/233–6854* ⊕ *www. andrewlowhouse.com* ⊠ *$10; $21 includes admission to Davenport House and Juliette Low House* ☉ *Mon.–Sat. 10–4, Sun. noon–4; last tour at 4* ☉ *1st 2 wks of Jan. and major holidays.*

Chippewa Square. Anchoring this square is Daniel Chester French's imposing bronze statue of General James Edward Oglethorpe, founder of both the City of Savannah and the State of Georgia. The bus-stop scenes of *Forrest Gump* were filmed on the northern end of the square. Savannah Theatre, on the corner of Bull and McDonough streets, claims to be the oldest continuously operated theater site in North America and offers a variety of family-friendly shows. ⊠ *Bull St., between Hull and Perry Sts., Historic District.*

Andrew Low House, **29**

Beach Institute African-American Cultural Center, **33**

Cathedral of St. John the Baptist, **32**

Christ Episcopal Church, **7**

Chippewa Square, **20**

City Hall, **5**

City Market, **3**

Colonial Park Cemetery, **19**

Ellis Square, **4**

Factors Walk, **11**

First African Baptist Church, **2**

Flannery O'Connor Childhood Home, **30**

Forsyth Park, **35**

Georgia State Railroad Museum, **24**

Green-Meldrim House, **26**

Isaiah Davenport House, **18**

Jepson Center for the Arts, **13**

Johnson Square, **6**

Juliette Gordon Low Birthplace, **16**

Lafayette Square, **31**

Madison Square, **28**

Mercer Williams House, **36**

Monterey Square, **37**

Olde Pink House, **8**

Owens-Thomas House and Museum, **17**

Ralph Mark Gilbert Civil Rights Museum, **34**

Reynolds Square, **9**

Rousakis Plaza, **10**

Savannah Children's Museum, **25**

Savannah History Museum, **23**

SCAD Museum of Art, **21**

Ships of the Sea Maritime Museum, **1**

St. John's Episcopal Church, **27**

Telfair Museum of Art, **14**

Temple Mickve Israel, **38**

Tricentennial Park & Battlefield, **22**

Waving Girl, **12**

Wright Square, **15**

Savannah River

0 ——— 1/4 mile
0 ——— 400 meters

River St.

10 Riverfront Plaza   River St.   **12**

11 Factors Walk

5

W. Bay St.   E. Bay St.

8

6   E. Julian St.   **9**
W. Julian St.   **7**   E. Bryan St.   Warren Sq.

E. Congress St.

Whitaker St.   E. Broughton St.   E. Broughton St.   Lincoln St.   Price St.   Houston St.

E. State St.
W. President   **15**   E.   President   **17**   **18**   Columbia Sq.   E. President St.

Oglethorpe Sq.

E. York St.

16   E.   Oglethorpe Ave.

Drayton St.

19
Colonial Park Cemetery   Habersham St.

W. Hull   E. Hull
Chippewa Sq.
20

E. Perry

Whitaker St.   Bull St.   E.   Liberty St.

32   **33**

E. Harris St.   Troup Sq.
26   **28**   **29**   **31**   E. Macon St.
27   E. Charlton St.   E. Charlton St.
30

E. Jones St.

Drayton St.   Lincoln St.

E. Taylor St.   Whitefield Sq.
Calhoun Sq.   E. Wayne St.
36   **37**   **38**
E. Gordon St.

Savannah
Historic District

35   Forsyth Park

City Market. Although the 1870s City Market was razed years ago, its atmosphere and character are still evident. Adjacent to Ellis Square, the area is a lively destination because of its galleries, boutiques, street performers, and open-air cafés. New to the block is Byrd Cookie Co., a popular local bakery with great edible souvenirs. City Market is also a good spot to purchase trolley tickets or take a ride in a horse-drawn carriage. ⊠ *W. St. Julian St., between Barnard and Montgomery Sts., Historic District* ☎ *912/232–4903* ⊕ *www.savannahcitymarket.com.*

Colonial Park Cemetery. Stroll the shaded pathways and read some of the old tombstone inscriptions in this park, the final resting place for Savannahians who died between 1750 and 1853. Many of those interred here succumbed during the yellow fever epidemic in 1820. Notice the dramatic entrance gate on the corner of Abercorn and Oglethorpe streets. Local legend tells that when Sherman's troops set up camp here, they moved some headstones around and altered inscriptions for their own amusement, which partially explains the headstones mounted against the far wall. This spooky spot is a regular stop for ghost tours. ⊠ *Oglethorpe and Abercorn Sts., Historic District* ⊙ *Daily 8–8.*

FAMILY Fodor'sChoice **Ellis Square.** Converted from a public square to a
★ parking garage in the 1970s, Ellis Square has been restored in recent years and is once again one of Savannah's most popular spots. Near the western end stands a statue of legendary songwriter Johnny Mercer, a Savannah native. Nearby is a visitor center with a touch-screen city guide, maps and brochures, and public restrooms. To the east is a lifesize chess board; the pieces can be requested at the visitor center. A treat for youngsters (and the young at heart) is the square's interactive fountain, which is entertaining and refreshing in the warmer months. ⊠ *Barnard St., between W. Congress and W. Bryan Sts., Historic District.*

Factors Walk. A network of iron crosswalks and steep stone stairways connects Bay Street to Factors Walk below. The congested area of multistory buildings was originally the center of commerce for cotton brokers, who walked between and above the lower cotton warehouses. Ramps lead down to River Street. ■ TIP→ **This area is paved in cobblestones, so wear comfortable shoes.** ⊠ *Bay St. to Factors Walk, Historic District.*

QUICK BITES. **Leopold's.** One of the best ice-cream parlors in the area is Leopold's, a Savannah institution since 1919. It's currently owned by Stratton Leopold, grandson of the original owner and the producer of films like *Mission Impossible 3*. Movie posters and paraphernalia make for an entertaining sideline to the selection of ice cream made with the old family recipe. Try the delicious lemon custard or honey, almond, and cream flavors, or unique seasonal inventions like lavendar, orange blossom, or rose petal. ⊠ *212 E. Broughton St., Historic District* ☎ *912/234–4442* ⊕ *www.leopoldsicecream.com.*

FAMILY Fodor'sChoice **Forsyth Park.** The heart of the city's outdoor life,
★ Forsyth Park hosts a number of popular cultural events, including film screenings, sports matches, and the annual Savannah Jazz Festival. Built in 1840 and expanded in 1851, the park was part of General Oglethorpe's original city plan and made possible by the donation of land from Georgia Governor John Forsyth. A glorious white fountain dating to 1858, Confederate and Spanish-American War memorials, a rose garden, multiple playgrounds, tennis and basketball courts, and an old fort are spread across this grand park. Recently restored, the fort now contains a café, an open-air stage, and lovely fountains. Be sure to stop by Saturday for the bustling farmer's market. The park's 1-mile perimeter is among the prettiest walks in the city and takes you past many beautifully restored historic homes. ⊠ *Gaston St., between Drayton and Whitaker Sts., Historic District.*

FAMILY **Georgia State Railroad Museum.** This museum preserves the legacy of the Central of Georgia Railway, an integral part of Savannah's industrial heritage. A step into a different era, the museum is home to numerous railcars and boxcars, working diesel and steam locomotives, and a rare functioning railroad turntable. Around the corner is an iconic 125-foot-tall smokestack and the original quarters for workers and managers. Children of all ages will appreciate the expansive model-train exhibit, a fully operable rendition of a train traveling through the region. Ride on a historic diesel or steam locomotive. ⊠ *303 Martin Luther King Jr. Blvd., Historic District* ☎ *912/651–6823* ⊕ *www. chsgeorgia.org/railroad-museum.html* ⌐ *$10* ⊙ *Daily 9–5.*

Famous Faces in Savannah

CLOSE UP

Here's a sampling of the figures who have etched themselves into Savannah's collective memory.

James L. Pierpont (1822–93) probably wrote a classic Christmas carol in Savannah, despite the total lack of snow. A native of Medford, Massachusetts, Pierpont became music director of Savannah's Unitarian church in the 1850s. In 1857 he obtained a copyright for "The One Horse Open Sleigh" (more popularly known as "Jingle Bells"). All was jolly until the 1980s: Tempers flared when Medford claimed that Pierpont had written the song there instead. The dispute over where he wrote the timeless tune remains unresolved.

John Wesley (1703–91), the founder of Methodism, arrived in 1735 and is commemorated by a statue in Reynolds Square. After returning to England, he became one of the towering figures in the history of Protestantism.

Johnny Mercer (1909–76), who penned such classic songs as "Moon River" and "Accentuate the Positive," was a fourth-generation Savannah native and helped found Capitol Records. He is buried in Bonaventure Cemetery next to his wife, Ginger.

Fiction writer **Flannery O'Connor** (1925–64) spent the first 13 years of her life in Savannah. Known for her Southern-Gothic style, her greatest achievement is found in her short stories, published in the collections *A Good Man Is Hard to Find* and *Everything That Rises Must Converge*.

Antwan "Big Boi" Patton (born 1975), best known as half of the legendary hip-hop duo OutKast, was born on the west side of the city and returns frequently to visit family and host events related to his nonprofit group, BigKidz.

Isaiah Davenport House. Semicircular stairs with wrought-iron railings lead to the recessed doorway of the red-brick Federal home constructed by master builder Isaiah Davenport for his family between 1815 and 1820. Three dormered windows poke through the sloping roof of the stately house, and the interior has polished hardwood floors and fine woodwork and plasterwork. The proposed demolition of this historic Savannah structure galvanized the city's residents into action to save their treasured buildings. The home endured a history of dilapidation that lingered since the 1920s, when it was divided into tenements. When someone proposed razing it to build a parking lot in 1955, a small group of neighbors raised $22,000 to buy and restore this property. This was the inception of the Historic Savannah Foundation and the first of many successful efforts to preserve the architectural treasure that is the city today. ⊠ *324 E. State St., Historic District* ☎ *912/236–8097* ⊕ *www.davenporthousemuseum. org* ⊠ *$9; $21 includes admission to Andrew Low House and Juliette Low Birthplace* ⊙ *Mon.–Sat. 10–4, Sun. 1–4; last tour at 4.*

★ Fodors Choice **Jepson Center for the Arts.** This contemporary
FAMILY building is one of a kind among the characteristic 18th- and 19th-century architecture of historic Savannah. The modern art extension of the Telfair Museum of Art, the Jepson was designed by renowned architect Moshe Safdie. Within the marble-and-glass edifice are rotating exhibits, on loan and from the permanent collection, ranging from European masters to contemporary locals. There's also an outdoor sculpture terrace and an interactive, kid-friendly area on the third level called the ArtZeum. ⊠ *207 W. York St., Historic District* ☎ *912/790–8802* ⊕ *www.telfair.org/ jepson* ⊠ *$12; $20 includes admission to the Owens-Thomas House and Museum and the Telfair Museum of Art* ⊙ *Sun. and Mon. noon–5, Tues., Wed., Fri., and Sat. 10–5, Thurs. 10–8.*

Johnson Square. The oldest of James Oglethorpe's original squares was laid out in 1733 and named for South Carolina Governor Robert Johnson. A monument marks the grave of Nathanael Greene, a hero of the Revolutionary War. The square has always been a popular gathering place: Savannahians came here to welcome President Monroe in 1819, to greet the Marquis de Lafayette in 1825, and to cheer for Georgia's secession in 1861. ■TIP→ **Locals call this Bank Square because of the plethora of nearby banks—perfect if you need an ATM.** ⊠ *Bull St., between Bryan and Congress Sts., Historic District.*

Juliette Gordon Low Birthplace. This early 19th-century town house, attributed to William Jay, was designated in 1965 as Savannah's first National Historic Landmark. "Daisy" Low, founder of the Girl Scouts, was born here in 1860, and the house is now owned and operated by the Girl Scouts of America. Mrs. Low's paintings and other artwork are on display in the house, restored to the style of 1886, the year of Mrs. Low's marriage. Droves of Girl Scout troops make the regular pilgrimmage to Savannah to see their founder's birthplace and earn merit badges. ⊠ *10 E. Oglethorpe St., Historic District* ☎ *912/233–4501* ⊕ *www.juliettegordon-*

lowbirthplace.org 🖅 *$10; $21 including admission to the Andrew Low House and the Isaiah Davenport House* ⊙ *Mar.–Oct., Mon.–Sat. 10–4, Sun. 11–4; Nov.–Feb., Mon., Tues., and Thurs.–Sat. 10–4, Sun. 11–4.*

Lafayette Square. Named for the Marquis de Lafayette, who aided the Americans during the Revolutionary War, the square contains a graceful three-tier fountain donated by the Georgia chapter of the Colonial Dames of America. The Cathedral of St. John the Baptist is located on this square, as are the Andrew Low House and the impressive Hamilton-Turner Inn. The childhood home of celebrated Southern author Flannery O'Connor also sits on this square. ⊠ *Abercorn St., between E. Harris and E. Charlton Sts., Historic District.*

Madison Square. Laid out in 1839 and named for President James Madison, this square is home to a statue depicting Sergeant William Jasper hoisting a flag, a tribute to his bravery during the Siege of Savannah. Though mortally wounded, Jasper rescued the colors of his regiment in the assault on the British lines. A granite marker denotes the southern line of the British defense during the 1779 battle. The Green-Meldrim House is here. ⊠ *Bull St., between W. Harris and W. Charlton Sts., Historic District.*

Mercer Williams House. A staple on the tourist circuit, this house museum has been the stuff of legend since the release of the longtime bestselling novel *Midnight in the Garden of Good and Evil.* The home was purchased in 1969 by Jim Williams, who purportedly killed his lover in the front den while sitting at the desk where, ironically, he later died. Scandal aside, Williams was an aficionado of historic preservation, and the Mercer House was one of some 50 properties that he purchased and restored. Designed by New York architect John S. Norris for General Hugh Mercer, great-grandfather of Johnny Mercer, the home was constructed in 1860 and completed after the end of the Civil War in 1868. Inside are fine examples of 18th- and 19th-century furniture and art from Jim Williams's private collection. ■**TIP➔** **Don't miss a look around the charming gift shop.** ⊠ *429 Bull St., Historic District* ☎ *912/236–6352* ⊕ *mercerhouse. com* 🖅 *$12.50* ⊙ *Mon.–Sat. 10:30–4:10, Sun. noon–4.*

Olde Pink House. Built in 1771, this is one of the oldest buildings in town. Now a restaurant, the portico pink-stucco Georgian mansion has also been a private home, a bank, and headquarters for a Yankee general during the

Full Steam Ahead

The first steam-powered ship to cross the Atlantic was the SS *Savannah*, which sailed from Savannah north to Newark and then finally to Scotland, England, and Russia during its maiden voyage in 1819. The ship was funded by local shipping magnate William Scarborough, whose home still stands on Martin Luther King Jr. Boulevard (formerly West Broad Street). While the SS *Savannah*'s first trip was a success as a major landmark in the evolution of maritime travel and commerce, the endeavor didn't work out so well for Scarborough as a businessman. He ended up bankrupt and eventually was forced to sell his newly constructed home, which is now the Ships of the Sea Maritime Museum—an appropriate homage to its original tenant. Before the building underwent substantial restorations prior to becoming the museum, it spent nearly a century as a school for African American children. Opened in the 1870s, the West Broad Street School was the first officially sanctioned school for African American children in the city.

Civil War. In its lower level is the city's most beloved piano bar, Planters Tavern, and on the southern side there's a bar and sidewalk café. ✉ *23 Abercorn St., Historic District* ☎ *912/232–4286*.

★ **Fodor's Choice Owens-Thomas House and Museum.** Designed by William Jay, the Owens-Thomas House is widely considered to be one of the finest examples of English Regency architecture in America. Built in 1816–19, the house was constructed with local materials. Of particular note are the curving walls of the house, Greek-inspired ornamental molding, half-moon arches, stained-glass panels, original Duncan Phyfe furniture, and the hardwood "bridge" on the second floor. The carriage house includes a gift shop and rare urban slave quarters, which have retained the original furnishings and "haint-blue" paint made by the slave occupants. This house had indoor toilets before the White House or Versailles. If you have time for just a single house museum, let this be the one. Owned and administered by the Telfair Museum of Art, this home gives an inside perspective on Savannah's history. ✉ *124 Abercorn St., Historic District* ☎ *912/790–8889* ⊕ *www.telfair.org/owens-thomas* 💲 *$15; $20 includes admission to Jepson Center for the Arts and the Telfair Museum of Art* ⊗ *Mon. noon–5, Tues.–Sat. 10–5, Sun. 1–5; last tour at 4:30.*

Reynolds Square. Anglican cleric and theologian John Wesley is remembered here. He arrived in Savannah in 1736 at the behest of General James Oglethorpe. During his short stay the future founder of the Methodist Church preached and wrote the first English hymnal in the city. His monument in Reynolds Square is shaded by greenery and surrounded by park benches. The landmark Planters Inn, formerly the John Wesley Hotel, is also located on the square. Ironically, though it was named after a man of the cloth, it was considered the best brothel in town at the turn of the century. ⊠ *Abercorn St., between E. Congress and E. Bryan Sts., Historic District.*

Rousakis Plaza. From River Street's main pavilion you can watch a parade of freighters and pug-nosed tugs glide by along the river. River Street is the main venue for several of the city's grandest celebrations, including the First Friday Fireworks and the Craft Beer Festival. The plaza is named for former Savannah mayor John Rousakis and fills with locals for Savannah's signature St. Patrick's Day festivities and Fourth of July celebration. Rousakis, like greater River Street, is flanked by an abundance of shops and restaurants and draws colorful street entertainers. ⊠ *River St., near Abercorn St., Historic District.*

FAMILY **Savannah Children's Museum.** Adhering to the principle of learning through doing, the Savannah Children's Museum has open green spaces with several stations geared for sensory play, including a water/sand play excavation station, sound station of percussion instruments, and an organic garden. The storybook nook is a partnership with the Savannah public library and encourages visiting youngsters to balance physical and mental recreation. One station includes costumes for stage performances. ⊠ *655 Louisville Rd., Historic District* ☎ *912/651–4292* ⊕ *www.savannahchildrensmuseum.org* ⊠ *$7.50* ⊙ *Tues.– Sat. 10–4, Sun. 11–4.*

FAMILY **Savannah History Museum.** This history museum houses exhibits on Savannah's cultural and military history. Inside you'll find much about the lives of early Native American settlers, including the development of tabby (crushed oyster shells with lime, sand, and water) for use in early construction. Subsequent historical periods are portrayed, including the Revolutionary and Civil War eras and the Industrial Revolution. More modern highlights include the city's countless Hollywood film appearances over the years, the most memorable of which might be *Forrest Gump*. The very bench that Tom Hanks sat on can be seen here. ⊠ *303 Martin Luther King Jr. Blvd., Historic District* ☎ *912/651–6825* ⊕ *www.chsgeorgia.org* ☑ *$7* ⊙ *Weekdays 8:30–5, weekends 9–5.*

★ Fodor'sChoice **SCAD Museum of Art.** This architectural marvel rose from the ruins of the oldest surviving railroad building in the United States. Appropriately, the architect chosen for the lofty design and remodel project was Christian Sottile, the valedictorian of Savannah College of Art and Design's 1996 graduating class and the current dean of the School of Building Arts. Sottile rose to the hearty challenge of merging the past with the present, preserving key architectural details of the original structure while introducing contemporary design elements. SCAD Museum of Art houses two main galleries with rotating exhibits by some of the most acclaimed figures in contemporary art: the Evans Gallery features works of African American arts and culture, while the André Leon Talley Gallery is devoted to fashion and high style. ⊠ *601 Turner Blvd., Historic District* ☎ *912/525–7191* ⊕ *scadmoa.org* ☑ *$10* ⊙ *Tues.–Fri. 10–5, weekends noon–5.*

Ships of the Sea Maritime Museum. This exuberant Greek-revival mansion was the home of William Scarborough, a wealthy early 19th-century merchant and one of the principal owners of the *Savannah,* the first steamship to cross the Atlantic. The structure, with its portico capped by half-moon windows, is another architect William Jay's notable contributions to the Historic District. These days it houses the Ships of the Sea Museum, with displays of model ships and exhibits detailing maritime history. The ambitious North Garden nearly doubled the original walled courtyard's size and provides ample space for naturalist-led walks and outdoor concerts. ⊠ *41 Martin Luther King Jr. Blvd., Historic District* ☎ *912/232–1511* ⊕ *www.shipsofthesea.org* ☑ *$8.50* ⊙ *Tues.–Sun. 10–5.*

Telfair Museum of Art. The oldest public art museum in the Southeast was designed by William Jay in 1819 for Alexander Telfair. Within its marble rooms are a variety of paintings from American and European masters, plaster casts of the Elgin Marbles and other classical sculptures, and some of the Telfair family furnishings, including a Duncan Phyfe sideboard and Savannah-made silver. It is the permanent home of the notable Bird Girl statue, made famous on the cover of John Berendt's *Midnight in the Garden of Good and Evil*. The Telfair hosts classical music performances during spring's Savannah Music Festival. ⊠ *121 Barnard St., Historic District* ☏ *912/790–8800* ⊕ *www.telfair.org* ✉ *$12; $20 includes admission to the Jepson Center for the Arts and the Owens-Thomas House and Museum* ⊙ *Mon. noon–5, Tues.–Sat. 10–5, Sun. 1–5.*

FAMILY **Tricentennial Park and Battlefield.** This 25-acre complex is home to the Savannah History Museum, the Georgia State Railroad Museum, and the Savannah Children's Museum, as well as Battlefield Memorial Park. This site offers an unbeatable introduction to the city and a full day of fun for the whole family. The battlefield was the site of the second bloodiest battle of the Revolutionary War where, on October 9, 1779, where 800 of the 8,000 troups who fought lost their lives. You can lunch inside an old dining car at the Whistle Stop Café. ⊠ *303 Martin Luther King Jr. Blvd., Historic District* ☏ *912/651–6825* ⊕ *www.chsgeorgia. org/tricentennial-park-sites.html.*

QUICK BITES. **Lulu's Chocolate Bar.** This is a great place to satisfy your sweet tooth. Full of freshly baked cakes, pies, and tarts, it's the place for some after-dinner indulgence. Lulu's also exhibits interesting work by local artists and hosts low-key live music on weekends. Don't miss the "drinkable chocolate," Lulu's twist on the classic hot chocolate. ⊠ *42 Martin Luther King Jr. Blvd., between Congress and Broughton Sts., Historic District* ☏ *912/480–4564* ⊕ *www.luluschocolatebar.net.*

WORTH NOTING

Beach Institute African-American Cultural Center. Works by African-American artists from the Savannah area and around the country are on display in this building, which once housed the first school for African-American children in Savannah. On permanent exhibit are more than 230 wood carvings by renowned folk artist Ulysses Davis. ⊠ *502 E. Harris St., Historic District* ☏ *912/234–8000* ⊕ *www.visit-historic-savannah.com/beach-institute.htm* ✉ *$5* ⊙ *Tues.–Sat. noon–5.*

Cathedral of St. John the Baptist. Soaring over the city, this French Gothic–style cathedral, with pointed arches and free-flowing traceries, is the seat of the Catholic diocese of Savannah. It was founded in 1799 by the first French colonists to arrive in Savannah. Fire destroyed the early structures; the present cathedral dates from 1876. Its architecture, gold-leaf adornments, and the entire edifice give testimony to the importance of the Catholic parishioners of the day. The interior spaces are grand and dramatic, including incredible stained glass and an intricately designed altar. ⊠ *222 E. Harris St., at Lafayette Sq., Historic District* ☎ *912/233–4709* ⊕ *www.savannahcathedral. org* ⊙ *Weekdays 9–5.*

Christ Episcopal Church. This was the first church—then Anglican—established in the Georgia colony in 1733. It is often called "The Mother Church of Georgia." Located on Johnson Square, the centuries-old building with its columns and wrought-iron railings is a pure white sight indeed. ⊠ *28 Bull St., Historic District* ☎ *912/236–2500* ⊕ *www. christchurchsavannah.org* ⊙ *Mon.–Thurs. 9–1.*

City Hall. Built in 1906 on the site of the Old City Exchange, this imposing structure is now home to the city council. Its landmark tower clock and bells played a significant role in the day-to-day business of Savannah in the days before everyone owned a pocket watch. City Hall is open to the public and visitors can admire the dramatic four-story rotunda crowned with a stained-glass inner dome, mosaic tiles, marble wainscoting, mahogany and live-oak pediments and banisters, and stately fountain. ⊠ *2 E. Bay St., Historic District* ☎ *912/651–6415* ⊕ *www.savannah. gov* ⊙ *Weekdays 8:30–5.*

First African Baptist Church. Slaves constructed this church at night by lamplight after having worked the plantations during the day. It is one of the first organized black Baptist churches on the continent. The basement floor still shows signs of its time as a stop on the Underground Railroad. Designs drilled in the floor are thought to actually have been air holes for slaves hiding underneath, waiting to be transported to the Savannah River for their trip to freedom. It was also an important meeting place during the civil-rights era. ⊠ *23 Montgomery St., Historic District* ☎ *912/233–6597* ⊕ *www.firstafricanbc.com* ⊿ *$7* ⊙ *Tours Tues. and Sat. at 11 and 2, Sun. at 1.*

Flannery O'Connor Childhood Home. Celebrated Southern author Flannery O'Connor lived in this austere Charlton Street home from her birth in 1925 until 1938 when the family moved to Milledgeville, Georgia. The beautifully renovated home includes oddities like the "kiddie coop," a cage for children designed by O'Connor's father. In fall, the home hosts a reception with lectures by academics and experts discussing different aspects of O'Connor's life and work. Events are free and open to the public. ✉ *207 E. Charlton St., at Lafayette Sq., Historic District* ☎ *912/233–6014* ⊕ *www.flanneryoconnorhome.org* 🖃 *$6* 🕐 *Fri.–Wed. 1–4.*

Green-Meldrim House. Designed by New York architect John Norris and built in 1850 for cotton merchant Charles Green, this Gothic-revival mansion cost $93,000 to build— a princely sum in those days. The house was purchased in 1892 by Judge Peter Meldrim, whose heirs sold it to St. John's Episcopal Church in the 1940s to use as a parish house. General Sherman lived here after taking the city in 1864. Sitting on Madison Square, the house has Gothic features such as oriels, a crenellated roof, and an external gallery with filigree ironwork. Inside are mantels of Carrara marble, carved black-walnut woodwork, and doorknobs and hinges of either silver plate or porcelain. ✉ *14 W. Macon St., Historic District* ☎ *912/233–3845* ⊕ *www.stjohnssav. org/green-meldrim-house* 🖃 *$10* 🕐 *Tues., Thurs., and Fri. 10–4, Sat. 10–1; last tour starts half an hour prior to close.*

Monterey Square. Commemorating the victory of General Zachary Taylor's forces in Monterrey, Mexico in 1846, this is the southernmost of Bull Street's squares. A monument honors General Casimir Pulaski, the Polish nobleman who lost his life in the Siege of Savannah during the Revolutionary War. On the square sit Temple Mickve Israel (one of the country's oldest Jewish congregations) and some of the city's most beautiful mansions, including the infamous Mercer House. ✉ *Bull St., between Taylor and Gordon sts., Historic District.*

Ralph Mark Gilbert Civil Rights Museum. This history museum has a series of engaging exhibits on segregation, from emancipation through the civil rights movement. The role of black and white Savannahians in ending segregation in their city is well detailed and includes archival photographs and videos. There's also a replica of a lunch counter where blacks were denied service. ✉ *460 Martin Luther King Jr. Blvd., Historic District* ☎ *912/777–6099* 🖃 *$8* 🕐 *Tues.–Sat. 9–5.*

St. John's Episcopal Church. Built in 1852, this church is famous for its whimsical chimes and stained-glass windows. The extraordinary parish house is the revered Green-Meldrim House. One interesting bit of trivia: on Christmas 1864, after General Sherman moved into the

Family-Friendly Savannah

Savannah has its share of kid-appropriate activities. Juliette Gordon Low's Birthplace is the original home of the founder of the Girl Scouts, and girls of scouting age flock here annually, especially during the summer. The house is full of period furnishings and memorabilia from the early days of the Girl Scouts. On the second floor is Juliette's childhood room with vintage toys and dolls and two dollhouses, one a Georgia Plains–style farmhouse.

City Market is always popular with younger children. Even if your child isn't keen on a horse-drawn carriage tour, they may enjoy petting the horses and taking pictures with them. A short stroll farther lands you at the Ellis Square fountain, a popular spot to run through the jets of water when the weather is warm.

Kids flock to Savannah's Tri-centennial Museums, which include the Savannah Children's Museum, Georgia State Railroad Museum, and Savannah History Museum, all within walking distance of one another. Entertaining and educational activities include story-time sessions, the backyard science program, rides on a historic steam engine, and programs about archaeology.

Forsyth Park is a great place to let kids run free, with wide-open fields, perfect for Frisbee or a game of catch, and two playgrounds—one for younger children and one for older. Next to the playground, housed in a former fort, is a café that sells coffee, snacks, and lunch.

The Jepson Center for the Arts is a terrific venue for children and helps instill an appreciation for art. ArtZeum, located on the upper levels, is an interactive, two-story space especially designed to entertain and educate.

Belles Ferry, the free water taxi that goes back and forth to the Westin, can also be a kid-pleasing opportunity to ride across the river. The trip offers great views of the old buildings lining the riverfront.

East of the Historic District is Oatland Island, a wildlife preserve that is popular with youngsters. Fenced habitats for wolves, bobcats, bison, and numerous birds are dotted along walking trails that run through the forest and marsh.

With long stretches of beach, quirky shops, and casual restaurants, Tybee Island is another popular destination for families.

Green-Meldrim House, his army chaplain conducted the church's Christmas service. ⊠ *1 W. Macon St., at Madison Sq., Historic District* ☎ *912/232–1251* ⊕ *www.stjohnssav. org* ⊙ *Mon.–Thurs. 9–4:30, Fri. 9–noon.*

Temple Mickve Israel. This unique Gothic-revival synagogue on Monterey Square houses the third-oldest Jewish congregation in the United States; its founding members settled in town only five months after the establishment of Savannah in 1733. The synagogue's permanent collection includes documents and letters (some from George Washington, James Madison, and Thomas Jefferson) pertaining to early Jewish life in Savannah and Georgia. ⊠ *20 E. Gordon St., Historic District* ☎ *912/233–1547* ⊕ *mickveisrael.org* ⊠ *$6 tour* ☉ *Tours weekdays 10–12:30 and 2–3:30.*

Waving Girl. This statue at River Street and East Broad Ramp is a beloved symbol of Savannah's Southern hospitality. It commemorates Florence Martus, a sister to the lighthouse keeper, who waved to ships in Savannah's port for more than 44 years. She would wave a white towel and, when young, always had her dog by her side. Late in her life, locals threw her a huge birthday party at Fort Pulaski with more than 5,000 guests. Despite having welcomed so many sailors to port, she died without ever having been wed. ⊠ *River St. near E. Broad Ramp, Historic District.*

Wright Square. Named for James Wright, Georgia's last colonial governor, this square has an elaborate monument in its center that honors William Washington Gordon, founder of the Central of Georgia Railroad. A slab of granite from Stone Mountain adorns the grave of Tomo-Chi-Chi, the Yamacraw chief who befriended General Oglethorpe and the colonists. ⊠ *Bull St., between W. State and W. York Sts., Historic District.*

THE SAVANNAH AREA

Bonaventure Cemetery. The largest of Savannah's municipal cemeteries, Bonaventure spreads over 160 acres and sits on a bluff above the Wilmington River. Once a plantation, the land became a private cemetery in 1846 and the public cemetery was established in 1907. The scenescape is one of lush natural beauty transposed against the elegant and almost eerie backdrop of lavish marble headstones, monuments, and mausoleums. John Muir reportedly camped at Bonaventure in 1867 on his legendary "thousand-mile walk." Local photographer Jack Leigh, novelist and poet Conrad Aiken, and singer/songwriter Johnny Mercer are among those interred here. ⊠ *330 Greenwich Rd., Thunderbolt* ☎ *912/651–6843* ⊕ *www.bonaventurehistorical. org* ☉ *Daily 8–5.*

2

CLOSE UP

Moss Mystique

Spanish moss—the silky gray garlands that drape over the branches of live oaks—has come to symbolize the languorous sensibilities of the Deep South. A relative of the pineapple, the moisture-loving plant requires an average year-round humidity of 70%, and thus thrives in subtropical climates—including Georgia's coastal regions.

Contrary to popular belief, Spanish moss is not a parasite; it's an epiphyte, or "air plant," taking water and nutrients from the air and photosynthesizing in the same manner as soil-bound plants. It reproduces using tiny flowers. When water is scarce, it turns gray, and when the rains come it takes on a greenish hue. Although it is tempting to grab handfuls of Spanish moss as a souvenir, be careful. It often harbors the biting menaces commonly known as chiggers.

Coastal Georgia Botanical Gardens. In 1890 Mrs. Herman B. Miller planted three clumbs of Japanese timber bamboo near her farmhouse 15 miles south of Savannah. As the bamboo took to the warm Southern climate, it spread to what now stands today at the Bamboo Farms at the Coastal Georgia Botanical Gardens. The gardens, deeded to the University of Georgia in 1983, now also boast a 4-acre bamboo maze, a children's garden, formal and shade gardens, and a water garden. Seasonally, visitors can enjoy the pick-your-own berries garden. ⊠ *2 Canebrake Rd.* ☎ *912/921–5460* ⊕ *www.coastalgeorgiabg.org* 🎫 *Free* ☉ *Weekdays. 8–5, Sat. 10–5, Sun. 12–5.*

Ebenezer. When the Salzburgers arrived in Savannah in 1734, General James Oglethorpe sent them up the Savannah River to establish a settlement. Their first homestead was assailed by disease, so they relocated closer to the Savannah River. They engaged in silkworm production and, in 1769, built the Jerusalem Church, which still stands. An important defensive position during the Revolutionary War, the town sustained heavy damage. After the war, the population dwindled and most of the settlement shifted toward nearby Springfield. Descendants of these Protestant religious refugees have preserved the church and assembled a few of the remaining buildings, moving them to this site from other locations. The town is 25 miles northwest of Savannah. ⊠ *2980 Ebenezer Rd., Rincon* ☎ *912/754–7001* ⊕ *www.georgiasalzburgers.com.*

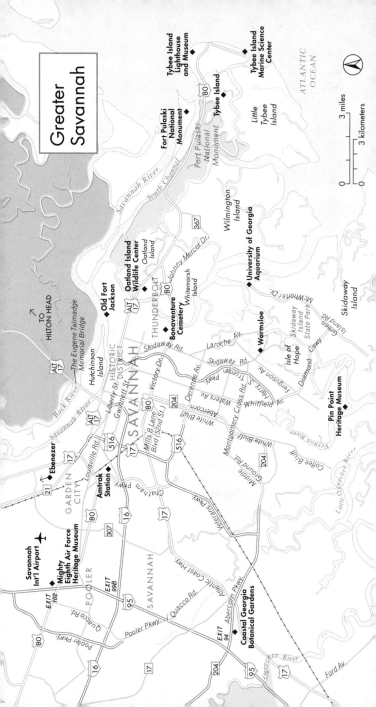

Greater Savannah

ATLANTIC OCEAN

Tybee Island Lighthouse and Museum

Tybee Island Marine Science Center

Fort Pulaski National Monument

Tybee Island

Little Tybee Island

3 miles

3 kilometers

Fort Pulaski National Monument

Savannah River

South Channel

Wilmington Island

367

Johnny Mercer Dr.

Oatland Island Wildlife Center

Oatland Island

Whitemarsh Island

University of Georgia Aquarium

Old Fort Jackson

THUNDERBOLT

ALT 17

80

Bonaventure Cemetery

McWhorter Dr.

Skidaway Island

The Eugene Talmadge Memorial Bridge

Hutchinson Island

Laroche. Av.

Wormsloe

Skidaway Rd.

Skidaway Island State Park

Green Island Rd.

TO HILTON HEAD

ALT 17

Liberty St.

Gwinnett St.

Victory Dr.

Skidaway Rd.

Isle of Hope

Diamond Cswy.

Ferguson Av.

Back River

HISTORIC DISTRICT

SAVANNAH

Harry S. Truman Pkwy.

Whitfield Av.

Pin Point Heritage Museum

Vernon River

Savannah River

ALT 17

Gwinnett St.

80

204

DeRenne Av.

Waters Av.

Abercorn St.

White Bluff

Montgomery Cross Rd.

White Bluff Rd.

Coffee Bluff

Little Ogeechee River

Ebenezer

21

17

GARDEN CITY

Louisville Rd.

516

Mills B. Lane Blvd (52nd St.)

17

516

Middle Ground Rd.

204

80

Amtrak Station

Chatham Pkwy.

16

307

Veterans Pkwy.

Savannah Int'l Airport

Mighty Eighth Air Force Heritage Museum

80

17

EXIT 102

Quacco Rd.

POOLER

EXIT 99B

95

Pooler Pkwy.

SAVANNAH

Atlantic Coast Hwy.

I Quacco Rd.

Abercorn Pkwy.

Coastal Georgia Botanical Gardens

EXIT 94

204

95

17

Ogeechee River

Ford Av.

16

17

Pooler Pkwy.

Quacco Rd.

80

★ Fodor'sChoice **Fort Pulaski National Monument.** Named for Casi-
FAMILY mir Pulaski, a Polish count and Revolutionary War hero,
this must-see sight for Civil War buffs was designed by
Napoléon's military engineer and built on Cockspur Island
between 1829 and 1847. Robert E. Lee's first assignment
after graduating from West Point was as an engineer here.
The fort was thought to be impervious to attack, but
as weapons advanced, it proved penetrable. During the
Civil War the fort fell after bombardment by newfangled
rifled cannons. The restored fortification, operated by the
National Park Service, has moats, drawbridges, massive
ramparts, and towering walls. The park has trails and
picnic areas. ✉ *U.S. Hwy 80* ☎ *912/786–5787* ⊕ *www.nps.
gov/fopu* 🖃 *$5* ⊙ *Daily 9–5.*

Isle of Hope. In 1736 General James Oglethorpe, who
founded the colony of Georgia, parceled out 1,500 acres
along the Intracoastal Waterway on the condition that
the owners would help defend the city. The northernmost
tract, today known as the Isle of Hope, was bequeathed
to Henry Parker, who became the first acting governor in
1752. In the 1840s the island had become a popular community for summer homes and, by 1875, the terminus for
the Savannah, Skidaway, and Seaboard railroads, three
major transit routes that transported travelers from far up
the East Coast and across the South. Today the horseshoe-
shape island provides sweeping views and cool breezes
from almost any point along the bluff, as well as an array
of beautiful, historic homes. ✉ *Thunderbolt.*

FAMILY **University of Georgia Aquarium.** On the grounds of the former
Modena Plantation, the University of Georgia runs this
aquarium with exhibits about the state's coastal wildlife
and ecosystems. Kids love seeing the tidal creeks of the
salt marshes, the ocean beaches, and the open waters of
the continental shelf up close. The sea turtles are especially
popular. Don't miss the nearby nature trails. ✉ *30 Ocean
Science Circle, 8 miles south of Savannah, Skidaway Island*
☎ *912/598–3325* ⊕ *marex.uga.edu/visit_aquarium/* 🖃 *$6*
⊙ *Weekdays 9–4, Sat. 10–5* ⊙ *Closed Sun. and holidays.*

Mighty Eighth Air Force Heritage Museum. A famous World
War II squadron called the Mighty Eighth was formed in
Savannah in 1942. Within one month, they answered the
call to arms and shipped out to the United Kingdom. Flying in Royal Air Force planes, the Mighty Eighth became
the largest air force of the period. Exhibits at this museum

begin with the prelude to World War II and the rise of Adolf Hitler, and continue through Desert Storm. You can see vintage aircraft, fly a simulated bombing mission with a B-17 crew, test your skills as a waist gunner, and view interviews with courageous World War II vets. The museum also has three theaters, an art gallery, and a 7,000-volume library. ⊠ *175 Bourne Ave.* ☎ *912/748–8888* ⊕ *www.mightyeighth.org* ⊠ *$10* ⊙ *Daily 9–5.*

FAMILY **Oatland Island Wildlife Center.** A few miles east of the Historic District, this wildlife preserve is home to a variety of animal habitats spread along a 2-mile-long path. Several coastal habitats are represented, including the wetlands that are home to alligators, herons, and cranes. Bobcats, wolves, buffalo, armadillo, and assorted birds of prey are also on exhibit. ■TIP→ **Be sure to bring a camera and comfortable shoes.** ⊠ *711 Sandtown Rd.* ☎ *912/395–1212* ⊕ *www.oatlandisland.org* ⊠ *$5* ⊙ *Daily 10–5; ticket booths close at 4.*

Old Fort Jackson. The oldest standing fort in Georgia was garrisoned in the War of 1812 and was the Confederate headquarters for the river batteries. Surrounded by a tidal moat, the brink fort guards Five Fathom Hole, the 18th-century deep-water port in the Savannah River. Inside you'll see exhibits that highlight the life of a soldier in the 19th century. Battle reenactments, blacksmithing demonstrations, and traditional music programs are among the attractions. ⊠ *1 Fort Jackson Rd.* ☎ *912/232–3945* ⊕ *www. chsgeorgia.org/old-fort-jackson.html* ⊠ *$7* ⊙ *Daily 9–5.*

QUICK BITES. **A-J's.** This island bar and grill resembles a fish camp that was expanded time and time again to accommodate its growing clientele. Colorful and laid back, the ambience is characteristic of Tybee Island itself, which perhaps explains why it is a favorite among locals. With a spacious patio overlooking the marsh, this is a great spot to watch the sunset. The food, mostly fresh seafood, is simple and delicious. ⊠ *1315 Chatham Ave., Tybee Island* ☎ *912/786–9533* ⊕ *ajsdocksidetybee.com.*

Pin Point Heritage Museum. The culturally rich community surrounding this museum has lived in relative isolation for nearly 100 years. Residents of Pin Point are Gullah/Geechee descendants of first-generation freed slaves from Ossabaw Island. Founded in 1890 on the banks of Moon River, this fishing community has a deep connection to the water. Many residents once worked at the A.S.

Varn & Son oyster and crab factory, which has been transformed into this museum to honor the life, work, and history of the community. ✉ *9924 Pin Point Ave.* ☎ *912/355–0064* ⊕ *www.pinpointheritagemuseum.com* ⊘ *Thurs. and Sat. 9–5.*

FAMILY **Tybee Island.** *Tybee* is an Indian word meaning "salt." The Yamacraw Indians came to this island in the Atlantic Ocean to hunt and fish. These days, the island is chock-full of seafood restaurants, chain motels, and souvenir shops—most of which sprang up during the 1950s and haven't changed much since. Fun-loving locals still host big annual parties like fall's Pirate Festival and spring's Beach Bum Parade. Tybee Island's entire expanse of taupe sand is divided into three public beach stretches: North Beach, the Pier and Pavillion, and the South End. Beach activities abound, including swimming, boating, fishing, sea kayaking, and parasailing. Newer water sports have gained popularity, including kiteboarding and stand-up paddle boarding. ✉ *U.S. 80, 18 miles east of Savannah, Tybee Island* ☎ *912/786–5444* ⊕ *tybeeisland.com.*

Tybee Island Lighthouse and Museum. Considered one of North America's most beautifully renovated lighthouses, the Tybee Light Station has been guiding Savannah River mariners since 1736. It's not the first lighthouse built on this site; the original was built on orders of General James Oglethorpe in 1732. You can walk up 178 steps for amazing views at the top. The lighthouse keeper's cottage houses a small theater showing a video about the lighthouse. The nearby museum is housed in a gun battery constructed for the Spanish-American War. ✉ *30 Meddin Dr., Tybee Island* ☎ *912/786–5801* ⊕ *www.tybeelighthouse.org* ⛶ *$9* ⊘ *Wed.–Mon. 9–5:30; last admission at 4:30.*

Tybee Island Marine Science Center. Don't miss the Tybee Island Marine Science Center's interesting exhibit on Coastal Georgia, which houses local wildlife ranging from Ogeechee corn snakes to American alligators. Schedule one of two guided walks along the beach and marshes if you're interested in the flora and fauna of the Lowcountry. There is also a "Turtle Talk," which consists of a classroom discussion and hands-on workshop. ■TIP→ **Arrive early, as parking near the center can be competitive in the busier months.** ✉ *1509 Strand Ave., Tybee Island* ☎ *912/786–5917* ⊕ *www. tybeemarinescience.org* ⛶ *$4; tours $10* ⊘ *Daily 10–5.*

Wormsloe. In 1736 General James Oglethorpe gave 500 acres to Noble Jones, who was required to build a small fort to protect Savannah from an attack up the Skidaway River. Wormsloe is the only property in Georgia remaining in the hands of descendants of the original owners. Over the years, the land was used to produce cotton, as well as fruits, vegetables, and silk. In later years it served as a dairy farm and rice mill. Many of the 400 oaks planted along the mile-and-a-half entry in 1891 still stand proud today— you might recognize them from the movie *Forrest Gump*. Today you can tour the tabby fort ruins, wander around the historic cemetery, and take in colonial plantation reenactments. ✉ *7601 Skidaway Rd* ☎ *912/353–3023* ⊕ *www. gastateparks.org/wormsloe* ⌨ *$10* ☉ *Tues.–Sun. 9–5.*

WHERE TO EAT

3

Updated
by
Summer
Teal
Simpson

SOUTHERN CUISINE IS RICH IN TRADITION, but the dining scene in Savannah is more than just fried chicken and barbecue. Many of the city's restaurants have been exploring locally sourced ingredients as a way to tweak their usual homespun offerings, a change that is now attracting chefs and foodies alike.

Although the farm-to-table trend was first spotted at upscale spots like the Sapphire Grill, Cha Bella, or Local 11ten, more neighborhood restaurants are now getting in on the action. Places like the Green Truck Pub utilize locally raised, grass-fed beef for their burgers, and after-dinner options now even include locally roasted coffee. New to Savannah in 2014, hot spots Pacci's and the Florence carry the farm-to-fork torch as well.

The arrival of some new kids on the block doesn't mean the old standbys have ridden off into the sunset just yet. For traditional, exquisitely prepared menus, be sure to visit Elizabeth's on 37th or the Olde Pink House, both of which have been pleasing local palates for decades. Or follow the crowds to either Paula Deen's famous Lady & Sons or the ever-popular Mrs. Wilkes' Dining Room (which even President Obama once visited), where you'll find all the fried chicken, collard greens, and mac and cheese you can handle. Or beat the lines at locals-only places like Sisters of the New South on the city's Eastside.

If you're looking for barbecue, several spots downtown can satisfy your urge for slow-cooked meats of all kind. For lunch, check out Angel's BBQ, a hole-in-the-wall spot with some of the city's best pork or brisket, as well as fried-bologna sandwiches. Another popular spot with local meat lovers is Wiley's Championship BBQ, located on nearby Wilmington Island. This relative newcomer is now regularly named as the locals' favorite place for barbecue.

That's just a few ideas to get you started. While exploring Savannah, you're sure to find any number of other exciting options as well, whether you're craving noodle bowls or a simple sandwich.

HOURS, PRICES, AND DRESS

Most popular restaurants serve both lunch and dinner, usually around 9 pm, later on Friday and Saturday night. Sunday brunch is a beloved institution, but be prepared to wait for a table at most of the popular spots.

Prices, although on the rise, are lower than in most major cities, especially on either coast.

Some locals and restaurant owners have a laid-back attitude about dressing for a night out. And if you are hitting a River Street tourist restaurant, a small neighborhood eatery, or a barbecue joint, jeans are just fine. However, if you are going to an upscale restaurant, dress in keeping with the environment, especially on weekend nights.

WHAT IT COSTS				
	$	$$	$$$	$$$$
Restaurants	under $15	$15–$19	$20–$24	over $24

Restaurant prices are for a main course at dinner, not including taxes (7.5% on food, 8.5% tax on liquor).

HISTORIC DISTRICT

★ Fodor'sChoice ✕ **22 Square Restaurant & Bar.** *American.* Off the
$$ lobby of the Andaz Hotel, this Ellis Square establishment is a far cry from your typical hotel restaurant. Combining the best local ingredients, pleasing modern decor, and great service, 22 Square offers a unique "farm-to-fork" experience. The Saturday brunch is unmatched by anything else in the city, offering seasonal seafood, choice cuts of meat, fresh produce, an omelet bar, and bottomless mimosas. Choose between a table in the refreshingly simple dining room or in one of the charming seating areas in the lobby. From the dinner menu, try the house-pickled vegetable platter, the tuna carpaccio, or pulled pork belly with corn cakes. ⑤ *Average main: $18 ⊠ Andaz Savannah, 14 Barnard St., Historic District* ☎ *912/629–9493* ⊕ *savannah.andaz.hyatt.com.*

$$$ ✕ **39 Rue de Jean.** *French.* Sister to the famous 39 Rue de Jean restaurant in Charleston, Rue de Jean Savannah also draws inspiration from the style of classic French brasseries. The dining room tranports you to Paris with high ceilings, a lively bar, and comfortable seating throughout. Lunch highlights include the onion soup topped with Gruyère, the traditional Niçoise salad with tuna, or the quiche of the day. At night the kitchen offers classic dishes like braised rabbit, steak topped with peppercorns, and a selection of mussels in your choice of six different boths. ⑤ *Average main: $24 ⊠ 605 W. Oglethorpe Ave.* ☎ *912/721–0595* ⊕ *www.39RuedeJean.com.*

$$$$ ✕ **45 Bistro.** *Modern American.* On the ground floor of the Marshall House, 45 Bistro has some of the best views of Broughton Street from the floor-to-ceiling windows that run the length of the room. The Marshall House might be a historic hotel, but this gem is all about updating old favorites: shrimp and grits married to fried Vidalia onion rings, or the grilled romaine hearts that ignite the exceptional Caesar salad. Most of the menu abounds with regional flavors: local crab, wild shrimp, spiced pecans, and Coca-Cola marinades. But standards like the marbled rib eye are equally as satisfying. Ⓢ *Average main: $34* ✉ *Marshall House, 123 E. Broughton St., Historic District* ☎ *912/234–3111* ⊕ *45bistro.com* ⊗ *Closed Sun. No lunch.*

$$$$ ✕ **700 Drayton Restaurant.** *American.* With its splashy interior, this is a one-of-a-kind spot in Savannah—a true anomaly amid the city's antebellum charms, but a welcome sign of its diverse dining scene. The former Keyton Mansion was converted into a lounge and restaurant that pairs fine dining with eccentric touches like Versace leopard-print chairs. Whether you're looking for a power lunch or a romantic dinner, you'll find it here. To start, the she-crab bisque is flawless, and the cooked-to-perfection Sapelo Island clams are a treat. Breakfast is served daily, and Sunday brunch is nice for special occasions. Ⓢ *Average main: $29* ✉ *Mansion on Forsyth Street, 700 Drayton St., Historic District* ☎ *912/721–5002* ⊕ *700drayton.com.*

$ ✕ **Angel's BBQ.** *Barbecue.* This cozy little spot is a favorite among barbecue fans and a regular stop for foodies. Serving up a simple menu of pork and brisket, either on a bun or with two sides as a plate, the quality and care put into the food is what keeps folks coming back for more. A wide variety of sauces representing all the major Southern styles (including Carolina's mustard base and Memphis's sweet red sauce) make it fun to experiment with flavors, but the house-made hot sauce is a winner. On the side, try the unique take on collard greens (which includes a peanut sauce) or some good old-fashioned mac and cheese. Wash it all down with a glass of sweet tea, or grab a long-neck bottle of Coca-Cola. Ⓢ *Average main: $10* ✉ *21 W. Oglethorpe La., Historic District* ☎ *912/495–0902* ⌔ *Reservations not accepted* ⊗ *Closed Sun. No dinner.*

$ ✕ **B&D Burgers.** *Burger.* Locally owned and operated B&D
FAMILY Burgers is a great bet for a quick, low-key bite to eat. The best offerings include the tempura-style chicken fingers and the grand assortment of locally themed burgers. Favorites include the Wormsloe burger, with pimento cheese and

CLOSE UP

Best Bets for Savannah Dining

With the many restaurants to choose from, how will you decide where to eat? Fodor's writers and editors have selected their favorite restaurants by price, cuisine, and experience in the Best Bets lists *below*. The Fodor's Choice properties represent the "best of the best." Peruse our reviews for details about the restaurants.

Fodor's Choice: 22 Square, Back in the Day Bakery, B. Tillman's, Circa 1875, Elizabeth's on 37th, Garibaldi's, Green Truck Pub, Jepson Café, Leoci's Trattoria, Local 11ten, Mrs. Wilkes' Dining Room, Olde Pink House, Sapphire Grill, Sundae Café, The Florence, Tybee Island Social Club, Wiley's Championship BBQ, Zunzi's

Best Budget Eats: Al Salaam Deli, Back in the Day Bakery, Green Truck Pub, Sundae Café, Vinnie VanGoGo's, Wiley's Championship BBQ, Zunzi's

Best Barbecue: Angel's BBQ, Wiley's Championship BBQ

Best Southern Food: Elizabeth's on 37th, Mrs. Wilkes' Dining Room, Vic's on the River

Best Brunch: B. Matthews Eatery, 22 Square, Huey's Southern Café

Best Lunch: Back in the Day Bakery, Kayak Café, Jepson Café, Sundae Café, Zunzi's

Child-Friendly: Crystal Beer Parlor, Green Truck Pub, The Pirates' House, Vinnie VanGoGo's, Zunzi's, The Crab Shack, B&D Burgers

Best for Foodies: The Florence, Elizabeth's on 37th, Green Truck Pub, Leoci's Trattoria, Local 11ten, Pacci's

Most Romantic: Circa 1875, Elizabeth's on 37th, Noble Fare, Olde Pink House

Outdoor Seating: Local 11ten, The Public Kitchen and Bar, B&D Burgers, Sushi Zen, Vinnie VanGoGo's, Zunzi's

---

fried green tomatoes, or the Fort Pulaski burger, topped with onion rings. Be forewarned that these come sturdy and piled high. The large, two-story dining room is decorated in Lowcountry flair, including faux trophy alligators and nets and buoys. But be encouraged to venture outside; this place has some of the best outdoor dining in the city. The expansive patio is equipped with a video screen for sports events and large umbrellas that protect against the rain and sun. There's a second location on Broughton Street that's usually less crowded. ⑤ *Average main: $11* ⊠ *209 W. Congress St., Historic District* ☎ *912/238–8315* ⊕ *bdburgers. net* ⌖ *Reservations not accepted.*

Where to Eat in Savannah

22 Square, **5**
39 Rue de Jean, **25**
45 Bistro, **20**
700 Drayton Restaurant, **38**
Al Salaam Deli, **43**
Angel's BBQ, **23**
B. Matthews Eatery, **14**
B. Tillman, **50**
B&D Burgers, **4**
Back in the Day Bakery, **34**
Bella's Italian Café, **41**
Bier Haus, **19**
Brighter Day, **33**
Cha Bella, **18**
Circa 1875, **8**
Collins Quarter, **22**
Crystal Beer Parlor, **30**
Dept. 7 East, **10**
Desposito's, **49**
Elizabeth on 37th, **37**
Fire Street Food, **26**
The Florence, **35**
Flying Monk, **9**
Garibaldi's, **3**
Green Truck Pub, **44**
Gryphon Tea Room, **32**
Huey's Southern Café, **12**
Jepson Cafe, **24**
Johnny Harris, **45**
Kayak Cafe, **47**
The Lady & Sons, **7**
Leoci's Trattoria, **42**
Local 11ten, **39**
Mrs. Wilkes'
Dining Room, **31**
Noble Fare, **29**
Olde Pink House, **13**
Pacci's, **16**
Pirates' House, **17**
The Public, **27**
Sapphire Grill, **6**
Savannah Squeeze, **48**
SoHo South Cafe, **28**

Sushi Zen, **1**
Toucan Café, **46**
Vic's on the River, **11**
Vinnie VanGoGo's, **2**
Wiley's Championship
BBQ, **15**
Yia Yia's Kitchen, **40**
Zunzi's, **21**

River St.

Williamson St.

W. Bay St.

W. Bryan St.

Ellis
Sq.

W. Julian St.

W. Congress St.

Ann St.

Martin Luther King Jr. Blvd

W. Broughton St.

Whitaker St.

W. State St.

Telfair
Sq.

W.
President

W. York St.

Montgomery St.

W. Oglethorpe Ave.

Jefferson St.

Barnard St.

W. Hull

Orleans
Sq.

W. Perry

Whitaker St.

Louisville Rd.

W. Harris St.

W. Harris St.

Pulaski
Sq.

W. Charlton St.

Jefferson St.

Tattnall St.

W. Jones St.

W. Taylor St.

Chatham
Sq.

W. Wayne St.

W. Gordon St.

W. Gaston St.

33 – 36

Savannah River

Riverfront Plaza

River St.

12

15 →

Factors Walk

11

E. Bay St.

14

16

17

E. Bryan St.

Johnson
Sq.

E. Julian St.

13

Reynolds
Sq.

Warren
Sq.

E. Congress St.

10

E. Broughton St.

E. Broughton St.

18

20

Lincoln St.

Price St.

Houston St.

East Broad St.

E. State St.

Wright
Sq.

E. President

Oglethorpe
Sq.

Columbia
Sq.

E. President St.

21

E. York St.

22

E. Oglethorpe Ave.

23

Drayton St.

Abercorn St.

Colonial
Park
Cemetery

Habersham St.

19

Chippewa
Sq.

E. Hull

E. Perry

26

E. Liberty St.

E. Liberty St.

27

Bull St.

E. Harris St.

Madison
Sq.

Lafayette
Sq.

E. Macon St.

Troup
Sq.

◆ St. John's Episcopal Church

E. Charlton St.

E. Charlton St.

32

East Broad St.

E. Jones St.

Lincoln St.

Monterey
Sq.

Drayton St.

Calhoun
Sq.

E. Taylor St.

Whitefield
Sq.

E. Wayne St.

E. Gordon St.

0

1/4 mile

0

400 meters

Forsyth
Park

E. Gaston Ln.

Price St.

49 **50**

37–**40**

41

43 **44**

45 **46**

47 **48**

42

$$ ✕**B. Matthews Eatery.** *Eclectic.* The freshly updated and expanded kitchen here offers a great menu that ranges from the familiar to the unexpected. Breakfast is a highlight, while lunch is known for being a great value, with most of the well-stuffed sandwiches going for around $9. Few can resist the fried green tomato and black-eyed pea cakes, served up with Cajun rémoulade and oregano aioli. Dinner entrées are more-upscale fare that won't break the bank, and the best bets include the inventive seafood dishes and the divine braised lamb shank. Ⓢ *Average main: $19* ⊠ *325 E. Bay St., Historic District* ☎ *912/233–1319* ⊕ *www.bmatthewseatery.com* ⊘ *Brunch only on Sun., 10 am–3 pm. No dinner Sun.*

$ ✕**Bier Haus.** *German.* This Belgian–German gastropub has made a name for itself with its generous pots of mussels steamed in your choice of beer. Other favorites include the Schweineschnitzel, a quintessentially German dish consisting of a breaded and fried pork cutlet, and the sausages made by Ogeechee Meat Market. The menu offers several vegetarian options as well, including mushrooms and artichokes with polenta. Aside from the food, Bier Haus rightfully boasts about its 20 rotating taps (10 are Belgian and 6 are German,), plus over 90 bottled beers. Ⓢ *Average main: $14* ⊠ *513 E. Oglethorpe St., Historic District* ☎ *912/349–1167* ⊕ *www.thebierhaus.com* ⊘ *No lunch Sun.*

MONEY-SAVING TIPS. **Purchase a Visitor VIP Dining Club Card for culinary savings during your stay in the Hostess City. It's plastic, just like a credit card, and costs $30. Some of the city's top restaurants are included in the list of more than 100 that honor the card. You might get a free appetizer or dessert, a bottle of wine, or a half-price entrée. Order the card online at** ⊕ *www.savannahmenu.com.*

$ ✕**Brighter Day.** *American.* The bakery and deli counter at Brighter Day Natural Foods is one of Savannah's best-kept secrets. This grocery store offers one of the city's best take-out lunches, and its location at the southern end of Forsyth Park makes it the perfect place to put together a picnic. The deli offers freshly made organic sandwiches with meat, vegetarian, and vegan options, as well as side dishes, salads, and cakes made right on the premises. Our favorites are the baked cheese and avocado sandwich and the stuffed grape leaves. Organic juices and smoothies and shots of organic wheat grass are also on offer. Ⓢ *Average*

CLOSE UP

Cooking School

700 Kitchen. Bring out your inner gourmet chef with a hands-on lesson in five-star food preparation at the 700 Kitchen. This educational and entertaining cooking school is part of the Mansion on Forsyth complex and boasts a state-of-the-art kitchen. No matter your skill level, you'll pick up tips and tricks from the pros. Be ready to get your hands dirty and enjoy tasting what you make. You will be given a little sparkling wine to smooth the palate, as well as a good-quality, long apron with the 700 Kitchen logo. The three-hour classes are held for a minimum of 10 persons, so you may have to buddy up with other people who register. ✉ *Mansion on Forsyth Park, 700 Drayton St., Historic District* ☎ *912/721–5006* ⊕ *www.700kitchen.com.*

main: $8 ✉ *1102 Bull St., Historic District* ☎ *912/236–4703* ⊕ *brighterdayfoods.com.*

$$$$ ✕ **Cha Bella.** *American.* The first farm-to-table restaurant in Savannah, Cha Bella continues to serve only dishes made with the finest local ingredients—the menu changes regularly based on what's fresh and available. Even if you've been here recently, there may be some surprises. A seared black grouper with seasonal veggies makes regular appearances, and it's definitely a highlight. Among the more recent additions is a delightful array of cocktails, including a light and refreshing cucumber mojito. The decor is contemporary and comfortable, but the real dining experience is found outside on the patio during the spring and fall. ⑤ *Average main: $27 ✉ 102 E. Broad St., Historic District* ☎ *912/790–7888* ⊗ *No lunch.*

★ **Fodor's**Choice ✕ **Circa 1875.** *French.* The closest thing you'll
$$$ find to a Parisian bistro in Savannah, this intimate gastropub offers a menu rich of traditional French dishes: escargots and pâté make excellent starters before you move on to main dishes like steak frites or cassoulet. Don't miss the mussels lovingly steeped in fennel, shallots, and white wine (and be sure to ask for extra bread to sop up the heavenly broth). Trust the well-trained staff to suggest a wine pairing for your meal. Head next door to the bar either for a nightcap, or if you're in the mood for a late-night bite, the kitchen stays open late for orders from the bar. ⑤ *Average main: $23 ✉ 48 Whitaker St., Historic District* ☎ *912/443–1875* ⊕ *www.circa1875.com* ⊗ *No lunch. Closed Sun.*

$$ ✕**Collins Quarter.** *Café*. Ideally situated to intercept passersby traversing busy Bull Street, the Collins Quarter offers a little something for everyone. Coffee afficionados appreciate the robust cups of joe made with innovative equipment, including cold-brew towers and a La Marzocco espresso machine. Foodies enjoy the curated menu—try the smoked and poached trout or the green gazpacho for a light bite. More substancial fare includes the crispy duck breast or the roasted eggplant with toasted pumpkin seeds and pomegranate. The beer selection includes favorites from craft breweries around the country, and the wines were carefully selected from some of the world's most storied regions to compliment the food. It's a sophisticated space where you can relax, enjoy a date night, or indulge in a business lunch. ⑤ *Average main: $17* ✉ *151 Bull St., Historic District* ☎ *912/777–4147* ⊕ *thecollinsquarter.com.*

$$ ✕**Crystal Beer Parlor.** *American*. This former speakeasy has
FAMILY been serving hungry locals since 1933. The back dining rooms are covered in historic newspaper clippings and local ephemera, while those around the bar maintains several of the original highback booths. As you can tell from the decor, this place is a landmark—and that goes for the menu, too. Anyone craving the basics heads here for delicious burgers, wings, and sandwiches. Be sure to try the creamy she-crab soup—it's not diet-friendly, but is well worth the indulgence. The homemade potato chips are an institution and the shrimp salad is some of the best you'll ever have. ⑤ *Average main: $15* ✉ *301 W. Jones St., Historic District* ☎ *912/349–1000* ⊕ *www.crystalbeerparlor. com* ⚐ *Reservations not accepted.*

$ ✕**Dept. 7 East.** *Southern*. This historic storefront has remained in the owner's family for nearly a century, and those familiar with the city may recognize it as the Savannah Tea Room. Although traditional tea service is no longer among the offerings here, you can stock up on local teas at the charming gift shop adjacent to the wine bar. Chef Meta Adler has designed a Southern fusion menu with charmers (and fillers) like the Redneck Reuben and the Deviled Eggs. For "supper," the Dixie Chicken and cornmeal waffles can't be beat. ⑤ *Average main: $14* ✉ *7 E. Broughton St., Historic District* ☎ *912/232–0215* ⊕ *dept7east.com* ⚐ *Reservations not accepted* ⊗ *Closed Sun.*

★ **Fodor's**Choice ✕**Elizabeth on 37th.** *Southern*. Set within the Vic-
$$$$ torian District, this elegant turn-of-the-20th-century mansion has been feeding Savannah's upper crust for decades. Regional specialties are the hallmark at this acclaimed

restaurant, which credits local produce suppliers on its menu. Chef Kelly Yambor has helmed the kitchen since 1996, and she replicates the blue-crab cakes that sit comfortably beside the Southern-fried grits and the honey-roasted pork tenderloin with roasted shiitake and oyster mushrooms. Splurge for the chef's seven-course tasting menu—you won't regret it. Don't be afraid to ask for wine recommendations, because the wine cellar is massive and the staff is knowledgeable. As might be imagined, the service is impeccable. ⑤ *Average main: $35* ⊠ *105 E. 37th St., Thomas Square* ☎ *912/236–5547* ⊕ *www.elizabethon37th. net* ⚐ *Reservations essential* ⊗ *No lunch.*

$ ✕**Fire Street Food.** *Modern Asian.* Restaurateurs Ele and Sean Tran opened Fire Street Food with the intention of bringing Asian-style street food to Savannah. The menu boasts everything from sushi rolls to noodle soups. The sweet-and-spicy chicken wings are some of the best in town, as is the signature salad with homemade ginger dressing. Occupying a bright, hypermodern space, this eatery offers an offbeat alternative to the slow-paced Southern Savannah feel. Enjoy a quick meal in the dining room, stop by when you have a late-night craving, or order a few of the small plates to go. ⑤ *Average main: $14* ⊠ *13 E. Perry St., Historic District* ☎ *912/234–7776* ⊕ *firestreetfood.com* ⚐ *Reservations not accepted.*

★ **Fodors**Choice ✕**The Florence.** *Modern Italian.* Housed in an **$$$** old Savannah ice factory, the Florence has lots of original architectural details and serves up some of the city's most innovative flavors. The Italian-influenced menu is crafted by Kyle Jacovino, who has worked in kitchens all over Atlanta and New York. The food speaks for itself, and you can't go wrong with anything on the menu. There are raves all around for the spicy diavolo pizza made with salami and Italian chilies, the farmer's egg starter served atop crispy polenta, and the squid-ink buccatini. Dont miss the cider-glazed ribs, rubbed in coffee, cooked for hours, and polished with a cider–pecan glaze. For cocktails, head to the upstairs bar and enjoy the signature Florence Cup—a twist on the Pimm's Cup—or an impressive array of amaros and other liqueurs. The adjacent coffee bar is open in the morning and offers small bites during lunch hours. ■TIP➔ **If you have trouble getting a table, grab a seat at the bar.** ⑤ *Average main: $21* ⊠ *1B W. Victory Dr., Historic District* ☎ *912/234–5522* ⊕ *theflorencesavannah.com* ⚐ *Reservations essential* ⊗ *Closed Mon. No lunch.*

BEST LOCAL SPECIALTIES

Barbecue. Whether it's part of a platter or served on a bun, the most common form of BBQ hereabouts is low-and-slow-cooked pulled pork. Running a close second are ribs (usually with dry rub), followed by brisket, which you'll only find at a handful of spots. The coastal Georgia style of sauce (best exhibited by the sauce from local favorite Johnny Harris) is a tomato base mixed with mustard, vinegar, and spices. Most places make their own sauce, so each will be a little different, but the mustard- or vinegar-based varieties found in the Carolinas are less common here. Wiley's BBQ, on the way out to Tybee, is a relative newcomer to the area, but has become a fast favorite, raking in loads of accolades. At Angel's the meats are cooked low and slow, and their homemade sauces, which run the gamut of regional styles, are top-notch.

Classic Lowcountry Cuisine. Traditional specialties like shrimp and grits are still menu mainstays at many restaurants, such as the ever-popular Huey's. Variations on she-crab soup abound; there are great ones at the Crystal Beer Parlor or the Olde Pink House, for example. The best ones are made with sinful amounts of butter and heavy cream but are worth the rare indulgence. Although a dish called Lowcountry Boil is more common at cookouts than on restaurant menus, keep an eye out for an opportunity to try it. This tantalizing mix of shrimp, smoked sausage, corn on the cob, and potatoes is boiled in huge pots with plenty of seasoning.

Reinvented Local Favorites. Although Southern cuisine has some of the longest-running food traditions in the country, young chefs are giving a number of the old favorites a new spin. At B. Matthews you might find black-eyed-pea cake with Cajun rémoulade or fried-green-tomato sandwiches with oregano aioli. The Olde Pink House serves an innovative shrimp 'n' grits with Andouille sausage and sweet-potato biscuits.

The Freshest Seafood. In most places worth your dining dollars, seafood is fresh off the Lowcountry boats. The most beloved local fruit of the sea is white shrimp, caught just off the shores of Tybee. You'll find them served all sorts of ways: in po'boy sandwiches, deep-fried, and mixed with grits. Keep an eye out for local grouper, red fish, and oysters. Perhaps the tastiest coastal mainstay is the blue crab, which flourishes in the marsh estuaries off the coast.

$ ✕**The Flying Monk Noodle Bar.** *Asian Fusion.* Noodle, rice, and soup dishes from across Asia come together on the eclectic, flavorful menu at the Flying Monk. The well-appointed space and laid-back atmosphere compliment the savory dishes. Start with vegetarian-friendly edamame dumplings or the meaty braised pork belly. Move on to the signature Vienamese pho or Japanese ramen noodle soups. For those interested in a traditional rice dish, the curry can't be beat. Ⓢ*Average main: $9* ✉*5 W. Broughton St., Historic District* ☎*912/232–8888* ⊕*eleandthechef.com.*

★ **Fodor's**Choice ✕**Garibaldi's.** *Modern Italian.* This well-
$$$ appointed restaurant is well known to locals and travelers alike for its contemporary cuisine. The original tin ceilings are a burnished gold, the bar and its fixtures are opulent, and the circular maple tables have leather booth seats. Renowned for well-priced Italian classics, the kitchen also sends out some much more ambitious offerings, albeit at slightly higher prices. There are such unforgettable appetizers as lamb ribs (slow-cooked with a sweet ginger sauce and pear-cabbage relish) or a salad with poached pear, arugula, walnuts, and goat-cheese fritters with a port-wine vinaigrette. The crispy flounder entrée is the stuff of local legend; the entire fish is drizzled with an incredible apricot and shallot sauce. Have your knowledgeable and professional server offer wine pairings from the intelligent and global wine cart. Ⓢ*Average main: $21* ✉*315 W. Congress, Historic District* ☎*912/232–7118* ⊕*www.garibaldisavannah.com* ⚖*Reservations essential* ☾*No lunch.*

$ ✕**Gryphon Tea Room.** *American.* Shimmering stained glass, stunning woodwork, and magnificent decor make this old-time pharmacy one of the handsomest settings in town, and the menu is as groomed as the atmosphere. Delectable sandwiches and salads are the main bill of fare, and winners include the classic chicken salad with mandarin orange souffle and the croque monsieur on challah bread. For more ambitious selections, opt for the ratatouille and shrimp orzo, served with locally caught wild Georgia shrimp. Of course, this is the place for traditional afternoon high tea, and few competitors can beat the expansive range of teas, from English breakfast to Black Dragon oolong. Ⓢ*Average main: $12* ✉*337 Bull St., Historic District* ☎*912/525–5880* ⊕*www.scad.edu/experience/gryphon* ⚖*Reservations not accepted* ☾*No dinner.*

$$ ✕**Huey's Southern Café.** *Creole.* Ideal for people-watching,
FAMILY this riverside spot also offers great views of passing ships. So far as Southern food goes, Huey's is decidedly more New

Orleans than Coastal Georgia, but it's not too far from home, as you'll discover with one bite of the sinfully rich beignets served with praline sauce—they are a taste of perfection. Although lunch and dinner items like po'boys and muffaletta accompanied by red beans and rice are delicious, the breakfast and brunch menu is the highlight. Pair one of the Bloody Marys (among the best in the city) with eggs Sardou, an eggs Benedict dish where the Canadian bacon is replaced by a garlicky spinach and artichoke concoction. The menu is definitely kid-friendly, too, so this can be a good option for families. ⑤ *Average main: $18 ✉ 115 E. River St.* ☎ *912/234–7385* ⊕ *hueysontheriver.net.*

★ **Fodor'sChoice** ✕ **Jepson Cafe.** *American.* Housed in the modern-
$ art extension of the Telfair Museum, the Jepson Cafe is an exquisite culinary experience. The small dining room is adorned with rotating temporary art installations. Overlooking the Jepson atrium, the space mimics the minimalist–modern feel of the building. Gourmands should look no further for lunch: Start with the tuna poke over sliced avocado, or the fresh summer rolls of local poached shrimp, fresh basil, and a peanut-hoisin sauce. The café uses lots of local purveyors, including Perc coffee, Savannah Bee Company honey, Savannah Tea Room mint tea, and Angel's BBQ for its pork shoulder. The proscuitto, fig, and brie panino is mouthwatering and perfectly melds these salty, sweet, and creamy flavors. ⑤ *Average main: $9 ✉ Jepson Center, 207 W. York St., Historic District* ☎ *912/790–8833* ⊕ *telfair.org/cafe* ⊘ *No dinner.*

$$$ ✕ **The Lady & Sons.** *Southern.* Line up to get a reservation for lunch or dinner because, y'all, this is the place that Paula Deen, high priestess of Southern cooking, made famous. Alas, the quality suffers these days because of the crowds. (Locals will tell you that in the early days, when Deen was doing her own cooking, it was decidedly better.) Nevertheless, everyone patiently waits to attack the buffet, which is stocked for both lunch and dinner with crispy fried chicken, mashed potatoes, collard greens, lima beans, and other favorites. Peach cobbler and banana pudding round off the offerings. You can order off the menu, too. The fried green tomatoes are a great starter, and long-time fans vouch for the crab-cake burger at lunch or chicken potpie or barbecue grouper at dinner. ⑤ *Average main: $23 ✉ 102 W. Congress St., Historic District* ☎ *912/233–2600* ⊕ *www.ladyandsons.com* ⌂ *Reservations essential* ⊘ *No dinner Sun.*

★ Fodor'sChoice ✕ **Leoci's Trattoria.** *Italian.* Chef Roberto Leoci
$$ learned his unique take on traditional Italian dishes the
old-fashioned way, while spending time with his grand-
mother in Sicily. He worked behind the line at several
prestigious spots around the Southeast before opening up
this place, a block east of Forsyth Park. Although a little
off the beaten path, Leoci's became an instant hit with local
food fanatics. Few can resist the carpaccio or the beet salad
with blue cheese and champagne tarragon vinagrette. The
orecchiette pasta tossed with broccoli and sausage and the
seafood fettucini are both great entrées. (If you think there's
no difference between fresh pasta and store-bought dry
pasta, prepare to learn an important lesson.) Save room for
homemade gelato for dessert. The relatively small dining
room is complemented by a large outdoor patio, which is
great when the weather's nice. ⑤ *Average main: $18* ⊠ *606
Abercorn St., Historic District* ☎ *912/335–7027* ⊕ *www.
leocis.com* ⚄ *Reservations essential.*

★ Fodor'sChoice ✕ **Local 11ten.** *Modern American.* Light years
$$$$ away from your average neighborhood watering hole,
this stark, minimalist place looks like it was transported
from a bigger, more sophisticated city. That also goes for
the upbeat and contemporary menu, a reason why young
chefs head here on their nights off. Seasonally driven, the
menu is continually changing depending on the local har-
vest and the chef's vision, but they are usually perfectly
prepared and presented. When available, the fried oyster
salad, charcuterie selection, and venison medallions are
highly recommended. Local has perfected its sea scallops,
which are fantastic when served over black rice with pickled
watermelon rind. With dessert, take in the fine-art instal-
lations on the walls, which rotate regularly to feature the
best local talent. ⑤ *Average main: $30* ⊠ *1110 Bull St.,
Historic District* ☎ *912/790–9000* ⊕ *www.local11ten.com*
⚄ *Reservations essential* ⊘ *No lunch.*

★ Fodor'sChoice ✕ **Mrs. Wilkes' Dining Room.** *Southern.* Everyone
$$ knows that this is the city's best Southern cuisine: When
FAMILY President Barack Obama was visiting Savannah, he and his
entourage had lunch here. Luckily he didn't have to join the
rest of the folks lined up outside in order to enjoy the fine
Southern fare, which is served family-style at big tables.
It's been in the same family for decades, and the original
Miz Wilkes really did run this historic place as a boarding house, serving three meals a day. Her granddaughter
and great-grandson are keeping it a family affair in more
ways than one (kids under 12 eat for half-price). These

days you can expect fried or roasted chicken, beef stew, collard greens, mashed potatoes, macaroni and cheese, sweet-potato soufflé, and corn bread, along with favorites like banana pudding for dessert. No alcohol is served, but you can get a lot of sweet tea. ⑤ *Average main: $18* ⊠ *107 W. Jones St., Historic District* ☎ *912/232–5997* ⊕ *www. mrswilkes.com* ⌖ *Reservations not accepted* ═ *No credit cards* ⊙ *Closed weekends and Jan. No dinner.*

$$$$ ✕ **Noble Fare.** *Eclectic.* In a gentrified neighborhood, this eatery's clientele ranges from thirtysomethings celebrating a special occasion to well-heeled older residents who love the elegant atmosphere. The decor is "dressy," a study in opulent black, white, and red. The bread service includes honey butter, pistachio pesto, olive oil, and balsamic vinegar for your biscuits, flat breads, rolls, and focaccia, all of which are artistically presented on contemporary dishes. Among the choice appetizers are tuna tartare with avocado and a fabulous shrimp bisque. The scallops are laudable, and the fish is so fresh it practically moves on your plate. The honey-cured pork chop melts in your mouth. A prix-fixe tasting menu is available as well. A savory meal can produce a chemical need for chocolate, so the molten-lava cake with raspberry sauce and custard ice cream may be a requirement, especially paired with a Zinfandel port. ⑤ *Average main: $33* ⊠ *321 Jefferson St., Historic District* ☎ *912/443–3210* ⊕ *www.noblefare.com* ⌖ *Reservations essential* ⊙ *No lunch. Closed Sun. and Mon.*

★ **Fodor'sChoice** ✕ **Olde Pink House.** *Southern.* This Georgian
$$$$ mansion was built in 1771 for James Habersham, one of the wealthiest Americans of his time, and the historic atmosphere comes through in the original Georgia pine floors of the tavern, the Venetian chandeliers, and the 18th-century English antiques. A more contemporary dining room has vintage pine floors and walls. A lovely bar has curvaceous doors that can be flung open on balmy nights for outdoor seating. Expect great service and amazing food. How about a classic chicken potpie with roasted veggies, porcini cream sauce, and a sweet-potato biscuit? ■**TIP**➔ **For a more intimate expereience, head downstairs to the Planter's Tavern, where the dining area is flanked by two large fireplaces.** ⑤ *Average main: $26* ⊠ *23 Abercorn St., Historic District* ☎ *912/232–4286* ⌖ *Reservations essential* ⊙ *No lunch Sun. and Mon.*

$$$ ✕ **Pacci's Kitchen + Bar.** *Italian.* Guests at this Savannah newcomer gather in the beautifully designed dining room or the open-air patio for signature cocktails like the Biarritz or the Negroni before moving on to some of the best charcuterie and crudites platters in the city. Breads, pastas, desserts, and pickled vegetables are all made in-house. The asparagus carbonara antipasti is richly fulfilling. Chef Roberto Leoci's kitchen is best known for its fish dishes, like the striped bass prepared in a white wine and caper sauce or the pan-seared flounder with herb-roasted potatoes. Pacci's has the look and taste of a high-end eatery, but with a laid-back and welcoming atmosphere. ⑤ *Average main: $22* ⊠ *Brice Hotel, 601 E. Bay St., Historic District* ☎ *912/233–6002* ⊕ *www.paccisavannah.com.*

$$$ × **Pirates' House.** *Southern.* A Savannah landmark, this 1753

FAMILY house is steeped in history, including scary tales of trap doors and secret passages leading down to the waterfront that were used to take inebriated patrons out to waiting boats (they'd wake up at sea and be given the choice between working on the boat or swimming several miles back to shore). Its popularity with tour groups has given it a reputation as a tourist trap, but the food is pretty good, with plenty of kid-pleasing choices. The lunch buffet has all the Southern standards, but the food is better on the à la carte menu. The baby back ribs and the honey-pecan chicken are highlights. There's no buffet for dinner, but the dessert menu is worth sticking around for. ⑤ *Average main: $22* ⊠ *20 E. Broad St., Historic District* ☎ *912/233–5757* ⊕ *www.thepirateshouse.com.*

$$ × **The Public Kitchen and Bar.** *American.* There is no handsomer space to dine in all of Savannah. Public Kitchen and Bar has it all: a prime location at the corner of Liberty and Bull streets, café-style outdoor dining, and a chic bar adorned with an industrial-style chandalier. Despite the upscale atmosphere, the food is approachable and affordable. The contemporary classics include a locally sourced burger, shrimp, and grits, and mussels steamed with chorizo and leeks. Not hungry? Don't be afraid to belly up to the bar for a finely crafted cocktail or a glass of wine. ⑤ *Average main: $16* ⊠ *1 W. Liberty St., Historic District* ☎ *912/790–9000* ⊕ *www.thepublickitchen.com* ⌳ *Reservations not accepted.*

★ Fodor'sChoice × **Sapphire Grill.** *American.* Savannah's foodies

$$$$ pack this trendy haunt with its surprisingly chic interior and artistic culinary creations. Downstairs, the decor is hip—think converted industrial loft—with gray brick walls and a stone bar; upstairs is quieter and a little more romantic. Chef Chris Nason focuses his seasonal menus on local ingredients, such as Georgia white shrimp, crab, and fish, all of it prepared with flair. Look for myriad interesting accompaniments, such as jalapeño tartar sauce, sweet soy-wasabi sauce, and lemongrass butter. The six-course chef's tasting menu, with fresh seafood and top-quality meats, is $100 and worth every penny. Chocoholics alert: you will find your bliss in the miniature cocoa gâteau with lavender-almond ice cream. From the bar, the hand-muddled mojito is a thing of beauty and delicious fortitude. If you and, say, nine of your favorite people want to celebrate, reserve the private wine room on the third floor. ⑤ *Average main: $36* ⌧ *10 W. Congress St., Historic District* ☎ *912/443–9962* ⊕ *www.sapphiregrill.com* ⌕ *Reservations essential* ☉ *No lunch.*

SUNDAY BRUNCH. On Sunday, Savannah's churches are packed to the choir loft, so follow the hungry, postservice crowds for some great cuisine. Given the local fishing traditions and the city's proximity to the ocean, it should be no surprise that seafood appears as brunch items more often in these parts than in other parts of the country. Keep an eye out for seafood omelets with hollandaise sauce, or eggs Benedict, served with a crab cake rather than Canadian bacon. Another local staple is shrimp and grits, which you'd be remiss not to try at least once while in town. If you're not a fan of seafood, don't fret: the ever-popular Southern tradition of sausage-gravy-smothered biscuits is a fine way to start the day, and there's always bacon and eggs, if you're not feeling adventurous.

$$$ ✕ **SoHo South Cafe.** *Eclectic.* A garage turned art gallery and, finally, a restaurant, this spot shares the aesthetic hallmarks of all its previous incarnations. Inside, the gallery roots are still strong thanks to the interesting art. But the food is the reason why people still make this a regular stop, especially for Sunday brunch. The playful menu includes a salmon BLT and a meat-loaf sandwich, as well as the signature tomato-basil bisque accompanying the grilled cheese on sourdough with pimento aioli—all best bets for lunchtime patrons. Dinner favorites include the Durrence Farms burger or the bourbon-glazed beef short ribs. There's also a small but well-rounded selection of craft beers and wine. ⑤ *Average main: $21* ⌧ *12 W. Liberty St., Historic District* ☎ *912/233–1633* ⊕ *www.sohosouthcafe. com* ⌕ *Reservations not accepted* ☉ *No dinner Sun–Wed.*

$$ ✕ **Sushi Zen.** *Japanese.* If you've had your fill of Southern cuisine, head to this downstairs spot that regularly wins awards for its sushi. That's not surprising, as chef and owner Kazumi Yoshimoto focuses on fresh ingredients and creative combinations, and his results are consistently delicious. The dining room's simple design and a mix of seating arrangements is only the beginning: The crown jewel is the patio, a wonderful spot to enjoy a pleasant evening, particularly in spring and fall. Check out the daily list of specialty rolls, or opt for something from the list of grilled meat and noodle dishes. For those burning the midnight oil, Sushi Zen is open past 3 am on weekends. ⑤ *Average main: $17 ⊠ 30 Martin Luther King Jr. Blvd., Historic District ☎ 912/233–1187 ⊕ www.sushizen-sav.com ⊘ Closed Mon. No lunch.*

$$$$ ✕ **Vic's on the River.** *Southern.* This upscale Southern charmer is one of the finest spots in town for well-executed Southern delicacies. The five-story brick building was designed by the famous New York architect John Norris as a warehouse and was painstakingly renovated into the elegant space you'll find these days. Reserve a window table for great views of the Savannah River. Lunch is popular with local business executives and out-of-towners looking for a quick and delicious seafood po'boy or Angus burger. The wine list is nothing short of formidable and suits every palate and price range. For dinner, herb-crusted grouper is accompanied by sautéed trumpet mushrooms, green apples, grape tomatoes, and fingerling sweet potatoes and topped with a leek cream sauce. The super-rich praline cheesecake is strongly recommended. Grab a copy of the eatery's cookbook to get a closer look at the kitchen. ⑤ *Average main: $26 ⊠ 26 E. Bay St., Historic District ☎ 912/721–1000 ⊕ www.vicsontheriver.com.*

$ ✕ **Vinnie VanGoGo's.** *Pizza.* With a secret dough recipe and
FAMILY a homemade sauce, Vinnie's is critically acclaimed by pizza and calzone enthusiasts from around the Southeast. There are only a few tables inside, along with a long stretch of stools at the bar. The heart of the restaurant is its plentiful outdoor seating, great for people-watching. Lots of visitors get a kick out of watching the cooks throw the dough in the air in the big open kitchen. Because of its prime City Market location, the wait for a table can be an hour or more, but you'll understand why with one bite of your pie. ■TIP→ **Vinnie's is cash only, but there is a nearby ATM.** ⑤ *Average main: $12 ⊠ 317 W. Bryan St., City Market ☎ 912/233–6394 ⊕ www.vinnievangogo.com ⌚ Reservations not accepted ⊟ No credit cards ⊘ No lunch Mon.–Thurs.*

★ Fodor's Choice ✕ **Zunzi's.** *South African.* The line out the door is
$ testament to the yummy flavors found inside this take-out restaurant. Owned and operated by Johnny and Gabriella

DeBeer, the place has a menu filled with South African, Dutch, Italian, and Swiss influences. A favorite sandwich is the Conquistador, French bread piled high with grilled chicken and the signature sauce. There's also a respectable selection of vegetarian options, including the vegetarian curry, which is especially delightful when washed down with Zunzi's unique sweet tea. Trust us: this place is worth every minute of the wait. ⑤ *Average main: $9* ✉ *108 E. York St., Historic District* ☎ *912/443–9555* ⊕ *zunzis.com* ⌦ *Reservations not accepted* ⊗ *Closed Sun. No dinner.*

ELSEWHERE IN SAVANNAH

$ × **Al Salaam Deli.** *Middle Eastern.* If your tastebuds are bored with the same old thing, head to one of Savannah's few restaurants specializing in Middle Eastern fare. Owned and operated by a husband and wife team, Al Salaam is celebrated for its moist and authentic falafel, spit-roasted lamb, and platters with hummus or baba ganoush. The food is plentiful and the prices are low. Take time to look around the small space, enticingly papered over with vintage covers of *National Geographic* and depicting cultures from the world over. ⑤ *Average main: $9* ✉ *2311 Habersham St., Thomas Square* ☎ *912/447–0400* ⌦ *Reservations not accepted* ⊗ *Closed Sun.*

★ Fodor'sChoice × **Back in the Day Bakery.** *Bakery.* From the folksy
$ artworks to the sweet splashes of pastels to the banners hanging from the ceiling, this corner bakery evokes a spirit of days gone by. A great place to start your day with a cup of coffee and a pastry, Back in the Day also serves fresh and yummy lunch selections. The chicken salad is delicious in both forms (rosemary or curried), and there's a good variety of both meaty and vegetarian sandwiches, each presented on homemade breads. Whenever you come here, don't miss the most famous delights on the menu: the city's most sinful cupcakes. A trip to this cheerful café will undoubtedly remind you, as the slogan goes, to "Slow down and taste the sweet life." ⑤ *Average main: $7* ✉ *2403 Bull St., Thomas Square* ☎ *912/495–9292* ⊕ *backinthedaybakery. com* ⊗ *Closed Sun. and Mon. No dinner.*

$$ × **Bella's Italian Café.** *Italian.* From its unpretentious location in a shopping center, this wildly popular eatery serves up simple Italian fare, including ziti, pizza, and panini, as well as particularly good manicotti. Just be sure not to fill up on the incredible breadsticks they serve with a choice of herb butter or marinara. Desserts are standout versions of clas-

sics, such as Italian wedding cake, tiramisu, and cannoli. Although a good choice for family dining, this spot has enough enough ambience to be romantic. Add in the genial, hospitable service, and this makes a perfect place to relax over a glass of wine. ⑤ *Average main: $15* ✉ *4420 Habersham St., Midtown* ☎ *912/354–4005* ⊕ *www.bellascafe. com* ⚲ *Reservations not accepted* ⊘ *No lunch weekends.*

★ **Fodor'sChoice** ✕ **B. Tillman.** *Southern.* This restaurant dates back
$$$ to 1924, when Ben T. Byrd began baking small batches of cookies in his Savannah bakery; today the Byrd Cookie Company distributes far and wide. Guests of the simple yet sophisticated restaurant, specializing in soups, salads, and sandwiches, can catch a peek inside the factory from the dining room. Countless menu items are made on the premises, from the breads to the pickles to the ricotta cheese. Savor the deviled eggs, roasted turnip bisque, or the thick-cut BLT with pesto aioli, each adding a refined twist to a Southern favorite. In the evening, the seared sheepsheads are a delectable selection. ⑤ *Average main: $21* ✉ *6700 Waters Ave., Southside* ☎ *912/721–1564* ⊕ *www. byrdcookiecompany.com* ⊘ *No lunch Sat. No dinner Sun.*

INTERNATIONAL EATS. Savannah's food offerings run deeper than just traditional Southern cooking. If you've got a taste for French, head to Circa 1875 (✉ *48 Whitaker St.* ☎ *912/443–1875* ⊕ *www. circa1875.com*), which serves traditional dishes like steak frites and cassoulet. If it's the islands you crave, head to the South-side of Savannah for a meal at Sweet Spice (✉ *5515 Waters Ave.* ☎ *912/335–8146* ⊕ *www.sweetspicerestaurant.com*). They serve up traditional favorites like jerk chicken and curried goat. For more exotic Korean flavors, make your way to Kim Chi II (✉149 *E. Montgomery Cross Rd.* ☎ *912/920–7273*). Try the fiery *kimchi banchan* or the bubbling-hot pork-and-tofu stew.

$ ✕ **Desposito's.** *Seafood.* This place is about as low key as it
FAMILY gets, as evidenced by the neon beer signs on the walls and the day-old newspapers doubling as tablecloths. Located just across the bridge from Savannah, Desposito's has been serving up cold beer and fresh fish for decades. The no-nonsense menu offers a small but tempting variety of seafood, including steamed oysters, boiled shrimp, and local blue crab. For the landlubbers, try the chili or sausage dog. No doubt about it: This is a great place to bring the kids. ⑤ *Average main: $9* ✉ *3501 Marye St., Whitemarsh Island* ☎ *912/897–9963* ⊘ *Closed Mon. No lunch on weekdays.*

★ Fodor'sChoice ✕ **Green Truck Pub.** *Burger.* Serving one of the best $ burgers in the state, this casual haunt draws diners from far FAMILY and wide for its grass-fed beef. Vegetarians find satisfaction with the hearty meatless patties. Everything from the coffee to the produce is locally sourced, and even the ketchup are made in-house. Little wonder this is one of the most popular restaurants in town. ■ TIP→ **Be prepared to wait at least 30 minutes for a table or grab a seat at the bar.** ⑤ *Average main: $10* ✉ *2430 Habersham St., Thomas Square* ☎ *912/234–5885* ⊕ *greentruckpub.com* ☾ *Closed Sun. and Mon.*

$$ ✕ **Johnny Harris.** *Southern.* It opened in 1924 as a small road-FAMILY side stand across from Grayson Stadium, and since then Johnny Harris has grown into one of the city's most beloved mainstays. Expect a trip down Memory Lane, as the ambience here is straight out of the 1950s. You'll have to go in the evening to check out the domed ceiling's twinkling lights, shedding a glow on the the 360-degree mural of rural landscapes below. The menu is pure Lowcountry, including favorites like Brunswick stew, Southern fried chicken, and barbecued meats spiced with the restaurant's famous barbecue sauce. The hickory-smoked pork (watch it cooking over the pits) is a particular treat. Don't forget to buy a bottle of sauce to take home with you. ⑤ *Average main: $17* ✉ *1651 E. Victory Dr., Eastside* ☎ *912/354–7810* ⊕ *www.johnnyharris.com.*

$ ✕ **Kayak Cafe.** *Vegetarian.* This palm-shaded eatery is hands down the best spot in town for vegetarian and vegan options. One of our favorite salads has a generous helping of hummus and tabbouleh. But there's also more than enough on the menu to keep a meat eater happy—consider the fried chicken tacos or the chicken and goat cheese enchiladas. If you have your mind on a cocktail, don't miss the Palm (made with muddled cucumber) or the Hot Derby (with spicy ginger ale from just over the South Carolina border). There's ample parking and a screen where you can watch the big game. ⑤ *Average main: $10* ✉ *5002 Paulsen St., Southside* ☎ *912/349–4371* ⊕ *www.eatkayak.com* ☾ *Closed Sun.*

$ ✕ **Savannah Squeeze.** *Vegetarian.* This is the city's first cold-pressed juice bar, with special equipment that extracts all the nutrients from fruits and vegetables. Each bottle contains two to three pounds of produce, most of it organic. A little outside town, Savannah Squeeze is well worth the trip for anyone interested in the healthiest juices. Try the carrot cake smoothie—it's as good as it sounds. Vegan snacks are also on offer. ⑤ *Average main: $9* ✉ *5002 Paulsen St., Southside* ☎ *912/349–4723* ⊕ *savannahsqueeze.com* ⬧ *Reservations not accepted* ☾ *Closed Sun.*

CLOSE UP

Savannah BBQ

Low and slow is the mantra of Savannah's barbecue pit masters who have perfected the region's tender, juicy, and mildly smoky style of pulled pork, traditionally served with sauce on the side. At **Wiley's Championship BBQ** (⊠ *4700 U.S. Hwy. 80 E* ☎ *912/201–3259* ⊕ *www.wileyschampionshipbbq. com*) a wall of awards testifies to Wiley's skill. The pulled pork and beef brisket are must-haves; make sure to save room for the bread pudding. **Angel's**

BBQ (⊠ *21 W. Oglethorpe La.* ☎ *912/495–0902* ⊕ *www. angels-bbq.com*) seats only 12 but prepares 10 times that of its juicy pulled-pork sandwiches for carryout. One of Savannah's original barbecue spots is **Johnny Harris** (⊠ *1651 E. Victory Dr.* ☎ *912/354–7810* ⊕ *www.johnnyharris.com*). Ribs, chicken, pulled pork, and Southern sides are served in a dining room that remains largely unchanged since its heyday in the 1930s and '40s.

$$ ✕**Toucan Café.** *Caribbean.* A bit off the beaten path, this colorful café has a light and cheery interior that invites good times with good food and good company. The menu, ranging from Caribbean to Mediterranean, is nothing if not eclectic. There are appealing options for both vegetarians and meat eaters, including deep-fried portobello mushrooms, wasabi-crusted tuna, and Jamaican-style jerk chicken. The regular menu is priced a little lower than the daily specials, but the latter usually have more flair. ⑤ *Average main: $16* ⊠ *531 Stephenson Ave., Southside* ☎ *912/352–2233* ⊕ *www.toucancafe.com* ⊗ *Closed Sun.*

★ **Fodor's**Choice ✕**Wiley's Championship BBQ.** *Barbecue.* Tucked **$** away in a strip mall on the way out to Tybee Island, this relative newcomer to the local BBQ scene has become an instant favorite with locals. The pulled pork is moist and flavorful, and the brisket is the best you'll find outside Texas. Try the BBQ sampler, which is enough to feed two people, and will let you sample just about everything they make. The small space is intimate and friendly and the staff is like long-lost family. There are only a few tables though, so you may have to choose between waiting for a seat and grabbing something to go. Be aware that Wiley's will close early if they run out of barbecue—so it doesn't hurt to show up early. ⑤ *Average main: $13* ⊠ *4700 U.S. Hwy. 80 E, Wilmington Island* ☎ *912/201–3259* ⊕ *www. wileyschampionshipbbq.com* ⊛ *Reservations not accepted* ⊗ *Closed Sun.*

$ ✕ **Yia Yia's Kitchen.** *Greek.* Drop by this neighborhood bakery and you'll hear Greek spoken as often as English. This is the real deal, an authentic eatery where grandmother's recipes inspired the menu. Most everything is made on the premises and perfectly blends the flavors of the Mediterannean. House favorites include Greek salads, savory spanakopita (spinach pie), and meat or vegetarian dolmades (stuffed grape leaves). For a sweet treat try the gooey baklava or the creamy tiramisu. Take-out items are great for picnics. $ *Average main: $10* ✉ *3113 Habersham St., Southside* ☎ *912/200–3796* ⌚ *Reservations not accepted* ⊙ *No dinner on weekends.*

TYBEE ISLAND

$$ ✕ **The Crab Shack.** *Seafood.* "Where the elite eat in their bare
FAMILY feet" is the motto of this laid-back eatery tucked away on a side street just over the bridge to Tybee Island. Out front is a large pool filled with baby alligators that is a huge hit with kids—a good way to keep them entertained if there's a wait for tables, which is possible on weekends when the weather's nice. Just inside is a huge patio lit with tiki torches and packed with picnic tables. Seating is available in screened-in dining areas if there's rain or sand gnats. The beer is cold, the vibe is relaxed, and items like the Lowcountry boil—a huge plate of shrimp, corn on the cob, and smoked sausage—are delicious. No wonder this place is a Jimmy Buffett fan's Shangri-la. $ *Average main: $15* ✉ *40 Estill Hammock Rd., Tybee Island* ☎ *912/786–9857* ⊕ *www.thecrabshack.com.*

$ ✕ **Fannie's on the Beach.** *Seafood.* A great place to grab a bite after a long day power-lounging on the beach, this beachside eatery is a favorite with locals and visitors alike. The menu lists simple favorites like sandwiches, burgers, and fried seafood, but all are prepared exceedingly well. The pizza menu includes some interesting choices, including pies topped with salmon or scallops and bacon. Chef Joel Worth does a nice Sunday brunch with great prebeach mimosas and eggs Benedict. Even after you finish your meal, Fannie's still has plenty to offer, thanks to the live music Wednesday to Saturday. At all times, you can enjoy a great view of the ocean from the third-story deck. $ *Average main: $13* ✉ *1613 Strand Ave., Tybee Island* ☎ *912/786–6109* ⊕ *www.fanniesonthebeach.com.*

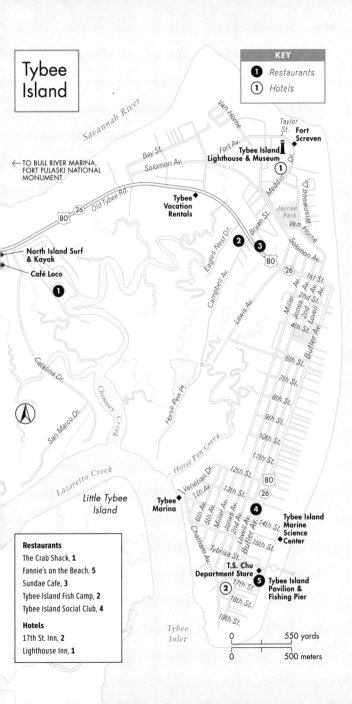

Tybee Island

KEY
- **1** Restaurants
- (1) Hotels

Savannah River

← TO BULL RIVER MARINA, FORT PULASKI NATIONAL MONUMENT

Van Horne

Taylor St.

Fort Screven

Fort Av.

Tybee Island Lighthouse & Museum

Meddin Dr.

Wirewood Dr.

Bay St.

Solomon Av.

(80) (26) Old Tybee Rd.

Tybee Vacation Rentals

Jaycee Park

Van Horne

Bryan St.

2 **3**

(80)

Solomon Av.

(26)

Eagles Nest Dr.

Campbell Av.

Lewis Av.

1st St.
2nd St.
Miller Av.
Jones Av.
2nd Av.
Lovell Av.
4th St.
Butler Av.

6th St.

North Island Surf & Kayak

Café Loco

1

Catalina Dr.

Chimney Creek

San Marco Dr.

Horse Pen Pt.

7th St.
8th St.
9th St.
10th St.
11th St.

Lazaretto Creek

Horse Pen Creek

Little Tybee Island

Venetian Dr.
7th Av.

12th St.
13th St.

(80)
(26)

Tybee Marina

5th Av.
Miller Av.
Jones Av.
2nd Av.
Lovell Av.
Butler Av.
14th St.

4

Tybee Island Marine Science Center

Chatham Av.

Tybrisa St.

15th St.

T.S. Chu Department Store

2

17th St.

5 **Tybee Island Pavilion & Fishing Pier**

18th St.

19th St.

Tybee Inlet

Restaurants
The Crab Shack, **1**
Fannie's on the Beach, **5**
Sundae Cafe, **3**
Tybee Island Fish Camp, **2**
Tybee Island Social Club, **4**

Hotels
17th St. Inn, **2**
Lighthouse Inn, **1**

0 ____ 550 yards

0 ____ 500 meters

★ Fodor'sChoice ✕ **Sundae Cafe.** *American.* Tucked into an unas-
$$ suming strip mall off the main drag on Tybee Island, this
gourmet restaurant is a diamond in the rough. Locals and
tourists alike enjoy the diverse menu, fresh seafood, and
brilliant food combinations—don't miss the unique sea-
food "cheesecake" starter, consisting of shrimp and crab
meat over greens with a hint of gouda. For lunch, the rich
fried green tomato BLT can stop your heart (in more ways
than one!), while the pork chops are always a sure bet at
dinner. This place has quite a following: Who can resist
generous portions at reasonable prices? Ⓢ *Average main:
$19* ✉ *101 U.S. Hwy. 80, Tybee Island* ☎ *912/786–7694*
⊕ *www.sundaecafe.com* ☉ *Closed Sun.*

$$$$ ✕ **Tybee Island Fish Camp.** *American.* The upscale sister to the
wildly successful Tybee Island Social Club, this restaurant
opened to raves in 2014. With great attention to detail, the
handsome eatery has a menu tailored to please even the
most critical foodie. Try the pork belly salad or the curried
mussels to start. For your entrée, you can't go wrong with
surf or turf. Local grouper is seared to perfection in a lemon
brown butter, and the bone-in rib eye will fill up the hungri-
est diners. Ⓢ *Average main: $27* ✉ *106 S. Campbell Ave.,
Tybee Island* ☎ *912/662–3474* ⊕ *www.tybeeislandfishcamp.
com* ⌕ *Reservations essential* ☉ *Closed Mon.*

★ Fodor'sChoice ✕ **Tybee Island Social Club.** *Modern American.*
$ This staple of the Tybee Island dining scene has successfully
updated some island favorites with a twist of contemporary
style. The small but flexible menu includes such entrées as
an elaborate array of gourmet tacos (a best bet is the one
with duck breast, sliced radish, and tomatillo salsa) or the
fish with pear puree, cilantro, and chorizo. Side dishes
like sweet-potato fries, collard greens, or black beans are
wonderful, too. The prices are surprisingly reasonable given
the quality. The menu also offers wine and beer pairings
with each item. Sunday brunch features local live blue-
grass music. There's a small children's menu for younger
travelers. Ⓢ *Average main: $10* ✉ *1311 Butler Ave., Tybee
Island* ☎ *912/472–4044* ⊕ *www.tybeeislandsocialclub.com.*

WHERE TO STAY

Updated by Summer Teal Simpson

THE HOSTESS CITY OPENS ITS DOORS every year to millions of visitors who are drawn to its historic and vibrant downtown. Because the majority of attractions are within the Historic District, most of the city's best hotels are there, too. Many are within easy walking distance of the city's premier restaurants and historic sites. In terms of accommodations, Savannah is best known for its many inns and B&Bs, which have moved into the stately antebellum mansions, renovated cotton warehouses, and myriad other historic buildings stretching from the river out to the Victorian neighborhoods in the vicinity of Forsyth Park. Most are beautifully restored with the requisite high ceilings, ornate carved millwork, claw-foot tubs, and other quaint touches. Some stay in close touch with the past and do not offer televisions or telephones; others have mixed in the modern luxuries that many travelers have grown accustomed to, including flat-screen TVs, Wi-Fi, and upscale bath amenities. Often, Southern hospitality is served up in the form of evening wine-and-cheese socials, decadent breakfasts, and pillow-top pralines.

A flush of newer boutique hotels has shaken some of the dust out of Savannah's lodging scene and raised the bar for competing properties. Properties like the Brice, the Cotton Sail, and the luxurious Mansion on Forsyth Park would be at home in a much larger city, but all have figured out how to introduce a sleek, cosmopolitan edge without bulldozing over Savannah's charm.

HOTEL PRICES

The central location and relatively high standards of quality in Savannah's Historic District hotels do drive up room rates, especially during peak seasons, holidays, and special events like St. Patrick's Day. The number of hotel rooms has more than doubled in the past 15 years, and occupancy rates have grown accordingly, even in the former slow season from September through January. October is another relatively busy time thanks to the pleasant temperatures and packed events calendar.

You will sometimes save by booking online or purchasing a package deal. Look for good last-minute deals when bookings are light. These are often available in late summer, when the heat and humidity are at their highest. If you're on a tight budget, there are plenty of nice, new, mid-range options from trusted hotel chains in less traveled but conveniently located areas a short drive from downtown, including midtown and the airport. Just be aware that what you are gaining in affordability you will often be losing in convenience and historic charm.

WHAT IT COSTS				
	$	**$$**	**$$$**	**$$$$**
Hotels	Under $150	$151– $200	$201– $250	over $250

Prices for two people in a standard double room in high season.

HISTORIC DISTRICT

$$$$ ☒ **Andaz Savannah.** *Hotel.* The interiors at the Andaz make quite a statement: The exposed-brick walls in the spacious lobby are offset by cozy, nested seating areas. **Pros:** knowledgeable concierge with extensive insider knowledge; excellent location. **Cons:** sounds of revelers on Congress Street can sometimes be heard in rooms. ⑤*Rooms from: $269* ✉*Ellis Square, 14 Barnard St., Historic District* ☎*912/233– 2116* ⊕*www.savannah.andaz.hyatt.com* ⇲*148 rooms, 3 suites. 2 lofts* ⍓*No meals.*

$$ ☒ **Azalea Inn & Gardens.** *B&B/Inn.* Expect a hospitable ambience, a wonderful breakfast, and afternoon wine service at this 1889 mansion built for a Cotton Exchange tycoon. **Pros:** rooms exude romance and luxury; baked goods are put out during the day; this is one of the few local B&Bs with a pool. **Cons:** just outside the heart of the Historic District, it's a bit of a walk to many attractions; less expensive rooms are small; the carriage house is not as distinctive. ⑤*Rooms from: $179* ✉*217 E. Huntingdon St., Historic District* ☎*912/236–6080, 800/582-3823* ⊕*www.azaleainn. com* ⇲*8 rooms, 2 suites* ⍓*Breakfast.*

BREAKFAST INCLUDED. When you are trying to decide on what kind of accommodation to reserve in Savannah, consider that B&Bs include breakfast (sometimes a lavish one), complimentary wine and cheese nightly, and even free bottled water. Hotels, particularly the major ones, usually do not even give you a bottle of water.

$$ ☒ **Ballastone Inn.** *B&B/Inn.* Step back into the Victorian era at this sumptuous inn on the National Register of Historic Places, which features fine antiques and reproductions, luxurious scented linens and down blankets on canopied beds; and a collection of original framed prints from *Harper's* scattered throughout. **Pros:** excellent location; romantic atmosphere; magnificently appointed suites. **Cons:** limited off-street parking; busy downtown area can be noisy. ⑤ *Rooms from: $179* ⊠ *14 E. Oglethorpe Ave., Historic District* ☎ *912/236–1484, 800/822–4553* ⊕ *www.ballastone.com* ⤱ *13 rooms, 3 suites* ⑩ *Breakfast.*

$ ⚑ **Bed & Breakfast Inn.** *B&B/Inn.* The rooms at this restored 1853 Federal-style row house on historic Gordon Row near Chatham Square aren't quite as luxe as some of Savannah's finer B&Bs, but they are handsomely appointed and retain many elements of the home's original charm, such as beamed ceilings and exposed-brick walls. **Pros:** cottages with kitchens are particularly well priced; free on-street parking; friendly for families. **Cons:** 20-minute walk to the river; front desk not staffed after 9 pm. ⑤ *Rooms from: $129* ⊠ *117 W. Gordon St., Historic District* ☎ *912/238–0518* ⊕ *www.savannahbnb.com* ⤱ *25 rooms, 5 suites, 4 cottages, 2 townhomes* ⑩ *Breakfast.*

★ Fodor'sChoice ⚑ **The Bohemian.** *Hotel.* Giving you easy access $$$$ to the hustle and bustle of River Street, this boutique hotel is a much-needed addition to the hotel landscape—instead of the Victorian decor that's so prevalent in Savannah; a stay at the Bohemian is like settling into a gentleman's study in a regal English manse. **Pros:** river-view rooms offer lovely vistas; pets are allowed for a nonrefundable fee of $100; access to spa at the Mansion on Forsyth Park. **Cons:** decor is a little over-the-top; the rooftop lounge stays open late and the noise can sometimes be heard in guest rooms; not very kid-friendly. ⑤ *Rooms from: $250* ⊠ *102 W. Bay St., Historic District* ☎ *912/721–3800, 888/213–4024* ⊕ *www.bohemianhotelsavannah.com* ⤱ *75 rooms* ⑩ *No meals.*

★ Fodor'sChoice ⚑ **The Brice.** *Hotel.* The Brice has been turning $$$ heads since it opened in 2014—no detail was spared in the remaking of this 1860s warehouse, which later served as a Coca-Cola bottling plant and then a livery stable. **Pros:** staff is genuinely warm and helpful; cruiser bikes are available to guests; great view of the secret garden from many of the second floor rooms. **Cons:** neighboring Bay Street can be loud, so request a room opposite the main thoroughfare. ⑤ *Rooms from: $209* ⊠ *601 E. Bay Street, Historic District* ☎ *912/238–1200* ⊕ *www.bricehotel.com* ⤱ *145 rooms, 26 suites* ⑩ *No meals.*

$$ ⚑ **Catherine Ward House Inn.** *B&B/Inn.* Elegance meets comfort at this bed-and-breakfast, applauded for warm and

Best Bets for Savannah Lodging

We offer a selective listing of quality lodging experiences in every price range, from a city's best budget motel to its most sophisticated luxury hotel. Here we've compiled our top recommendations by price and experience. The very best properties—those that provide a particularly remarkable experience—are designated with the Fodor's Choice logo.

Fodor's Choice: Andaz, Bohemian, Cotton Sail, Gastonian, Hamilton-Turner Inn, Kehoe House, Lighthouse Inn, Mansion on Forsyth Park, Marshall House, The Brice, Westin Savannah Harbor Golf Resort & Spa

Best Budget Stay: Bed & Breakfast Inn, Holiday Inn Express Historic District, Thunderbird

Best Celebrity Retreat: Hamilton-Turner Inn, Mansion on Forsyth Park, The Marshall House

Best Hotel Bars: Andaz, Bohemian, Cotton Sail, The Brice, The Marshall House

Best for Romance: Gastonian, Hamilton-Turner Inn, Kehoe House, Mansion on Forsyth Park

Best B&Bs: Ballastone Inn, Dresser-Palmer House, Foley House Inn, Gastonian, Hamilton-Turner Inn, Kehoe House

Best Pool: Holiday Inn Express Historic District, Mansion on Forsyth Park, Westin Savannah Harbor Golf Resort & Spa

Best Views: Bohemian, Cotton Sail, The Marshall House, Westin Savannah Harbor Golf Resort & Spa

Pet-Friendly: East Bay Inn, Hampton Inn, Olde Harbour Inn, The Brice, Westin Savannah Harbor Golf Resort & Spa

Best Interior Design: Andaz, Bohemian, Cotton Sail, Dresser Palmer House, Hamilton-Turner Inn, Kehoe House, The Brice

Best Location: Andaz, Bohemian, Cotton Sail, Foley House Inn, Mansion on Forsyth Park

---

inviting touches like soft music, cozy lighting, and smoldering fires in period fireplaces. **Pros:** rooms have antique mantels and fireplaces, some of which work; some rooms have two-person whirlpool tubs; tasty breakfasts. **Cons:** less expensive rooms are small; carriage-house rooms are not as atmospheric as the main house; two-night minimum usually required for weekends. ⑤ *Rooms from: $179* ✉ *118 E. Waldburg St., Historic District* ☎ *912/234–8564,* *800/327–4270* ⊕ *www.catherinewardhouseinn.com* ⌖ *9 rooms* ⚏ *Breakfast.*

Where to Stay in Savannah

Azalea Inn & Gardens, **32**

Ballastone Inn, **18**

Bed & Breakfast Inn, **29**

The Bohemian, **3**

The Brice, **12**

Catherine Ward House Inn, **34**

Cotton Sail, **2**

The Dresser-Palmer House, **31**

East Bay Inn, **8**

Eliza Thompson House, **27**

Foley House Inn, **19**

Gastonian, **30**

Green Palm Inn, **14**

Hamilton-Turner Inn, **25**

Hampton Inn & Suites, **22**

Hampton Inn Historic District, **7**

Hilton Savannah Desoto, **24**

Holiday Inn Express Historic District, **6**

Hyatt Regency Savannah, **4**

Inn at Ellis Square, **1**

Kehoe House, **15**

Mansion on Forsyth Park, **33**

Marshall House, **17**

Olde Harbour Inn, **10**

Planters Inn, **13**

The Presidents' Quarters, **16**

Residence Inn, **23**

River Street Inn, **5**

Savannah Marriott Riverfront, **11**

SpringHill Suites, **20**

Suites on Lafayette, **26**

Thunderbird Inn, **21**

Westin Savannah Harbor Golf Resort & Spa, **9**

Zeigler House Inn, **28**

Indian St.

Williamson St.

W. Bay St.

W. Bryan St.

Ellis Sq.

W. Julian St.

W. Congress St.

Ann St.

W. Broughton St.

Whitaker St.

Martin Luther King Jr. Blvd

W. State St.

W. Telfair Sq. President

W. York St.

W. Oglethorpe Ave.

Jefferson St.

Barnard St.

Montgomery St.

W. Hull

Orleans Sq.

W. Perry

Whitaker St.

Louisville Rd.

W. Harris St.

W. Harris St.

Pulaski Sq.

St. John's Episcopal ◆ Church

W. Charlton St.

W. Jones St.

W. Jones St.

W. Taylor St.

Jefferson St.

Tattnall St.

Chatham Sq.

W. Wayne St.

W. Gordon St.

167AB

W. Gaston St.

W. Huntingdon St.

$$$ � **Cotton Sail.** *Hotel.* One of the newer hotels dotting the landscape, this locally owned and operated establishment is perched over River Street and offers expansive views of the Savannah River. **Pros:** hints of period charm; great location; bar is a great place to meet locals and out-of-towners. **Cons:** bar gets busy on the weekends, so early birds should ask for rooms away from the noise. ⑤ *Rooms from: $240* ✉ *126 W. Bay St., Historic District* ☎ *912/200–3700* ⊕ *cottonsailhotel.com* ➪ *56 rooms* ⑩ *No meals.*

$$ ☐ **The Dresser Palmer House.** *B&B/Inn.* This rambling Italianate town house from the late 19th century is a standout for its ornate exterior, relaxing front porch, and comfortable ambience. **Pros:** two back gardens with fountains are lovely; evening social offers wine, cheese, and guest camaraderie; one room is wheelchair accessible. **Cons:** lacks the privacy of a large property. ⑤ *Rooms from: $179* ✉ *211 E. Gaston St., Historic District* ☎ *912/238–3294, 800/671–0716* ⊕ *www.dresserpalmerhouse.com* ➪ *16 rooms* ⑩ *Breakfast.*

$$ ☐ **East Bay Inn.** *B&B/Inn.* Built in 1852, this charming inn has a handsome brick exterior, hunter-green shutters and awnings, and soaring 12- to 18-foot ceilings adorned with intricate crown molding. **Pros:** hospitality and service get very high marks; nightly turndown service; routinely offers free tour tickets to guests. **Cons:** not enough parking spaces for the number of rooms; hallways and bathrooms are not as wonderful as the rooms. ⑤ *Rooms from: $169* ✉ *225 E. Bay St., Historic District* ☎ *912/238–1225, 800/500–1225* ⊕ *www.eastbayinn.com* ➪ *28 rooms* ⑩ *Breakfast.*

$$ ☐ **Eliza Thompson House.** *B&B/Inn.* Afternoon wine, cheese, and appetizers and luscious evening desserts and sherry are served in the atmospheric main parlor of this fine town house built by Eliza Thompson's loving husband, Joseph, for her and their seven children in 1847. **Pros:** on one of Savannah's most beautiful streets; in a lively residential neighborhood; flat-screen TVs in every room. **Cons:** must purchase parking passes; breakfast can be hit or miss; some of the back rooms are small. ⑤ *Rooms from: $159* ✉ *5 W. Jones St., Historic District* ☎ *912/236–3620, 800/348–9378* ⊕ *www.elizathompsonhouse.com* ➪ *25 rooms* ⑩ *Breakfast.*

$$ ☐ **Foley House Inn.** *B&B/Inn.* In the center of the Historic District, this elegant inn is made up of two town houses built 50 years apart. **Pros:** pets of all breeds and sizes allowed for a fee; luxury bath products; complimentary cocktails at night. **Cons:** no Wi-Fi in the carriage house; fee

SAVANNAH LODGING TIPS

■ **Do Your Research.** Don't hesitate to call the innkeepers and chat; you'll quickly gauge their attitude and sense of hospitality. And know the parking situation; many of these B&Bs provide only on-street parking, which can be tricky on busy weekends; though they usually pay for your parking pass, you still have to move the car on days when the streets need to be cleaned.

■ **Know What Historic Really Means.** Among the negatives can be antique beds, albeit beautifully canopied, that are short, not even as big as today's doubles. If you are tall or are used to a California King, this could be a definite issue. Rooms can be small, especially if they were originally backrooms meant for children or servants; rooms below street level—often called garden or courtyard rooms—can be damp. Windows aren't usually soundproof, and some squares are noisy in the morning or late at night,

depending on the proximity to bars. Many B&Bs in old homes require patrons to share bathrooms.

■ **Savannah Has Hotels, Too.** Full-service hotels such as Hyatt Regency, Marriott, Westin, and Hilton—as well as several boutique hotels—may be more appealing to visitors who actually prefer a larger, more anonymous property, or at least one with an elevator, swimming pool, or flat-screen TV.

■ **Don't Forget the Chains.** Mid-range chain hotels and motels that normally would not excite or even interest you can be surprisingly appealing in Savannah. Some in the Historic District are creatively renovated historic structures. If you can't afford to stay downtown, you'll find many mid-range chains in midtown and the Southside (still less than 7 miles from downtown), as well as near the airport. The farther out you go, the less expensive your lodging will be.

for parking pass; no elevator. ⓢ *Rooms from: $150 ⊠ 14 W. Hull St., Historic District* ☎ *912/232–6622, 800/647–3708* ⊕ *www.foleyinn.com* ⌕ *19 rooms* ⦿ *Breakfast.*

★ **Fodor's**Choice ⌧ **Gastonian.** *B&B/Inn.* Guest rooms—many
$$$$ of which are exceptionally spacious—in this atmospheric Italianate inn dating from 1868 all have fireplaces and are decorated with a mix of funky finds and antiques from the Georgian and Regency periods. **Pros:** cordial and caring staff; hot breakfast is hard to beat; afternoon tea and wine

Savannah's Spooky Stays

CLOSE UP

In 2003 the American Institute of Paranormal Psychology christened Savannah the "most haunted city in America." And there have been countless reports of run-ins with spirits and specters in Savannah's many inns and B&Bs.

Some adventurous travelers even request haunted rooms, and you'll find that many properties wear their supernatural reputations like badges of honor. The East Bay Inn, for instance, lovingly refers to their resident ghost, Charlie, like a harmless extended houseguest.

You might occasionally hear the wooden floorboards squeaking; is it Charlie pacing the halls or a 200-year-old building settling in for the night?

At the Eliza Thompson House visitors have reported doors spontaneously locking and ghostly figures appearing in guest rooms. The Marshall House and Olde Harbour Inn also proudly tout their resident ghosts. Whether you consider it a selling point or a deterrent may depend on how superstitious you are, but don't say you haven't been warned.

and cheese at night. **Cons:** accommodations on the third floor are a climb; some of the furnishings are less than regal. *⑤ Rooms from: $259 ⊠ 220 E. Gaston St., Historic District ☎ 912/232–2869, 800/322–6603 ⊕ www.gastonian. com ⌨ 15 rooms, 2 suites ⓘ Breakfast.*

$$ **⚁ Green Palm Inn.** *B&B/Inn.* This gingerbread inn built in 1897 is a pleasing little discovery with its spacious, high-ceilinged, and elegantly furnished cottage-style rooms inspired by Savannah's British Colonial heritage. **Pros:** innkeeper is knowledgeable about Savannah's history; quiet location with a garden patio; affordable rates. **Cons:** with only four guest rooms, it might be too intimate for some; location on the eastern edge of the Historic District isn't as convenient as other hotels. *⑤ Rooms from: $169 ⊠ 548 E. President St., Historic District ☎ 912/447–8901, 888/606–9510 ⊕ www.greenpalminn.com ⌨ 4 suites; 1 cottage ⓘ Breakfast.*

★   **Fodor's Choice ⚁ Hamilton-Turner Inn.** *B&B/Inn.* With bathrooms
$$$ the size of New York City apartments, this French-Empire mansion is celebrated, if not in song, certainly in story, and certainly has a "wow" effect, especially the rooms that front Lafayette Square. **Pros:** wonderfully furnished rooms; breakfast is a treat; pets are allowed in the ground-level rooms with a deposit. **Cons:** sedate atmosphere won't

appeal to everyone; no guest elevator (except for accessible Room 201); street parking only. ⑤ *Rooms from: $214 ✉ 330 Abercorn St., Historic District* ☎ *912/233–1833, 888/448–8849* ⊕ *www.hamilton-turnerinn.com* ☞ *11 rooms, 6 suites, 1 carriage house* ⦿ *Breakfast.*

$ ☷ **Hampton Inn & Suites.** *Hotel.* The rooms and suites at this well-known chain hotel are a remarkably good value for Savannah's Historic District. **Pros:** spacious accommodations; continental breakfast with plenty of hot options; suites start at only $10 more than a standard room. **Cons:** avoid the suite next to the noisy boiler; charge for parking; noise from nearby traffic. ⑤ *Rooms from: $139 ✉ 603 W. Oglethorpe Ave., Historic District* ☎ *912/721–1600, 800/426–7866* ⊕ *www.hamptoninn.com* ☞ *124 rooms, 30 suites* ⦿ *Breakfast.*

$$ ☷ **Hampton Inn Historic District.** *Hotel.* Directly across the street from Factors Walk, this former cotton warehouse has antique heart-pine floors that extend the length of the lobby. **Pros:** cushy bedding and duvets; friendly staff; very child-friendly. **Cons:** pool and deck are not high enough for river views. ⑤ *Rooms from: $159 ✉ 201 E. Bay St., Historic District* ☎ *912/231–9700, 888/231–9706* ⊕ *www. hotelsavannah.com* ☞ *144 rooms* ⦿ *Breakfast.*

$$ ☷ **Hilton Savannah Desoto.** *Hotel.* Expect tasteful contemporary furnishings at this 15-story property with a rooftop pool, convenient restaurant and pub, and a downtown location in the heart of a thriving shopping and dining neighborhood. **Pros:** overlooking Madison Square; nice skyline views from the upper floors; complimentary Wi-Fi. **Cons:** on-street parking or pricey valet. ⑤ *Rooms from: $185 ✉ 15 E. Liberty St., Historic District* ☎ *912/232–9000, 800/426–8483* ⊕ *www.desotohilton.com* ☞ *246 rooms, 5 suites* ⦿ *No meals.*

$ ☷ **Holiday Inn Express Historic District.** *Hotel.* Since all buildings in the Historic District must conform to the local charm, Holiday Inn went all-out, creating a handsome interior design in the public spaces, with tasteful animal-print settees, leather club chairs, fireplaces, and classy chandeliers—so this hotel may change your perception of what is generally thought of as a modest, limited-service chain with no notable atmosphere. **Pros:** impressive Wi-Fi throughout; soundproof rooms; on-site fitness center. **Cons:** rates are higher than at most similar properties. ⑤ *Rooms from: $115 ✉ 199 E. Bay St., Historic District* ☎ *912/231–9000, 877/834–3613* ⊕ *www.staysmartsavannah.com* ☞ *143 rooms, 3 suites* ⦿ *Breakfast.*

FAMILY

4

$$ ⊡ **Hyatt Regency Savannah.** *Hotel.* A study in modernity amid the history of River and Bay streets, the seven-story Hyatt Regency Savannah has marble floors, glass elevators, and a towering atrium. **Pros:** modern decor; comfortable bedding; views from everywhere. **Cons:** valet parking is very expensive; many large groups. Ⓢ *Rooms from: $169* ⊠ *2 W. Bay St., Historic District* ☎ *912/238–1234, 866/899–8039* ⊕ *www.savannah.hyatt.com* ⌁ *351 rooms* ⦿ *No meals.*

$ ⊡ **Inn at Ellis Square.** *Hotel.* Tucked inside the Guckenheimer

FAMILY Building, the Inn at Ellis Square received a historic preservation award for its attention to detail in renovating the nationally registered landmark that once housed one of Savannah's central grocery stores. **Pros:** complimentary deluxe continental breakfast; fitness center, and lounge; free Wi-Fi. **Cons:** parking in the parking garage under Ellis Square; the understated lobby and room furnishings leave much to be desired. Ⓢ *Rooms from: $129* ⊠ *201 W. Bay St., Historic District* ☎ *912/236–4440* ⊕ *www.innatellissquare.com* ⌁ *195 rooms* ⦿ *Breakfast.*

★ **Fodor's**Choice ⊡ **Kehoe House.** *B&B/Inn.* Known for its remark-

$$$ ably friendly and attentive staff, this handsomely appointed house, dating from the 1890s, was originally the family manse of William Kehoe. **Pros:** a popular wedding and anniversary venue; the two elevators are a rarity in a B&B; you definitely won't leave hungry. **Cons:** a few rooms have the sink and shower in the room; soundproofing in guest rooms could be better. Ⓢ *Rooms from: $229* ⊠ *123 Habersham St., Historic District* ☎ *912/232–1020, 800/820–1020* ⊕ *www.kehoehouse.com* ⌁ *13 rooms* ⦿ *Breakfast.*

★ **Fodor's**Choice ⊡ **Mansion on Forsyth Park.** *Hotel.* Sitting on the

$$$ edge of Forsyth Park, this Kessler property has dramatic design, opulent interiors with a contemporary edge, and a magnificently diverse collection of some 400 pieces of American and European art, all of which create a one-of-a-kind experience—sophisticated, chic, and artsy only begin to describe it. **Pros:** stimulating environment transports you from the workaday world; full-service spa; complimentary shuttle to River Street. **Cons:** very pricey; some of the art from the early 1970s is not appealing. Ⓢ *Rooms from: $215* ⊠ *700 Drayton St., Historic District* ☎ *888/213–3671, 912/238—5158* ⊕ *www.mansiononforsythpark.com* ⌁ *125 rooms* ⦿ *No meals.*

★ **Fodor's**Choice ⊡ **Marshall House.** *B&B/Inn.* With original pine

$$ floors, handsome woodwork, and exposed brick, this is a hotel that provides the charm and intimacy of a B&B. **Pros:** great location near stores and restaurants; exceptional restaurant; balconies offer great bird's-eye views of Broughton Street. **Cons:** no free parking; no room service; the sounds of bustling Broughton Street can be noisy. ⑤*Rooms from: $152* ✉*123 E. Broughton St., Historic District* ☎*912/644–7896, 800/589–6304* ⊕*www.marshallhouse.com* ☜*65 rooms, 3 suites* ❍|*Breakfast.*

$$$ 🖥 **Olde Harbour Inn.** *B&B/Inn.* Dating from 1892, this riverfront lodging tries hard to please even if it doesn't always hit the heights; nevertheless, it's a good option for those who want to be near the action of River Street. **Pros:** hearty breakfast menu; welcomes families and pets; all suites have views of river. **Cons:** not luxurious; location has some negatives, including hard-partying crowds and late-night noise. ⑤*Rooms from: $215* ✉*508 E. Factors Walk, Historic District* ☎*912/234–4100, 800/553–6533* ⊕*www.oldeharbourinn.com* ☜*24 rooms* ❍|*Breakfast.*

$$ 🖥 **Planters Inn.** *Hotel.* A Savannah landmark, the Planters Inn makes sure its guests mix and mingle—the evening wine-and-cheese reception is a house party where the concierge introduces fellow guests, a good cross-section of leisure and business travelers, many of whom are repeats. **Pros:** management and staff truly make you feel at home; great architectural details in the lobby; convenient location near the Olde Pink House, where the kitchen provides for room service. **Cons:** decor and bathrooms could benefit from an update. ⑤*Rooms from: $159* ✉*29 Abercorn St., Historic District* ☎*912/232–5678, 800/554–1187* ⊕*www.plantersinnsavannah.com* ☜*60 rooms* ❍|*Breakfast.*

$$$ 🖥 **The Presidents' Quarters.** *B&B/Inn.* You'll be impressed even before you enter this lovely historic inn, which has an exterior courtyard so beautiful and inviting that it's popular for wedding receptions. **Pros:** central-but-quiet location; private parking and some private entrances; romantic atmosphere. **Cons:** inn books up fast in spite of ghost rumors; some might not like the contemporary carpeted floors in guest rooms. ⑤*Rooms from: $229* ✉*225 E. President St., Historic District* ☎*912/233–1600, 800/233–1776* ⊕*www.presidentsquarters.com* ☜*16 rooms* ❍|*Breakfast.*

🖥 **Residence Inn.** *Hotel.* Some of the architecture at this reasonably priced lodging re-creates the 19th-century cottages that were used to house executives of the Central of Georgia Railroad. **Pros:** outdoor pool; complimentary hot breakfast; Wi-Fi throughout the hotel. **Cons:** location on the western edge of Historic District isn't the best; looks and feels like a chain hotel; parking for a fee. ⑤*Rooms from: $189* ✉*500 W. Charlton St., Historic District* ☎*912/233–9996* ⊕*www.marriott.com* ☜*109* ❍|*Breakfast.*

$$ ⛴ River Street Inn. *Hotel.* Housed in a five-story converted warehouse, this 1817 lodging has a harbor-from-yesteryear theme, with nautical murals and model schooners. **Pros:** fitness center; fifth-floor library; complimentary wine and hors d'oeuvres are laid out almost every evening. **Cons:** could use a renovation; no private parking (city garage across the street); beware of the wildly uneven floors. Ⓢ*Rooms from: $159* ✉ *124 E. Bay St., Historic District* ☎ *912/234–6400* ⊕ *www.riverstreetinn.com* ⤴ *86 rooms, 1 suite* ⒶNo meals.

$$ ⛴ Savannah Marriott Riverfront. *Hotel.* One of the city's few high-rise hotels—and the major anchor of the east end of the River Street area—the Savannah Marriott Riverfront delivers the professional management demanded by business travelers while offering some of the resort amenities that vacationers crave. **Pros:** atmospheric waterfront location; indoor and outdoor pools; great spa. **Cons:** conventions often dominate the main floor, limiting access to the indoor pool; a fair walk to the hot spots up on River Street; pedicabs can't come here on the cobblestones. Ⓢ*Rooms from: $179* ✉ *100 General McIntosh Blvd., Historic District* ☎ *912/233–7722, 800/285–0398* ⊕ *www.marriott.com* ⤴ *341 rooms, 46 suites* ⒶNo meals.

$ ⛴ SpringHill Suites. *Hotel.* Holding its own beside any of the city's boutique hotels, the SpringHill Suites has a lobby that's a study in sleek, contemporary design, with shimmery aqua drapes lining its windows and ultramodern light fixtures. **Pros:** suites include refrigerators and microwaves; on-site gym; free Wi-Fi and hot buffet breakfast. **Cons:** some bathrooms are small and stark; parking is pricey. Ⓢ*Rooms from: $139* ✉ *150 Montgomery St., Historic District* ☎ *912/629–5300* ⊕ *www.marriott.com* ⤴ *160 suites* ⒶBreakfast.

$$ ⛴ Suites on Lafayette. *B&B/Inn.* Originally the home of a Confederate officer who died at nearby Fort McAllister, this charming inn consists of three historic buildings: the main house was built in 1852, and two adjacent buildings were constructed in the 1890s. **Pros:** location on Lafayette Square can't be beat; beautiful antique claw-foot tubs in some bathrooms; fully equipped kitchens in each suite. **Cons:** minimal off-street parking; two-night minimum stay. Ⓢ*Rooms from: $169* ✉ *201 E. Charlton St., Historic District* ☎ *912/596–1506* ⤴ *10 rooms.*

$ ⛴ Thunderbird Inn. *Hotel.* A stay in this throwback motor lodge will transport you back to the 1960s, with pop music in the parking lot, white leather chairs in the rooms, and

Moon Pies on your pillow with the complimentary turn-down. **Pros:** free parking; hip furnishings; great location. **Cons:** as far as the towels go, you get what you pay for; traffic noise can be a little loud. ⑤ *Rooms from: $87* ✉ *611 W. Oglethorpe Ave., Historic District* ☎ *912/232–2661, 866/324–2661* ⊕ *www.thethunderbirdinn.com* ⇌ *42 rooms* ⑩ *No meals.*

$$$ ⊡ **Zeigler House Inn.** *B&B/Inn.* Enjoy a romantic stay in a beautifully appointed room or, better yet, a suite with contemporary style at the Zeigler House Inn. **Pros:** on one of Savannah's most beautiful streets; lovely slate fireplaces and heart-pine floors and staircase. **Cons:** no hot breakfast; two-night minimum for weekends or holidays. ⑤ *Rooms from: $199* ✉ *121 W. Jones St., Historic District* ☎ *912/233–5307, 866/233–5307* ⊕ *www.zeiglerhouseinn. com* ⇌ *7 suites* ⑩ *Breakfast.*

ELSEWHERE IN SAVANNAH

★ Fodor'sChoice ⊡ **Westin Savannah Harbor Golf Resort & Spa.**
$$$ *Resort.* Within its own fiefdom, this high-rise property
FAMILY with more resort amenities than any other property in the area—including tennis courts, a full-service spa, and a golf course—presides over Hutchinson Island, five minutes by water taxi from River Street and just a short drive over the Talmadge Bridge. **Pros:** heated outdoor pool boasts a great view of River Street; dreamy bedding; great children's program. **Cons:** you are close, but still removed, from downtown; lacks atmosphere; an expensive and annoying resort fee. ⑤ *Rooms from: $235* ✉ *1 Resort Dr., Hutchinson Island* ☎ *912/201–2000, 800/937–8461* ⊕ *www.westinsavannah.com* ⇌ *390 rooms, 13 suites* ⑩ *No meals.*

TYBEE ISLAND

$ ⊡ **Tybee Vacation Rentals.** *Rental.* If renting a five-star beach house, a pastel island cottage, or a waterfront condo in a complex with a pool and tennis courts is your coastal-Georgia dream stay, check out Tybee Vacation Rentals. ⑤ *Rooms from: $129* ✉ *1010 Hwy. 80 E, Tybee Island* ☎ *912/786–5853, 855/651–1840* ⊕ *www.tybeevacationrentals.com* ⇌ *10-plus properties* ⊙ *Mon.–Sat. 9–6, Sun. 10–4.*

A SIDE OF TYBEE ALMOST GONE. You may hear some wild stories about Tybee Island: that it is a veritable Margaritaville, a kitschy resort area right out of the 1950s, or a hideout for eccentric beach bums. All the rumors are true, but that doesn't mean the island hasn't changed some over the years. If you want to keep in the traditional Tybee vibe, check out **Mermaid Cottages** (⊕ *www.mermaidcottages.com*), which rents a variety of funky, colorful bungalows—with names like the Crabby Pirate and the Pink Flamingo. They are a trip back to nostalgic beach communities of old and a fun way to experience the pleasures of life on the island.

$$ ☒ **17th Street Inn.** *B&B/Inn.* You're steps from the beach at
FAMILY this Tybee Island inn dating from 1920. **Pros:** very child-friendly; a half-block to the beach; a labyrinth of contemporary decks has been built to incorporate shade trees. **Cons:** art in some rooms leaves much to be desired; no breakfast. ⑤ *Rooms from: $165* ⊠ *12 17th St., Tybee Island* ☎ *912/786–0607, 888/909–0607* ⊕ *www.tybeeinn.com* ➷ *8 rooms, 2 condos* ⦿ *No meals.*

★ Fodor'sChoice ☒ **Lighthouse Inn.** *B&B/Inn.* This yellow-and-
$$$ white frame house is a quiet getaway, a place to unplug and renew, to sit on the front porch and make the rocker creak while watching the sun drop. **Pros:** lovely breakfast entrées; charming claw-foot tubs in the vintage baths. **Cons:** no water views; it is a relatively small, close environment; house rules are strictly enforced. ⑤ *Rooms from: $209* ⊠ *16 Meddin Dr., Tybee Island* ☎ *912/786–0901, 866/786–0901* ⊕ *www.tybeebb.com* ➷ *3 rooms* ⦿ *Breakfast.*

NIGHTLIFE AND PERFORMING ARTS

Updated
by
Summer
Teal
Simpson

ALONG WITH HOT, HUMID EVENINGS, Savannah's nightlife has a lot in common with that of New Orleans. Although Savannah's musical traditions may not run as deep as in the Big Easy, there's no shortage of entertainment in the Hostess City, whether you're looking for a live band, a crowded dance floor, or any number of more laid-back options. In both cities you can carry alcoholic beverages with you on the street, adding a festive touch to life after dark.

Congress Street and River Street have the highest concentrations of bars with live music, especially if you're looking for rock, heavy metal, or the blues. Many of the most popular dance clubs are scattered across the same area. If you're in the mood for something more sedate, there are plenty of chic enclaves known for their creative cocktails and cozy nooks that encourage intimate conversation.

As the old saying goes, "In Atlanta, they ask you what you do. In Macon, they ask what church you go to. And in Savannah, they ask you what you drink." But just because the city enjoys its liquor doesn't mean that there's nothing going on for those who'd rather not imbibe. There are coffee shops that serve up live music and film screenings, as well as arts venues offering theater, films, and comedy.

NIGHTLIFE

THE HISTORIC DISTRICT

BARS AND NIGHTCLUBS

★ Fodor'sChoice **Circa 1875.** In a beautifully renovated space with pressed-tin ceilings and a gorgeous antique bar, this is the place to come for a bottle of wine or champagne by the glass. Recordings of jazz legends like Billie Holiday or Django Reinhardt are usually the soundtrack, and the bar area is filled with tucked-away nooks for couples on a date. The gastropub next door offers a full menu of French fare that can also be ordered late into the night. The gourmet burgers and the mussels are highly recommended. ✉ *48 Whitaker St., Historic District* ☎ *912/443–1875* ⊕ *www. circa1875.com* ☉ *Closed Sun.*

Ampersand. One of the newest venues in town, this three-level corner spot features well-made cocktails (don't pass up the Sweet Legs, a blend of bourbon, honey syrup, and lime juice) accompanied by nibbles that foodies fawn over.

Upstairs you'll find an array of live performances and other events. Weekends add DJ action to the mix. ✉ *36 Martin Luther King Jr. Blvd., Historic District* ☎ *912/665–6373* ⊕ *andsavannah.com.*

Club One. Savannah's mainstay gay bar has also won praise from locals as one of the city's best dance clubs. It's also your destination for entertaining cabaret and drag shows. The notorious Lady Chablis (famous for her role in *Midnight in the Garden of Good and Evil*) makes regular appearances here, lip-synching disco tunes, shimmering in sequins, and bumping and grinding her way down the catwalk. Although the decor is a little tacky, the scene is wildly fun when the lights go down and the music starts. ✉ *1 Jefferson St., Historic District* ☎ *912/232–0200* ⊕ *www.clubone-online.com.*

Congress Street Social Club. Part sports bar, part music venue, the Congress Street Social Club is always jam-packed on weekend nights. Popular with a younger crowd, this is a great place to grab a drink on a pleasant evening and stroll out to the patio. There are three bars on the three levels, along with a stage for live music. Take advantage of the old-fashioned photo booth near the bathrooms to help commemorate the evening out. Enjoy tasty nibbles with your draft beer. ✉ *411 W. Congress St., Historic District* ☎ *912/238–1985* ⊕ *congressstreetsocialclub.com.*

Hang Fire. This place was once a strip club, and the original stripper pole still hangs horizontally above the bar. The owner gave the space a warm, homey feel, creating the bar out of metal shavings from a machine shop. On weekends this is a big hangout for young hipsters who like cheap beer and live rock music. The staff is friendly, and the jukebox is awesome. ✉ *37 Whitaker St., Historic District* ☎ *912/443–9956* ⊗ *Mon.–Sat. 5 pm–3 am* ⊗ *Closed Sun.*

Kevin Barry's Irish Pub. One of the city's most venerable drinking establishments, Kevin Barry's Irish Pub has a friendly vibe, a full menu, and traditional Irish music seven days a week. This is one of the most authentic pubs you'll find this side of the Atlantic, making it a great place to be on St. Patrick's Day. The rest of the year there's a mix of locals and out-of-towners of all ages. The corned beef and cabbage is hearty and delicious. ✉ *114 W. River St., Historic District* ☎ *912/233–9626* ⊕ *www.kevinbarrys.com.*

★ Fodor'sChoice **Lulu's Chocolate Bar.** This laid-back spot invites you to indulge your sweet tooth. Walking through the door, you're immediately greeted by a dessert case full of freshly baked specialties—try some of the homemade truffles. The menu also includes a spectacular list of specialty drinks, including delectable champagne cocktails, alongside a modest selection of beers and wines. Don't miss the truly divine "drinkable chocolate," an especially fulfilling twist on hot chocolate. ⊠ *42 Martin Luther King Jr. Blvd., Historic District* ☎ *912/480–4564* ⊕ *www.luluschocolatebar.net.*

Molly MacPherson's Scottish Pub & Grill. This Scottish pub near City Market is a must for Scotch lovers, who'll find a selection of more than 100 single malts. Well-prepared Scottish and American specialties include bangers and mash and fish-and-chips. Local rock and folk bands perform Friday and Saturday night. ⊠ *311 W. Congress St., Historic District* ☎ *912/239–9600* ⊕ *macphersonspub.com.*

Moon River Brewing Company & Beer Garden. Savannah's first microbrewery, Moon River occupies a historic building that once served as a hotel and a lumber and coal warehouse. In 2013 it opened an adjacent outdoor beer garden known for great people-watching, live music, and cool breezes. Check out the amazing variety of handcrafted lagers, ales, and wheat beers, compliments of award-winning brewmaster John Pinkerton. Pinkerton monitors the large steel vats of beer, which you can see through the glass partition. Soak up the first few rounds with a good variety of pub food. ⊠ *21 W. Bay St., Historic District* ☎ *912/447–0943* ⊕ *www. moonriverbrewing.com.*

Pinkie Masters. It might not be the oldest bar in Savannah, but Pinkie Masters could be the most historically significant. This dive bar's biggest claim to fame is that Georgia's own Jimmy Carter stood up on the bar to announce that he would run for president. Photos of Southern politicians and public figures adorn the walls. The jukebox plays anything under the sun. ⊠ *318 Drayton St., Historic District* ☎ *912/238–0447* ⊕ *pinkiemasters.net* ⊗ *Closed Sun.*

★ Fodor'sChoice **Planters Tavern.** Lighted by flickering candles, this tavern in the basement of the Olde Pink House is one of Savannah's most romantic late-night spots. There's a talented piano player setting the mood, two stone fireplaces, and an array of fox-hunt memorabilia. The upstairs menu is available, with the same quality of service but a slightly less formal approach. ■TIP→ **The handful of tables**

NIGHTLIFE TIPS

■ **Drinking on the Street Is Allowed.** You can take your drink out onto the street, but it has to be in a plastic cup—no cans or bottles. Barkeeps and door staff usually have a supply of plastic cups on hand, known locally as "to-go cups." As long as your drink is less than 16 ounces and you're somewhere north of Jones Street, then it's perfectly legal to stroll around.

■ **Stay in on Sunday Night.** To abide with the state's blue laws, most bars and clubs are closed on Sunday. There are a few exceptions, because some places that serve food remain open, but the choices are slim compared with Friday and Saturday. Thanks to a change of state and local laws in 2011, it is now possible to buy alcohol from retailers on Sunday, which had previously been prohibited.

■ **Try a Pub Crawl.** The same way taking a tour during the day will help you get your bearings, there are plenty of tours geared toward the nightlife. Several companies offer haunted pub crawls and other "spirited" walking tours to acquaint you with some local "haunts." It can be both entertaining and a good way to find places you might want to revisit on subsequent nights.

■ **No Smoking in Bars.** After heated discussions between elected officials and bar owners, the city banned smoking in bars in 2010. There are still a few places where smokers can get their fix, including a handful of open-air patios, but don't light up inside or within 10 feet of the front door.

■ **See What's Brewing.** Local breweries like Southbound and Service Brewing Co. have popped up in recent years. They offer tours of their facilities, where a tasty array of craft beers are brewed on-site and ripe for the sipping.

fill up fast, but the staff will serve you on your lap anywhere in the place. ⊠ *23 Abercorn St., garden level, Historic District* ☎ *912/232–4286.*

★ **Fodor's**Choice **Rocks on the Roof.** Atop the trendy Bohemian Hotel, this rooftop bar offers some of the city's best sunset and river views. Taking full advantage of Savannah's beautiful weather, the north and south walls of the bar open onto well-appointed outdoor areas with comfortable seating. The limited menu includes pizzas, sandwiches, and a cheese plate. ⊠ *Bohemian Hotel, 102 W. Bay St., Historic District* ☎ *912/721–3901* ⊕ *www.bohemianhotelsavannah.com.*

COFFEEHOUSES

★ Fodor'sChoice **The Coffee Fox.** The newest addition to the local coffeehouse scene, the Coffee Fox is downtown's answer to Foxy Loxy. Specializing in locally roasted coffee, homemade baked goods, and craft beers, the Coffee Fox is a great stop whether you're on the run or looking to perch. The cold brew will win the hearts of coffee aficionados in the hot summer months. The popular Mexican Mocha is a sweet and spicy twist on the traditional mocha. ⊠ *102 W. Broughton St., Downtown* ☎ *912/401–0399* ⊕ *thecoffeefox.com.*

★ Fodor'sChoice **Foxy Loxy.** A little south of Downtown Savannah, this charming coffeehouse and café provides the cozy comfort lacking in many other Savannah coffee shops. Purveying a variety of coffee drinks—many made with locally roasted Perc Coffee—craft beers, and wine, Foxy Loxy is a staple in the lives of loyal customers of all ages. Try delicious baked treats like kolaches or bourbon-bacon brownies. Don't forget to admire the decor and the rotating art exhibits. Owner Jen Jenkins was a professor printmaker, so her space doubles as a gallery. Leashed pets are welcome in the expansive courtyard in the rear. ⊠ *1919 Bull St., Historic District* ☎ *912/401–0543* ⊕ *www.foxyloxycafe.com.*

Gallery Espresso. This long-established coffee haunt and art enclave features a steady rotation of local artists. The staff can be curt, but it is a real neighborhood joint and a popular destination for art students. The comfortable vintage couches and chairs are a great place to curl up with a book. ⊠ *234 Bull St., Historic District* ☎ *912/233–5348* ⊕ *www.galleryespresso.com.*

Sentient Bean. On the southern edge of Forsyth Park, this hangout was one of Savannah's best-kept secrets until it was written up by the *New York Times.* It is a favorite gathering spot for locals of all stripes, who are drawn by its welcoming atmosphere and organic fare. The Bean offers a small but delectable menu of breakfast and lunch options, along with a variety of fair-trade coffees, teas, and smoothies. In the evening, customers can enjoy poetry readings, film screenings, and live music over a beer or glass of wine at happy-hour prices. ■ TIP→ **The place is cash only, but there's an ATM on-site.** ⊠ *13 E. Park Ave., Historic District* ☎ *912/232–4447* ⊕ *www.sentientbean.com.*

LIVE MUSIC CLUBS

Casimir Lounge. This sleek nightspot regularly features live jazz and blues—keep an eye out for local favorites like vocalist Roger Moss. The decor is luxe, perhaps even a bit over the top. There's a great balcony on the side where you can have a drink while enjoying a view of the park. The mussels and burgers are highly recommended. ✉ *Mansion on Forsyth Park, 700 Drayton St., Historic District* ☎ *912/721–5002* ⊕ *www.mansiononforsythpark.com/dining/lounge* ⊘ *Closed Sun.–Tues.*

Dollhouse Studios. Besides being home to its own recording studio, this 1940s-era factory building hosts fashion, art, and live music events. Run by a young couple hailing from New York City, the place attracts up-and-coming and known national touring artists alike, including some big names like Art Garfunkel. The vibe is offbeat and indie, a mirrored stage and hipster patrons, all in an expansive old warehouse with impressive high ceilings and exposed brick walls. It's open only when there's a show, so check the calendar. ✉ *980 Industry Dr., Historic District* ☎ *912/582–1903* ⊕ *www.dhouseproductions.com.*

Jazz'd Tapas Bar. This chic subterranean venue attracts a crowd of young professionals who belly up to the industrial-style bar for some of Savannah's best martinis. Local jazz and blues artists perform most evenings. The nicely presented tapas are tasty and easy on the budget. ✉ *52 Barnard St., Historic District* ☎ *912/236–7777* ⊕ *jazzdtapasbar.com.*

The Jinx. There's live music almost every night of the week at the Jinx. Weekends could feature anything from heavy metal or punk to outlaw country. The house special is a Pabst Blue Ribbon and a shot of Wild Turkey. Tuesday is the hugely popular hip-hop night, and Saturday happy hour regularly features beloved local bands. If you like tattoos, you will see some of the best in the city. ✉ *127 W. Congress St., Historic District* ☎ *912/236–2281* ⊘ *Closed Sun.*

The Warehouse. An old-school dive bar that claims to have "the coldest beer in town," the Warehouse's River Street location means more tourists than locals. The service is friendly, and lots of different local bands play everything from original rock and country to classic covers. The kitchen serves Southern standbys if you get a hankering for something to snack on. ✉ *18 E. River St., Historic District* ☎ *912/234–6003* ⊕ *thewarehousebarandgrille.com.*

5

BARS AND NIGHTCLUBS

Coach's Corner. This is the place to be if you're trying to catch the big game. Although it's a few miles east of downtown, Coach's Corner serves burgers and other traditional pub grub and is known for some of the best wings in all of Savannah. There's live music on the patio on the weekends. ✉ *3016 E. Victory Dr., Thunderbolt* ☎ *912/352–2933* ⊕ *www.coachs.net.*

Savannah Smiles. Reminiscent of an old roadside honky tonk, Savannah Smiles features dueling piano players that take requests via napkins, and a tip will get your song bumped up in the playlist. Patrons are encouraged to participate in the onstage antics. The kitchen is open late. ✉ *314 Williamson St., Historic District* ☎ *912/527–6453* ⊕ *www. savannahsmilesduelingpianos.com* ⊘ *Closed Sun.–Tues.*

Sandfly Bar & Grill. A favorite neighborhood watering hole, Sandfly is also one of the town's great sports bars. Worth the drive for anyone at home amid pool tables and wall-to-wall TVs displaying a wide range of sports events. Sandfly is also loved for the great (if not so great for you) comfort food. Children and groups are welcome. ✉ *7360 Skidaway Rd., Eastside* ☎ *912/354–8288.*

PERFORMING ARTS

FESTIVALS AND SPECIAL EVENTS

At various times during the year, particularly during spring and fall, Savannah hosts an array of festivals and celebrations.

FAMILY **First Friday Art March.** This creative collaborative event takes place on the first Friday evening of each month from 6 to 9 at various galleries and studios around Savannah's Midtown neighborhood. Sponsored by the local organization Art Rise, the event includes food, music, and multiple art receptions and exhibits. A free trolley helps shuttle participants from gallery to gallery. ✉ *Historic District* ⊕ *artmarchsavannah.com.*

Savannah Book Festival. Held each February, the festival jump-starts the city's spring cultural season with dozens of high-profile authors, many with a connection to the region. The literary event, which takes place in bookstores and other locations around downtown Savannah, is marked by book signings, discussions, and plenty of activities for kids. ✉ *Historic District* ☎ *912/598–4040* ⊕ *www.savannahbookfestival.org.*

Savannah Craft Brew Festival. Held every Labor Day weekend along the Savannah River, the Craft Brew Festival is a buzz-worthy annual event for beer connoisseurs. Featuring dozens of small breweries from around the country, the weekend festival features educational seminars, gourmet meals, live music, and a grand tasting event. ✉ *1 International Dr., Downtown* ⊕ *www.savannahcraftbrewfest.com.*

★ **Fodor's Choice Savannah Film Festival.** This star-studded affair, hosted by the Savannah College of Art and Design in late October and early November, offers multiple daily screenings of award-winning films in various venues on or near Broughton Street. John Goodman, Alec Baldwin, and Aaron Eckhart are among the celebrities who've attended in recent years. Academy-Award winner Jeremy Irons accepted a lifetime achievement award in 2013. Q&A sessions with visiting celebrities are always popular. ✉ *Downtown* ⊕ *filmfest.scad.edu.*

FAMILY **Savannah Folk Music Festival.** For three days in mid-October (usually the second weekend), the free Savannah Folk Music Festival celebrates the legacy of traditional folk music and countless newer variations. The family-friendly event unfolds in various local schools and churches, but the big events take place in Ellis Square and Grayson Stadium and feature performances by a mix of local and national musicians and old-time country dancing. ⊕ *www.savannahfolk.org.*

Savannah Jazz Festival. A local favorite since 1982, this free outdoor musical event is held annually in late September. Thousands of concertgoers pack Forsyth Park's expansive lawn with chairs, blankets, and picnic spreads for several nights of live jazz performances. Given the ideal weather this time of year, this festival puts Savannah's foremost greenspace to great use. ✉ *Forsyth Park, Gaston St., between Drayton and Whitaker Sts., Historic District* ⊕ *www.savannahjazzfestival.org.*

★ **Fodor's Choice Savannah Music Festival.** Georgia's largest and most acclaimed music festival brings together musicians from around the world for more than two weeks of unforgettable performances. The multigenre entertainment ranges from foot-stomping gospel to moody blues to mainstream rock to new takes on classical music. Performances take place in Savannah's premier music venues, as well as non-traditional venues like the rotunda of the Telfair Museum of Art. Festival honcho Rob Gibson spent several years with Jazz at Lincoln Center, so there is no shortage of amazing players. ⊠ *Downtown* ⊕ *www.savannahmusicfestival.org.*

Savannah Stopover Music Festival. This intimate indie music festival is a yearly "stopover" for bands headed to the massive South by Southwest event in Austin. The event features almost 100 acts in about a dozen different venues, providing indie music fans with an unmatched opportunity to experience their favorite up-and-coming acts. ⊠ *Historic District* ⊕ *www.savannahstopover.com.*

★ **Fodor'sChoice Sidewalk Arts Festival.** Sponsored by the Savannah College of Art and Design, the Sidewalk Arts Festival a great opportunity to experience Forsyth Park in abundant glory. At no other time in the year is the park so packed with people of all ages, coming out in droves to see students past and present take to the park's winding sidewalks with rainbow colors of chalk. By the day's end, the park is lined with out-of-this-world drawings as far as the eye can see, plus fun stains of chalk throughout the grass and on scraggling artists. ⊠ *Forsyth Park, Gaston St., between Drayton and Whitaker Sts., Historic District.*

St. Patrick's Day Parade. The city's largest annual festival has evolved over the past two centuries to be one of the largest of its kind in the country. Each March, roughly 700,000 participants tip their hats (and their glasses) to the rolling hills of Ireland. River Street becomes a sea of green: clothes, beer, food, and even the water in city fountains is dyed the color of the clover. ■TIP→ **Hotel rates during this period can be as much as three times the norm, so reserve well in advance.** ⊠ *River St., Downtown* ⊕ *www.savannahsaint-patricksday.com.*

FAMILY **Tybee Island Pirate Festival.** Swashbucklers and wenches descend on Tybee Island each Columbus Day weekend for the Pirate Festival. Don your best pirate-themed costumes for the Buccaneer Ball at the Crab Shack to kick off the weekend's festivities. Saturday is the popular Pirate Parade, where Butler Avenue becomes a sea of ships filled with buccaneers tossing beads and booty. Venture over to the Thieves Market, where vendors from across the country peddle their pirate wares and arts and crafts. Fun for the whole family, the festival includes magicians, puppet shows, and storytellers. Live entertainment rounds

Did You Know?

Savannah's photogenic side has long served as a popular backdrop for movies. In the 1970s, some scenes from the legendary television miniseries *Roots* were shot at various spots around Savannah. In 1989 the Academy Award–winning film *Glory*, starring Denzel Washington and Morgan Freeman, was filmed near Fort Pulaski. One of Savannah's most famous film appearances came in 1994, when scenes for *Forrest Gump* were set on the north end of Chippewa Square. *Midnight in the Garden of Good and Evil* was filmed in the Historic District in 1997, and

two years later *The General's Daughter* was shot at Wormsloe Plantation. *The Legend of Bagger Vance,* starring Will Smith, brought film crews to Savannah and Jekyll Island in 2000. Robert Redford's historical drama about Mary Surratt, *The Conspirator,* used Savannah for its backdrop in 2009. Most recently, parts of the city were transformed into 1970s New York City for a biopic about the early days of the legendary CBGB's nightclub. Shot in 2012, the movie featured Rupert Grint and Alan Rickman, who both had prominent roles in the Harry Potter movies.

out the experience with concert headliners like Vince Neil and Eddie Money. ⊠ *Strand Ave., between Tybrisia St. and 17th Pl., Tybee Island* ⊕ *tybeepiratefest.com* ⊟ *From $10 per day or $22 for weekend.*

VENUES

Johnny Mercer Theater. Named for the city's most famous songwriter, the Johnny Mercer Theater in the Savannah Civic Center hosts numerous events and performances throughout the year, including big-ticket concerts, sporting events, and the circus. ⊠ *301 W. Oglethorpe Ave., Orleans Sq., Historic District* ☎ *912/651–6550* ⊕ *www.savannahcivic.com.*

★ Fodor'sChoice **Lucas Theatre.** Slated for demolition in 1921, the Lucas Theatre is now one of Savannah's most celebrated spaces. The beautifully renovated space hosts a variety of performances throughout the year, from ballet to bluegrass bands. It's a go-to venue for events hosted by the Savannah College of Art and Design, the Savannah Film Festival, and the Savannah Music Festival. ⊠ *32 Abercorn St., Historic District* ☎ *912/525–5050* ⊕ *www.lucastheatre.com.*

Muse Arts Warehouse. A relative newcomer to Savannah's cultural scene, this converted warehouse is home to one of the city's most vibrant arts spaces. Hosting theater, comedy, music, film, and other events, this intimate black-box theater offers a little bit of everything. ✉ *703 Louisville Rd.* ☎ *912/713–1137* ⊕ *www.musesavannah.org.*

Savannah Theatre. One of the country's oldest continuously operating theaters, the beautifully maintained Savannah Theatre presents family-friendly comedies and musical revues. The 600-seat theater is a throwback to the glory days of the stage. Don't miss the *Savannah Live* variety show. ✉ *222 Bull St., at Chippewa Sq., Historic District* ☎ *912/233–7764* ⊕ *www.savannahtheatre.com.*

★ Fodor'sChoice **Trustees Theater.** When it opened in 1946, the Trustees Theater was one of the largest movie screens in the South. Now run by the Savannah College of Art and Design, it hosts a variety of events, including the Savannah Film Festival. It's also a popular venue for concerts and lectures. ✉ *216 E. Broughton St., Historic District* ☎ *912/525–5050* ⊕ *www.trusteestheater.com.*

SPORTS AND THE OUTDOORS

Updated
by
Summer
Teal
Simpson

SAVANNAH RESIDENTS TAKE ADVANTAGE of life on the coast. The neighboring areas and barrier islands of the Lowcountry are conducive to nearly all types of water sports. Swimming, sailing, kiteboarding, fishing, kayaking, parasailing, and surfing are popular pastimes. The Savannah River flows alongside the city on its way to the Atlantic Ocean and is easily accessible by boat. A multitude of tidal creeks and marshlands intertwine the river and the barrier islands, most notably Tybee, where you can enjoy the sun-drenched beaches, friendly people, and a quirky vibe. The water here is generally warm enough for swimming from May through September.

For those who would prefer to stay on land, bicycling and jogging, golf and tennis, and arena sports dominate. During the hot and humid summer months, limit the duration of strenuous activity, remember to drink lots of water, and protect your skin from the sun.

SPORTS AND ACTIVITIES

BASEBALL

FAMILY **Savannah Sand Gnats.** The Class-A Savannah Sand Gnats play at Grayson Stadium, one of the oldest minor-league ballparks in the country. (Babe Ruth played a few games here back in the day.) Since this is a New York Mets farm team, you might catch sight of a future star on the diamond. Much more affordable than catching a big league game, this is good old-fashioned family fun with on-field activities, traditional ballpark refreshments, and a full bar. Gnate the Gnat, the team's goofy mascot, is popular with kids. A fireworks display follows every Saturday evening game. ⊠ *1401 E. Victory Dr., Daffin Park* ☎ *912/351–9150* ⊕ *www.sandgnats.com.*

BEACHES

North Beach. Tybee Island's North Beach is an all-in-one destination for beachgoers of every age. Located at the mouth of the Savannah River, the scene is generally low-key and is a great vantage point for viewing the cargo ships making their way to the Port of Savannah. A large, metered parking lot gives you convenient access to the beach, Fort Screven, and the adjacent Tybee Island Lighthouse and Museum, a 178-step lighthouse with great views of the surrounding area. The North Beach Grill, located in the

BEST OUTDOOR ACTIVITIES

■ **Baseball.** A baseball game under a summer sky is an all-American pleasure. It is a family-bonding opportunity, and, happily, ticket prices for the Savannah Sand Gnats (a New York Mets farm-system affiliate) start at just $8. Buy a hot dog and join in the fun. On Friday nights kids get to run the bases after the game, and on Saturday nights there are fireworks, so you can double your fun for the cost of admission.

Biking. Forsyth and Daffin parks are favored destinations for locals. Rails-to-Trails is a 3-mile route that starts 1 mile east of the Bull River Bridge on Highway 80 and ends at the entrance to Fort Pulaski. Tom Triplett Park, east of town on U.S. 80, offers three bike loops—3.5 miles, 5 miles, and 6.3 miles. You can explore quaint Tybee Island by bike for nearly half of what it costs to rent a bike downtown.

■ **Golf.** The weather here, particularly in the spring and fall, is custom ordered for a round or two of golf. Though the courses aren't as well regarded as those on Hilton Head, players looking for a challenge can count on gems like the Westin's Club at Savannah Harbor and the Wilmington Island Club, both of which are more moderately priced than the Hilton Head courses.

■ **Water Sports.** Water sports are the obvious choice for a city surrounded by rivers, creeks, marshes, and the Atlantic Ocean. Kayaking, sailing, stand-up paddleboarding, and kiteboarding are all popular, and there are plenty of options for guided tours, charter boats, and equipment rental (if you haven't brought your own).

6

parking lot, is perfect for an ice-cold beverage or bite to eat. To get here from Highway 80, turn left on Campbell Street and follow the signs to the Tybee Island Lighthouse. ■TIP→ **The local police are notorious for parking tickets, so make sure you feed the meter. Amenities:** food and drink; lifeguard; parking (fee); toilets. **Best for:** solitude; sunrise; swimming; walking. ⊠ *Meddin Dr. at Gulick St., north of 1st St., Tybee Island.*

South End. If your idea of a good beach day involves empty stretches of sand, unobstructed views, plenty of privacy, and the sound of crashing waves, then you should test the waters at the South End. As its name suggests, the South End is located at the southern tip of the island where Tybee's

Back River meets the Atlantic Ocean. △ **Riptides and strong currents are prevalent here, so use extreme caution when swimming.** At low tide the waters recede to expose a stunning system of sandbars that are great for shelling and spotting sea life. Check the tides to make sure you don't get stranded on the sandbars. This is one of Tybee's prettiest beaches, and is worshipped by locals for its seclusion. There are no restaurants in the immediate vicinity, so it's a good idea to bring a cooler packed with snacks and beverages. Parking is tough—just two very small metered lots. In high season, arrive on the early or the late side, when crowds are thinner. **Amenities:** parking (fee). **Best for:** sunset; walking; windsurfing; sea kayaking. ✉ *Butler Ave., at 19th St., Tybee Island.*

Tybee Island Pier and Pavilion. This is Tybee's "grand strand," the center of the summer beach action. Anchored by a 700-foot pier that is sometimes host to summer concerts, this stretch of shoreline is your best bet for people-watching and beach activities. Just off the sand at the bustling intersection of Tybrisa Street and Butler Avenue, a cluster of watering holes, souvenir shops, bike shacks, and oyster bars makes up Tybee's main business district. ■ TIP→ **There's metered street parking as well as two good-size lots. Both fill up fast during the high season, so arrive early.** There are public restrooms at the Pier and at 15th and Tybrisa streets. The pier is popular for fishing and is also the gathering place for fireworks displays. **Amenities:** food and drink; lifeguard; parking (fee); toilets. **Best for:** partiers; sunrise; surfing; swimming. ✉ *Tybrisa St. at Butler Ave., Tybee Island.*

BIKING

Savannah is table-flat, to the enjoyment of many bicyclists. Like many towns and cities across the country, Savannah has introduced a bike-share program, allowing daily or weekly access to bikes at several solar-powered stations downtown. The city has also added a number of bike racks around the Historic District to make it easier for cyclists to find adequate parking without blocking foot traffic.

Sunday is the best day for riding downtown, but be aware that throughout much of downtown there are restrictions for bikers. Riding through the middle of squares and on the sidewalks of Broughton Street is illegal and carries a stiff fine if you're busted.

Bikers should always ride with traffic, not against it, and obey the lights. Riding after dark requires bicycles to display a white light visible from 300 feet on the front and a red reflector on the back. Helmets are legally required for those under the age of 16 (and a good idea for everyone). Be sure to lock up your bike securely if you're leaving it unattended, even for a few minutes.

CAT Bike. Keeping pace with booming metropolises like New York and Washington D.C., the City of Savannah and Chatham Area Transit introduced a public bike-share program in 2014. Two solar-powered stations are located at Ellis Square and Rivers Exchange. Rates start at $5 for a 24-hour pass or $20 for a weekly pass. ⊠ *Historic District* ☎ *912/233–5767* ⊕ *catbike.bcycle.com.*

Motorini. See the sights of Savannah aboard a Vespa—a fun and stylish scooter. Rates at Motorini start at $30 for the first hour. ⊠ *236 Drayton St., Historic District* ☎ *912/201– 1899* ⊕ *www.vespasavannah.com* ⊗ *Daily 10–6.*

Perry Rubber Bike Shop. At the pulsing corner of Bull and Liberty streets, Perry Rubber is the go-to shop for repairs and your best bet for rentals. It offers trendy Pure City or Pure Fix bikes at $20 for a half-day or $35 for the full day—helmet, lock, and basket included. ⊠ *240 Bull St., Downtown* ☎ *912/236–9929* ⊕ *www.perryrubberbikeshop. com* ⊗ *Mon.–Sat. 10–6, Sun. noon–5.*

Sekka Bike. Stop by this popular storefront shop for hourly or daily bike rentals. Take an afternoon spin at $10 for three hours, or opt for a weekly rental for only $60. ⊠ *206 E. Broughton St., Historic District* ☎ *912/233–3888* ⊕ *sekk- abike.com* ⊗ *Mon.–Sat. 10–6, Sun. noon–6.*

Tim's Bike & Beach Gear. Filled with ocean-view trails, Tybee Island offers a bike-friendly environment and rentals at half the cost of downtown. Tim's Beach Gear rents bikes for adults and kids, as well as pull-behind carriers and jogging strollers. The shop offers free delivery and pickup on the island. Daily rates are $10 and include helmets and cup holders. And talk about one-stop shopping: umbrellas, beach chairs, towels, and games like bocce ball and horseshoes are also available. ⊠ *1101 U.S. Hwy 80 E, Tybee Island* ☎ *912/786–8467* ⊕ *www.timsbeachgear.com* ⊗ *Daily 9–5.*

6

BOATING AND FISHING

Bull River Yacht Club Marina. This is your one-stop-shop for all your boating needs. Bull River offers rentals, tours, and charters in boats big and small. Starting at $20 per person, expert guides will take you to hunt sharks' teeth; on a sightseeing tour of area forts and lighthouses; or on a 90-minute dolphin tour. For the more adventuresome, inshore and offshore charters start at $325 and $475, respectively, for four people. If you prefer to captain your own boat, pontoon rentals start at $175 for two hours. Kayak rentals are $30 for a half day. ✉ *8005 U.S. Hwy. 80, Wilmington Island* ☎ *912/897–7300* ⊕ *www.bullriver-marina.com* ⊗ *Daily 8–6.*

★ Fodor'sChoice **Captain Mike's Dolphin Tours.** If boat-bound
FAMILY adventure is what you seek, look no further than Captain Mike. Widely popular with tourists and locals alike, Captain Mike's tours have been featured on the Discovery Channel, *Good Morning America,* and in the pages of *Southern Living.* Choose from a 90-minute dolphin tour from $15 per person, or an $18 sunset tour (available May to September). Captain Mike's has a 32-foot cabin cruiser in his fleet and offers inshore and offshore fishing charters. This business is family-owned and operated, and kids are welcome. ✉ *Lazaretto Creek Marina, 1 Old U.S. Hwy. 80, Tybee Island* ☎ *912/786–5848* ⊕ *tybeedolphins.com.*

FAMILY **Dolphin Magic Tours.** Explore the natural beauty of Savannah's coastal waters on a narrated boat tour with Dolphin Magic Tours. From River Street you cruise out to the marshlands and tidal creeks near Tybee Island. The search for dolphin encounters lasts two hours and costs $30; sightings are guaranteed. Departure times vary according to the tides and the weather. ✉ *312 E. River St., Historic District* ☎ *912/897–4990* ⊕ *www.reelemn.com/dolphinmagic.*

Miss Judy Charters. Captain Judy Helmey, a longtime fishing guide and legendary local character, heads up Miss Judy Charters. The company offers packages ranging from 3-hour sightseeing tours to 14-hour deep-sea fishing expeditions. Inshore rates start at around $350 for three to four people for three hours; offshore rates start at $400 for up to six people for three hours. ✉ *124 Palmetto Dr., Wilmington Island* ☎ *912/897–4921* ⊕ *www. missjudycharters.com.*

Moon River Kayak Tours. Setting out from either Wilmington or Skidaway islands, Moon River Kayak offers a different experience than many of the tours originating on Tybee Island. Paddling Turner's Creek, Skidaway Narrows, and Johnny Mercer's Moon River gives you a more inland perspective rich with sightings of such spectacular birds as ospreys and eagles. Be sure to bring your binoculars. ⊠ *Rodney J. Boat Ramp & Park, 45 Diamond Causeway, Skidaway Island* ☎ *912/897–3474* ⊕ *www.moonriver kayak.com.*

North Island Surf & Kayak. Virtually unsinkable and great for navigating the shallowest of creeks, sit-on-top kayaks are available at North Island Surf & Kayak. All rentals include paddles, lifejackets, and seat backs. Prices are $45 per day for a single, $55 for a double. Paddle to the beautiful uninhabited island of Little Tybee or to Cockspur Beacon. Discounts are available for multiday rentals, so you can even camp on one of the islands. Stand-up paddleboards are $40 for the day. If you've always wanted to learn how to surf, $50 will get you a board rental and a two-hour lesson. ⊠ *1C Old Hwy. 80, Tybee Island* ☎ *912/786–4000* ⊕ *www.northislandkayak.com* ☉ *Daily 9–6.*

★ Fodor'sChoice **Savannah Canoe and Kayak.** Leading you through inlets and tidal creeks, Savannah Canoe and Kayak has highly skilled guides that provide expert instruction for newbies and challenges for seasoned paddlers. You'll also learn about the history of these historic waterways. Half-day tours start at $55 for three hours. ⊠ *414 Bonaventure Rd.* ☎ *912/341–9502* ⊕ *www.savannahcanoeandkayak.com.*

Sea Kayak Georgia. Owned by professional paddlers and instructors Marsha Henson and Ronnie Kemp, Sea Kayak Georgia provides gear, tours, and courses for beginners and advanced kayakers alike, not to mention stand-up paddleboard rentals and the unique experience of teacher-led stand-up paddleboard yoga. Seasoned guides and naturalists lead half-day salt-marsh paddle tours beginning at $55. ⊠ *1102 U.S. Hwy. 80, Tybee Island* ☎ *912/786–8732* ⊕ *www.seakayakgeorgia.com* ☉ *Daily 10–6.*

FAMILY **Tele-Caster Charters.** Captain Kevin Rose leads fishing excursions on his 18-foot Pioneer flats boat for speckled trout, black drum, redfish, sheepshead, whiting, and even sharks. Fully licensed and insured, his four-hour trips start from one of several locations. The excursions start at $325 for two people and include bait and licenses. Rose also offers

CLOSE UP

Georgia Football

This is the Deep South, so naturally locals can't get enough of Georgia football. They eat it for breakfast. Many locals take a couple of days off from their busy schedules to attend one of the first University of Georgia Bulldogs football games of the season.

If you want to make friends fast, express an interest in the Bulldogs—or "Dawgs," as they're better known in these parts. The famous mascot, nicknamed "Uga," hails from a line of white bulldogs that has been owned since the 1950s by Savannah resident Sonny Seiler. Once an attorney so prominent that he was featured in Hollywood's adaptation of *Midnight in the Garden of Good and Evil*, he is a local celebrity in his own right. And don't be surprised if your waiter raises the sleeve of his T-shirt to show you his symbolic University of Georgia tattoo—"One big G!"

island shuttles and nature tours. Children are welcome. ☎ 912/308–4622 ⊕ www.telecasterscharters.com.

Tybee Jet Ski & Watersports. For those who enjoy more fast-paced activities, little compares to the rush of jet skiing on the island waterways or riding the swells of the beach. Tybee Jet Ski & Watersports rents Jet Skis/waverunners starting at $99 per hour. In addition, this shop offers everything you need for sea kayaking excursions. Rates for a single kayak start at $35 for a full day. If you'd like a guided tour of the coastal marshes and tidal streams, the cost is $38 for 90 minutes. ⊠ 1C Old Hwy. 80, Tybee Island ☎ 912/786–5554 ⊕ tybeejetski.com ⊙ Daily 7–7.

GOLF

Bacon Park Golf Course. Completely renovated in 2014, Savannah's municipal golf club offers three 9-hole courses played in different 18-hole configurations. The Live Oak course debuted in 1926, making it one of the area's oldest; the Cypress and Magnolia courses were added in the '70s and '80s. Located on Savannah's Southside, Bacon Park is the best bang for your golfing buck in the area. ⊠ 1 Shorty Cooper Dr. ☎ 912/354–2625 ⊕ baconparkgolf.com ⛳ 9 holes, $21; 18-hole combination, $36 ⅃ Live Oak Course: 9 holes, 3423 yards, par 36; Cypress Course: 9 holes, 3256 yards, par 36; Magnolia Course: 9 holes, 3317 yards, par 36 ⊙ Daily 7–6.

★ Fodor's Choice **The Club at Savannah Harbor.** The area's only PGA course, this resort property on Hutchinson Island is a free ferry ride from Savannah's riverfront. The lush championship course winds through pristine wetlands and has unparalleled views of the river and downtown. It is also home to the annual Liberty Mutual Legends of Golf tournament, which attracts golfing's finest each spring. A bit pricier than most local clubs, it's packed with beauty and amenities. ⊠ *Westin Savannah Harbor, 2 Resort Dr., Hutchinson Island* ☎ *912/201–2240* ⊕ *www.theclubatsavannahharbor. com* ⊒ *$145* ⚲ *Reservations essential* ⚑ *18 holes, 7288 yards, par 72* ⊙ *Mon.–Sat. 6:30–10, Sun. 11:30–2.*

Crosswinds Golf Club. This 18-hole championship course features parkland-style play in an isolated setting 12 miles from downtown Savannah. Crosswinds has a reputation for being exceedingly well maintained; a nice, lighted 9-hole executive course is available, as is a driving range. ⊠ *232 James Blackburn Dr.* ☎ *912/966–1909* ⊕ *www.crosswinds-golfclub.com* ⊒ *Championship Course, $53; Par-3 Course, $20* ⚲ *Reservations essential* ⚑ *Championship Course: 18 holes, 6748 yards, par 72; Par-3 Course: 9 holes, 1126 yards, par 27.* ⊙ *Sat.–Mon. 7:30–dusk, Tues.–Fri. 7–9.*

Henderson Golf Club. Located 15 miles from downtown, Henderson Golf Club might not be Savannah's biggest course, but its abundance of natural beauty makes it a draw for locals and visitors alike. This lush municipal course is surrounded by live oaks and wandering wetlands. You can rent a cart, or walk it if the weather's cool. ⊠ *1 Al Henderson Dr.* ☎ *912/920–4653* ⊕ *www.hendersongolfclub.com* ⊒ *$39* ⚲ *Reservations essential* ⚑ *18 holes, 6700 yards, par 71* ⊙ *Daily 7:30–6.*

Southbridge Golf Club. Nestled within one of Savannah's most exclusive private housing communities, Southbridge is a popular Bermuda grass course. ⊠ *415 Southbridge Blvd.* ☎ *912/651–5455* ⊕ *www.southbridgegolfclub.com* ⊒ *$60* ⚲ *Reservations essential* ⚑ *18 holes, 6922 yards, par 72* ⊙ *Mon.–Thurs. 7–7, Fri.–Sun. 7–dusk.*

Wilmington Island Club. Designed by Donald Ross in 1927, this gorgeous property is dotted with palms and live oaks. It's just east of downtown across the Wilmington River. ⊠ *501 Wilmington Island Rd., Wilmington Island* ☎ *912/897–1612* ⊕ *thewilmingtonislandclub.com/* ⊒ *$69* ⚲ *Reservations essential* ⚑ *18 holes, 6715 yards, par 71* ⊙ *Weekdays 8–5, weekends 10–5.*

6

ROLLER DERBY

Savannah Derby Devils. This women's flat-track roller derby team, the Derby Devils, is composed of an all-volunteer squad, coaches, medics, refs, and jeer-leaders. They play in "bouts" several times a year against worthy Southeastern opponents. The truly daring might try "suicide seating," on the edge of the rink, just inches away from bone-checking, jaw-dropping action. ⊠ *Savannah Civic Center, 301 W. Oglethorpe Ave., Historic District* ☎ *912/220–9744* ⊕ *www.savannahderby.com* ⊐ *$13.*

SPORTS BARS. Don't forget the sport of cheerleading! If you can't get tickets to the game, the next best thing is joining locals around a neighborhood bar to root for the home team. Spots like Congress Street Social Club and Coach's Corner make an art out of it.

WATER SPORTS

AOK Watersports. Kiteboarding has already taken coastal communities by storm. On Tybee Island you too can learn to kiteboard (on land or in the water) from certified instructors at AOK. Lessons begin at $100 per hour. AOK also offers gear rental to experienced riders. The online shop carries beachwear, sunglasses, and sells top adventure sport gear for kiteboarding, skateboarding, longboarding, paddleboarding, and even snowboarding. ⊠ *1510 Butler Ave., Tybee Island* ☎ *912/786–8080* ⊕ *www.aok-watersports.com.*

SHOPPING

Updated
by
Summer
Teal
Simpson

ANYONE WITH EVEN THE SLIGHTEST INCLINATION toward shopping would be hard pressed to leave Savannah empty-handed. The downtown streets are alive with an array of boutiques and shops running the gamut from kitschy to glamorous, locally owned to nationally renowned.

A 2014 infusion of capital into Broughton Street has seen the city's "main street" come full circle over the past 30 years, and what was once a string of abandoned storefronts has been transformed into a world-class shopping district. As you stroll along Broughton, note the original tenant names etched into historic facades and the sidewalk entries.

Antiques malls and junk emporiums with eye-catching facades and eclectic offerings beckon you to take home treasures from the city's rich past. Meanwhile, contemporary design shops feature the latest lighting and sleek designer furnishings. Some of the newest additions to the shopping landscape are specialty food stores that offer tastings throughout the day. And don't miss trendy boutiques that offer modern fashions with a Southern twist.

Since a great many of the city's attractions are centrally located, a day of shopping can go hand-in-hand with visits to nearby museums or long meals at one of the well-regarded restaurants. The tree-lined streets promise a vista at every turn, so be sure to bring along your camera and a comfortable pair of walking shoes. Should you tire along the way, horse-drawn carriages, trolley tours, or pedicabs abound to help you get off your feet without sacrificing a full itinerary.

SHOPPING DISTRICTS

Broughton Street. Savannah's "main street" has long served as an indicator of the city's changing economic and demographic trends. The first of Savannah's department stores, Adler's and Levy's, emerged on Broughton, followed by the post-WWII introduction of national chains Sears & Roebuck, JCPenney, and Kress. During the 1950s, ladies donning white gloves and heels did their shopping, while kids gathered at the soda counter or caught the matinee. Downtown's decline began in the late 1950s and continued through the '70s, when boarded-up storefronts were the norm rather than the exception. Today Broughton is again thriving, not only with local boutiques and world-class shops, but with theaters, restaurants, and coffeehouses. A

BEST BETS FOR SHOPPING

■ **Art Galleries.** The Savannah College of Art and Design has indelibly imprinted the city with a love of fine arts. Numerous galleries are associated with the school, and many more feature works by some of the many successful alums.

■ **Clothing and Accessories.** Broughton Street is the place for designer clothing, chic shoes, and one-of-a-kind jewelry and accessories to outfit the most discerning shoppers. J. Parker Ltd. is where Savannah's Southern gentlemen pick up their seersucker suits.

■ **Eclectic Gifts.** The Savannah Bee Company's flagship store is a haven of honey-based delights. Pair that with a gift box from Savannah Tea Company and homemade biscuits from Byrd Cookie Company for a take-home taste of Savannah.

■ **Home Decor and Antiques.** The charming Paris Market & Brocante occupies two floors with a feel reminiscent of a turn-of-the-20th-century French bazaar. But don't neglect the city's many antiques shops, including Habersham Antiques and Alex Raskin's.

2014 facelift attracted more upscale boutiques and high-end fashion retailers. ✉ *Broughton St., between Congress and State Sts., Historic District.*

City Market. Dating from the 1700s, the four-block-long City Market is a pedestrian-friendly emporium that has experienced a magnificent renaissance. The city's original farmers' market contains an eclectic and concentrated mix of artist studios, sidewalk cafés, bars, and shops. On weekends the sounds of live music drift throughout the flower-adorned market. A great stop for a quick ice-cream cone or a leisurely lunch, City Market is also ground zero for trolley and horse-carriage tours. ✉ *W. St. Julian St., between Ellis and Franklin Sqs., Historic District* ☎ *912/232–4903* ⊕ *www.savannahcitymarket.com.*

Downtown Design District. Renowned for its array of fine antiques shops and interior design boutiques, the Downtown Design District is worth a visit. Stop in some of Savannah's trendier fashion stores, many of them housed in charming historic storefronts. Nearby are the famed Mercer-Williams House and the landmark Mrs. Wilkes' Dining Room, known for some of the area's best family-style Southern food. The picturesque surrounding neighborhoods are also amenable for a nice afternoon stroll. ✉ *Whitaker St., between Charlton and Gaston Sts., Historic District.*

Madison Square. You'll discover an array of unique local shops nestled around historic Madison Square. Grab lunch on the rooftop of the Public Kitchen and Bar before stopping in longtime favorites like the Christmas Shop and E. Shaver Booksellers. ShopSCAD offers some of the finest gifts, clothing, and home decor items designed and produced by students of the highly regarded Savannah College of Art and Design. Take afternoon tea at the college's Gryphon Tea Room, located inside a remodeled old-time pharmacy. ✉ *Bull St., bordered by Liberty and Charlton Sts., Historic District.*

Riverfront/Factors Walk. Though it's often crowded and a little rowdy after dark, no visit to Savannah would be complete without a stroll through Riverfront/Factors Walk. These nine blocks of renovated waterfront warehouses were once the city's cotton exchange. Today you'll discover more than 75 boutiques, galleries, restaurants, and pubs, as well as a spectacular view of the Savannah River. Glimpse impressive cargo ships as they head to port while you shop for souvenirs, specialty treats, and local art. Tired of shopping? Catch a dolphin tour or dinner boat and see the waterfront from a different perspective. ■TIP→ **River Street's cobblestones and Factors Walk's steep stairwells can be rough, so be sure to wear comfortable footwear.** ✉ *River St., Historic District.*

SHOPPING REVIEWS

HISTORIC DISTRICT

ANTIQUES

37th @ Abercorn Antique & Design. Filled with antiques and collectibles spanning 200 years, this one-stop shop lets you peruse the area's largest collection of vintage children's clothes and museum-quality quilts, clocks, and costume jewelry. Visit a primitive country kitchen displaying gadgets, enamelware, and 1950s-era linens. Original Persian rugs and antique sterling-silver accessories are among other items on display. ✉ *201 E. 37th St., Thomas Square* ☎ *912/233–0064* ⊕ *www.37aad.com* ☉ *Mon.–Sat. 10–5, Sun. 11–4.*

★ Fodor'sChoice **Alex Raskin Antiques.** This shop is inside the four-story Noble Hardee Mansion, a gilded Italianate home. You can wander through almost all 12,000 square feet of the former grand residence and see how the landed gentry once lived. The building is a bit musty, with peeling wallpaper and patches of leaky ceiling, but the antiques within are in great condition and represent a colorful scrapbook of Savannah's past. They specialize in furniture, rugs, and paintings, but take note of more uncommon artifacts like tramp art frames and antique doll furniture. Take in the view of Forsyth Park from one of the upper-level porches. ■TIP➔ **The building lacks air conditioning, so avoid the heat of midday or bring along a fan.** ⊠ *441 Bull St., Historic District* ☎ *912/232–8205* ⊕ *www.alexraskinantiques.com* ⊙ *Mon.– Sat. 10–5.*

Habersham Antiques. With more than 70 vendors under one roof, this shop's sprawling hodgepodge of antique styles has a growing emphasis on the mid-century modern designs of the '50s and '60s. In one booth you'll find funky Lucite chairs and teak sideboards, and in another you'll find slinky costume jewelry and handbags. It is always fun to browse the ever-changing collections, and prices are among the most reasonable you can find in a city known for its antiques. ⊠ *2502 Habersham St., Historic District* ☎ *912/238–5908* ⊕ *habershamantiquesmarket.com* ⊙ *Weekdays 9:30–5:30, Sat. 10–5.*

ART GALLERIES

The Butcher Art Gallery. Half gallery, half tattoo studio, the Butcher is a true original. Its rotating exhibitions feature younger, more contemporary artists. The staff is hip, friendly, and knowledgable, and the space is a modern twist on a vintage storefront. ⊠ *19 E. Bay St., Historic District* ☎ *912/234–6505* ⊕ *www.whatisthebutcher.com* ⊙ *Tues.– Thurs. noon–9, Fri. and Sat. noon–10, Sun. noon–8.*

Grand Bohemian Gallery. Neatly tucked inside the Mansion on Forsyth Park, one of the city's most luxurious hotels, this gallery showcases the Kessler Collection, acquired by the gallery's owner and hotelier, native Georgian Richard Kessler. You'll find more than 400 works by acclaimed artists, especially contemporary paintings, blown glass, whimsical sculptures, and some incredibly innovative jewelry. ⊠ *The Mansion on Forsyth Park, 700 Drayton St., Historic District* ☎ *912/721–5007* ⊕ *www.grandbohemiangallery.com* ⊙ *Mon.–Sat. 10–7, Sun. 10–5.*

★ Fodor's Choice **Gutstein Gallery.** The Savannah College of Art and Design has masterfully restored dozens of historic buildings throughout Savannah, but the Gutstein Gallery, in a former cafeteria, is one of the most noteworthy. The gallery displays rotating exhibitions of fine art by students, professors, and visiting artists. If you're walking around downtown, stop by this and other student galleries, including Pinnacle, Hall Street, Alexander Hall, Fahm Hall, May Poetter, and Pei Ling Chan. ⊠ *201 E. Broughton St., Historic District* ☎ *912/525–4743* ⊕ *www.scad.edu/exhibitions* ⊙ *Weekdays 10–6, Sat. noon–5.*

★ Fodor's Choice **Kobo Gallery.** Between the bustling hubs of Broughton Street and City Market sits the city's foremost cooperative art gallery. Near Ellis Square, the tasteful space is teeming with fine art across countless mediums. Noteworthy are the industrial-style jewelry by Meredith Sutton, large and small colorful abtract paintings by Ikeda Feingold, and Dicky Stone's intricate wordworking. ⊠ *33 Barnard St., Historic District* ☎ *912/201–0304* ⊕ *kobogallery.com* ⊙ *Mon.–Sat. 10:30–5:30, Sun. 11–5.*

★ Fodor's Choice **Roots Up Gallery.** Opened in 2014 by longtime Savannah residents Leslie and Francis Allen, Roots Up is a testament to the charm and mystique of Southern folk art. On the parlor level of an 1854 mansion, Roots Up is home to such artists as Howard Finster, Willie Tarver, Jimmy Lee Sudduth, Antonio Estevez, and Mr. Imagination. The collection includes everything from handmade dolls to vintage pieces. ⊠ *6 E. Liberty St., Historic District* ☎ *912/677-2845* ⊕ *www.rootsupgallery.com* ⊙ *Tues.–Sat. 10–6.*

Tiffani Taylor Gallery. Renowned local artist Tiffani Taylor's textured paintings are romantic yet bold, influenced by nature and her extensive travels. Her work has been exhibited in the Salvador Dalí Museum in St. Petersburg, Florida, and her clients include Oprah Winfrey and Diane von Furstenberg. In addition to her paintings, Taylor's original pottery and stationery make great gifts. ⊠ *11 Whitaker St., Historic District* ☎ *912/507–7860* ⊕ *www.tiffaniart.com* ⊙ *Tues.–Sat. 10–5.*

BOOKS

The Book Lady. On the garden level of a Liberty Street row house, the Book Lady stocks around 50,000 new, used, and vintage books spanning 40 genres. The shop also offers Wi-Fi access, a reading garden, and bookbinding repairs. The friendly staff is always available for a lively literary discussion, and the shop hosts the occasional book signing by noted authors. ✉ *6 E. Liberty St., Historic District* ☎ *912/233–3628* ⊕ *www.thebookladybookstore.com* ⊗ *Mon.–Sat. 10–5:30.*

★ **Fodor's**Choice **E. Shaver Booksellers.** Among the city's most beloved bookshops, E. Shaver is the source for 17th- and 18th-century maps and new books on local history, recipes, artists, and authors. This shop occupies 12 rooms of a historic building, which alone is something to see. The whole family can explore the children's book sections. The booksellers are welcoming and knowledgeable about their wares. ✉ *326 Bull St., Historic District* ☎ *912/234–7257* ⊕ *eshaverbooks.com* ⊗ *Mon.–Sat. 9:30–5:30.*

V&J Duncan. An intricate iron sign and gate point the way to V&J Duncan, an off-the-beaten path Savannah relic on the garden level of a historic home on Monterey Square. The shop specializes in antique maps and prints and carries a vast collection of engravings, photographs, and lithographs. There are also rare books on Southern culture. Their hours aren't strictly observed, so call ahead to make sure they're open. ■TIP➔ **With so much to see, plan to spend some time here.** ✉ *12 E. Taylor St., Historic District* ☎ *912/232–0338* ⊕ *vjduncan.com* ⊗ *Mon.–Sat. 10:30–4:30.*

CLOTHING

Copper Penny. Venture to this Broughton Street mainstay for women's clothing and footwear that is, as they say, "curated with the Southern eye." You'll find seasonal looks by Elizabeth and James, Trina Turk, Alice & Trixie, French Connection, and Julie Brown, as well as shoes and accessories by Rebecca Minkoff, Michael Kors, and Chanel. The owners have their own renowned shoe line, Rowen, that's sold here and at their flagship shop in Charleston. ✉ *22 W. Broughton St., Historic District* ☎ *912/629–6800* ⊕ *www.shopcopperpenny.com* ⊗ *Mon.–Sat. 10–6.*

J. Parker Ltd. This is where savvy gentlemen go to suit up. Look for outerwear, sportswear, and dresswear by top men's designers like Filson, Southern Tide, Corbin, and Mountain Khakis. If you need a seersucker suit on short notice, this is your best bet. ✉ *20 W. Broughton St., Historic District* ☎ *912/234–0004* ⊕ *www.jparkerltd.com* ⊗ *Mon.–Sat. 10–6, Sun. 12:30–5.*

James Hogan. Savannah's resident fashion designer and his shop, tucked in a storefront in the Historic District, have brought a touch of glamour to the city. Featured here is

7

apparel designed by Hogan himself, as well as upscale women's fashions from well-regarded American and European designers like Etro and Charles Chang Lima. ⊠ *412B Whitaker St., Historic District* ☎ *912/234–0374* ⊕ *www. jameshogan.com* ⊘ *Weekdays 10–5:30, Sat. 10–5.*

Red Clover. This is the place to be if you want fashionable and affordable apparel, shoes, and handbags. It features sharp looks from up-and-coming designers, all at under $100. It's also a great place to search for unique jewelry. ⊠ *244 Bull St., Historic District* ☎ *912/236–4053* ⊕ *www. shopredclover.com* ⊘ *Mon.–Sat. 10:30–6, Sun. noon–5.*

FOOD AND WINE

★ **Fodor's Choice Form.** A self-proclaimed "tastery," this food shop offers one of the area's finest selections, with more than 60 artisan cheeses and almost 400 wines, including budget offerings. It also offers a selection of gourmet food items prepackaged for takeout—the perfect option for picnics. If you sample only one thing from the kitchen, make sure it's the perfectly prepared cheesecake, distributed to many of the city's fine-dining establishments. ⊠ *1801 Habersham St., Historic District* ☎ *912/236–7642* ⊘ *Weekdays 8–7, Sat. 10–6.*

Le Chai Galerie du Vin. This is a long-cherished establishment for Savannah's wine aficionados. Once off the beaten path, its new central location makes this expansive spot a good bet for visitors as well. With a devoted following, proprietor Christian Depken has a trained palate for old-world wines—trust him to recommend the perfect accompaniment to any dish. ⊠ *15 E. Park St., Historic District* ☎ *912/713–2229* ⊕ *www.lechai.com* ⊘ *Mon.–Sat. 11–7, Sun. 10–7.*

Paula Deen Store. The "First Lady of Southern Cooking" sells her wares at this shop on Congress Street. You can find some very Southern spices and sauces, such as a smokin' barbecue sauce, and salad dressings—like peach-pecan and blueberry-walnut—that are so sweet they could double as dessert toppings. Two full floors of Paula's own label of cooking goodies and gadgets are cleverly displayed against bare brick walls. The shop is adjacent to Deen's famous Southern-style restaurant. ⊠ *108 W. Congress St., Historic District* ☎ *912/232–1579* ⊕ *www.pauladeenstore.com* ⊘ *Mon.–Sat. 10–10, Sun. 10–5.*

Pie Society. This British-style bakery sells everything from traditional meat pies to savory quiches to crusty bread, all of it baked fresh daily. The owners hail from Staffordshire and make remarkable and authentic meat pies in such varieties as steak and ale, chicken and thyme, and steak and kidney. ✉ *19 Jefferson St., City Market* ☎ *912/856–4785* ⊕ *www.britishpiecompany.com* ⊗ *Mon.–Thurs. 7–6; Fri.–Sat. 7 am–2 am; Sun. 8-5.*

River Street Sweets. Savannah's self-described "oldest and original" candy store, River Street Sweets opened in 1973 as a mother-daughter operation. The aroma of creamy homemade fudge will draw you in, and once you're inside you won't be able to resist the piping-hot pralines, made all day long. The store is also known for milk-chocolate bear claws. The old-fashioned taffy machine pulls 50 different flavors. You'll always receive excellent customer service here. ✉ *13 E. River St., Historic District* ☎ *912/234–4608* ⊕ *www.riverstreetsweets.com* ⊗ *Daily 9 am–11 pm.*

The Salt Table. More than 200 flavors of salts are on offer here, as well as specialty sugars, peppers, and teas. Noteworthy are the popular black truffle, smoked bacon, and ghost pepper sea salts. Gourmands should not miss the Himalayan pink salt plates. These solid salt bricks or slabs come in various sizes and can be used as cutting boards for preparing meats, vegetables, seafood, or even cheeses. They can also be placed directly on the stovetop, adding flavor to every dish. ✉ *51 Barnard St., Downtown* ☎ *912/447-0200* ⊕ *www.salttable.com* ⊗ *Mon.–Sat. 10–6, Sun. 11–6.*

FAMILY **Fodor'sChoice** ★ **Savannah Bee Company.** Ted Dennard's Savannah Bee Company has been featured in such national magazines as *O, Vogue, InStyle,* and *Newsweek,* and with good reason—the locally cultivated honey and bath products are simply wonderful. You can sample and buy multiple varieties of honey and even raw honeycombs. Don't miss the delicate mead (honey wine) or the decadent honey lattes. Though there is a new location on River Street, be sure to stop in the flagship store on Broughton Street. Children enjoy the full-size beehive. ✉ *104 W. Broughton St., Historic District* ☎ *912/233-7873* ⊕ *www.savannahbee.com* ⊗ *Mon.–Sat. 10–7, Sun. 11–5.*

Savannah Candy Kitchen. One of the largest candy stores in the South, Savannah Candy Kitchen has made its home on historic River Street for more than 30 years. Owner and head confectioner Stan Strickland grew up in Woodbine, Georgia, watching his mother bake pecan log rolls, pralines, and peanut brittle. You'll find every scrumptious delight imaginable here, but don't miss the world-famous praline layer cake. There's a second location in City Market ⊠*225 E. River St., Historic District* ☎*912/233–8411* ⊕*www.savannahcandy.com* ☉*Sun.–Thurs. 9:30–10, Fri. and Sat. 9:30–11.*

GIFTS AND SOUVENIRS

The Christmas Shop. In a neo-Gothic storefront rich with architectural detail, the Christmas Shop features hand-smocked children's clothing, German pewter, and hard-to-find seasonal accessories and collectibles. Even though it's hard to imagine sleigh bells in the tropical heat of summer, these items are so special you may not be able to resist a souvenir nutcracker. ⊠*307 Bull St., Historic District* ☎*912/234–5343* ⊕*thechristmasshop.homestead.com* ☉*Mon.–Sat. 9:30–6, Sun. noon–3.*

La Paperie. Gorgeous stationery, journals, and writing implements are on offer at this shop in the Downtown Design District. It also carries an impressive array of designer wrapping paper and handpressed botanical prints. Don't forget the final touches: embossers, stamps, and wax seals are all available. ⊠*409 Whitaker St., Historic District* ☎*912/443–9349* ⊕*www.lapaperie.net* ☉*Mon.–Sat. 10–5:30.*

Prospector Co. Occupying a historic storefront, this shop goes for a minimalist, industrial decor. The highly stylized space makes for a chic shopping experience. Stop here for high-end shaving gear, skincare products, or fragrances. It's a great place for softly scented candles, trendy sunglasses, or home accessories. ⊠*320 W. Broughton St., Historic District* ☎*912/721–7745* ⊕*www.prospectorco.com* ☉*Mon.–Sat. 11–7, Sun. noon–6.*

★ **Fodor's**Choice **ShopSCAD.** Inside historic Poetter Hall, the Savannah College of Art and Design's shop is filled with handcrafted items guaranteed to be one of a kind. Handmade and hand-dyed silk accessories are cutting-edge, as are original fashion pieces and experimental purses by design students. Just remember that these originals do not come cheap. ⊠*340 Bull St., Historic District* ☎*912/525–5180* ⊕*www.shopscadonline.com* ☉*Weekdays 9–5:30, Sat. 10–5:30, Sun. noon–5.*

HOME DECOR

★ **Fodor's**Choice **24e.** Owner Ruel Joyner has a keen eye for design, and stocks the best items from such revered design houses as Alessi, Knoll, and Kartell. The shop has also made a name for itself with custom-built furniture. Simply perusing the two stories of spectacular specimens is an inspiring way to spend some time—even if the store's big-ticket items are a little out of your price range. Fans of Savannah should not pass up on the handprinted lattitude pillows by local artists Lovelane Designs, featuring the coordinates of the Hostess City. ⊠ *24 E. Broughton St., Historic District* ☎ *912/233–2274* ⊕ *www.24estyle.com* ⊘ *Mon.–Thurs. 10:30–7, Fri. and Sat. 10:30–8, Sun. noon–5.*

One Fish Two Fish. Whimsically named for the classic Dr. Seuss book *One Fish Two Fish* is a high-end home decor shop located in the Downtown Design District. Look for contemporary furnishings, fine linens, and bedroom and bathroom accessories. Every corner of the store has something charming to offer, including elegant handbags and jewelry amd colorful modern lighting fixtures. For fine wearables, cross over Whitaker Street to visit the Annex, its sister store. ⊠ *401 Whitaker St., Historic District* ☎ *912/447–4600* ⊕ *onefishstore.com* ⊘ *Daily 10–5:30, Sun. noon–5.*

★ Fodor'sChoice **The Paris Market & Brocante.** A Francophile's dream, this two-story emporium hung with glittering chandeliers is a classy reproduction of a Paris flea market, selling elegant furnishings, vintage art, garden planters, and home decor items. Although the staff is happy to ship your purchases, there are numerous treasures that can be easily carried away, like soaps, candles, vintage jewelry, and dried lavender. New in 2014, a café serves baguette sandwiches from Back in the Day Bakery, locally roasted Cup-to-Cup coffee, macarons from Maison de Macarons, and candies by local chocolatier Adam Turoni. ⊠ *36 W. Broughton St., Historic District* ☎ *912/232–1500* ⊕ *www.theparismarket. com* ⊘ *Mon.–Sat. 10–6, Sun. noon–5.*

Villa Savannah. Broughton's newest high-end retail store features a wide array of everything from quirky home accessories and furnishings to elegant clothing and jewelry. For your home, expect luxe fabrics, opulent lighting, and unusual accessories with which to decorate your pad. The clothing and accessories are fun, flirty, and affordable. ⊠ *109 W. Broughton St., Historic District* ☎ *912/233– 2870* ⊕ *www.shopvillasavannah.com* ⊘ *Mon.–Wed. 11–6, Thurs.–Sat. 10–6, Sun. noon–5.*

JEWELRY AND ACCESSORIES

ZIA. Savannah's most-lauded jewelry boutique features pieces designed by artists around the world and assembled by owner Zia Sachedina. The opulent and eye-catching wearable art—including magnificent necklaces, rings, and bracelets made from such unexpected materials as titanium, amber, quartz, and even Hawaiian lava—is individually made. The jewelry represents a broad array of styles, materials, and price points. ✉ *325 W. Broughton St., Historic District* ☎ *912/233–3237* ⊕ *www.ziaboutique.com* ⊘ *Mon.– Thurs. 11–6, Fri.–Sun. 10–6.*

SHOES, HANDBAGS, AND LEATHER GOODS

Globe Shoe Co. Hands down Savannah's best shoe store, Globe has served both well-heeled women and well-soled men since 1892. There's an expansive storefront display, so it's easy to window shop for the perfect pair. It features footwear and accessories by Stuart Weitzman, Donald Pliner, Cole Haan, Sam Edelman, VanElli, Thierry Rabotin, Gentle Souls, and Jeffrey Campbell, to name a few. ✉ *17 E. Broughton St., Historic District* ☎ *912/232–8161.*

★ **Fodor's**Choice **Satchel.** This artisan leather studio and shop is owned by Elizabeth Seegar, a New Orleans native and graduate of the Savannah College of Art and Design. The store specializes in custom leather clutches, handbags, travel bags, and accessories and offers a wide selection of leathers to choose from, including python and alligator. At lower price points are the sharp and handy beverage cozies, cuff bracelets, and wallets. ✉ *4 E. Liberty St., Historic District* ☎ *912/233–1008* ⊕ *shopsatchel.com* ⊘ *Mon.–Sat. 10–6.*

SPAS

★ **Fodor's**Choice **Glow Medical Spa & Beauty Boutique.** Consistently ranked by locals as the best in Savannah, this sparkling day spa is known for its extensive menu of services. Specializing in the latest treatments for face and skin, this full-service facility offers exceptional massages and a wide selection of high-end cosmetics that are hand-selected by owner Courtney Buntin Victor. It's about 8 miles from downtown, but the excellent customer service makes it worth the drive. ✉ *415 Eisenhower Dr., Suite 1, Midtown* ☎ *912/303–9611* ⊕ *www.glowsavannah.com* ⊘ *Tues.–Sat. 10–6.*

JW Salon & Spa. One of the most attractive spas in Savannah, the JW Salon & Spa is a must for brides-to-be. The range of services includes massages, hydrotherapy, facials, manicures, and pedicures. The treatment area is two levels of a 19th-century brick row house that was renovated into a soothing, contemporary loftlike setting. ✉ *19 E. York St., Historic District* ☎ *912/236–7577* ⊕ *www.jwsalonandspa. com* ⊗ *Tues. and Thurs.–Fri. 10–7, Weds. 10–6, Sat. 9–4.*

Poseidon Spa. The very chic Poseidon Spa offers a number of rejuvenating treatments, including manicures, pedicures, massages, and skin and body treatments. Included in the rates is access to the white-marble courtyard and pool, a 24-hour fitness center, and a relaxation area. One wet and three dry treatment rooms, separate women's and men's locker rooms, and a steam shower make up the facilities. This is the town's glamour spa, though in truth prices run only a bit more than the rest. It's also a beautiful, calming place to relax. ✉ *The Mansion on Forsyth Park, 700 Drayton St., Historic District* ☎ *912/721–5004* ⊕ *www. mansiononforsythpark.com* ⊗ *Mon.–Thurs. 9–6, Fri. and Sat. 9–7, Sun. 9–4.*

Savannah Day Spa. In addition to traditional spa services, Savannah Day Spa offers a complete line of skin-care products, accessories for home, and a line of vegan body products. This former mansion is a delightful place to take your treatments, be it one of the creative massages or a therapeutic facial for your particular skin type. It's also one of the more romantic settings for couples messages. ✉ *18 E. Oglethorpe St., Downtown* ☎ *912/234–9100* ⊕ *www. savannahdayspa.com* ⊗ *Mon.–Thurs. 10–8, Fri. 10–7, Sat. 9–6, every other Sun. 11–5.*

Spa Bleu. Consistently ranked as one of Savannah's top ways to pamper yourself, Spa Bleu offers a more contemporary feel. In keeping with trends of the "New South," Spa Bleu offers true Southern comfort in a modern space. The signature Organic Thermal Body Treatments are not to be missed, and neither are spa night where you can stay late and indulge in hors d'oeuvres and champagne. ✉ *101 Bull St., Historic District* ☎ *912/236–1490* ⊕ *www.spableu-sav. com* ⊗ *Mon.–Sat. 10–7, Sun. noon–6.*

ELSEWHERE IN SAVANNAH

CLOTHING

★ Fodor'sChoice **BleuBelle Boutique.** A favorite among local fashionistas, BleuBelle offers high-end women's fashions in an inspiring downtown setting. The boutique carries lines by designers such as Diane von Furstenberg, Milly, and Alice & Olivia. It's Savannah's go-to destination for everything from cocktail dresses to fashion denim. Owner Heather Burge is often on hand to give style guidance. ✉ *5500 Abercorn St., Midtown* ☎ *912/355–3554* ⊕ *www.bleubelle.com* ⊗ *Mon.–Sat. 10–6.*

Cohen's Retreat. Savannah's newest design mecca, Cohen's Retreat includes a gallery, boutique, café, and craft workshops. Built in 1934 as Cohen's Old Men Retreat, the main building is resplendent with historic charm as well as noteworthy high-end modern upgrades. Inside, you will find local art, crafts, home decor items, and designer furniture. ✉ *5715 Skidaway Rd., Eastside* ☎ *912/355-3336* ⊕ *www. cohensretreat.com* ⊗ *Weekdays 8–5, Sat. 10–4.*

FOOD

Byrd Cookie Company & Gourmet Marketplace. Founded in 1924, this shop sells picture tins of Savannah and gourmet foodstuffs such as condiments and dressings. This shop—along with a newer location in City Market—is the best place to buy benne wafers ("the seed of good luck") and trademark Savannah cookies, notably key lime, and other house-made crackers. Free samples of all are available. ✉ *6700 Waters Ave., Southside* ☎ *912/355–1716* ⊕ *www. byrdcookiecompany.com* ⊗ *Weekdays 9–6, Sat. 10–5, Sun. noon–5.*

SPAS

Westin Heavenly Spa. Across the Savannah River from downtown, the Westin Heavenly Spa feels a world away. Housed in a country club, the spa features the standard menu of services and then some. The "quiet room," with its solarium-like setting, is a highlight. It's a little on the pricey side, but it's worth it for the relaxing, luxurious environment. It's also a great destination for bridal parties. ■**TIP**→ **If you're coming from downtown, consider traveling by water taxi.** ✉ *Westin Savannah Harbor Golf Resort & Spa, 1 Resort Dr., Hutchinson Island* ☎ *912/201–2250* ⊕ *www. westinsavannah.com* ⊗ *Daily 9–6.*

8

HILTON HEAD
AND THE
LOWCOUNTRY

Updated
by Sally
Mahan

HILTON HEAD ISLAND IS A UNIQUE and incredibly beautiful resort town that anchors the southern tip of South Carolina's coastline. What makes this semitropical island so unique? At the top of the list is the fact that visitors won't see large, splashy billboards or neon signs. What they will see is an island where the environment takes center stage, a place where development is strictly regulated.

There are 12 miles of sparkling white-sand beaches, amazing world-class restaurants, top-rated golf courses—Harbour Town Golf Links annually hosts the Heritage Golf Tournament, a PGA Tour event—and a thriving tennis community. Wildlife abounds, including loggerhead sea turtles, alligators, snowy egrets, wood storks, great blue heron, and, in the waters, dolphins, manatees, and various species of fish. There are lots of activities offered on the island, including parasailing, charter fishing, kayaking, and many other water sports.

The island is home to several private gated communities, including Sea Pines, Hilton Head Plantation, Shipyard, Wexford, Long Cove, Port Royal, Indigo Run, Palmetto Hall, and Palmetto Dunes. Within these you'll find upscale housing (some of it doubling as vacation rentals), golf courses, shopping, and restaurants. Sea Pines is one of the most famous of these communities, as it is known for the iconic candy-cane-striped Hilton Head Lighthouse. There are also many areas on the island that are not behind security gates.

ORIENTATION AND PLANNING

GETTING ORIENTED

Hilton Head is just north of South Carolina's border with Georgia. The 42-square-mile island is shaped like a foot, hence the reason locals often describe places as being at the "toe" or "heel" of Hilton Head. This part of South Carolina is best explored by car, as its points of interest are spread across a flat coastal plain that is a mix of wooded areas, marshes, and sea islands. The more remote areas are accessible only by boat or ferry.

Hilton Head's neighbor, Bluffton, is an artsy town rich with history. In the last several years the tiny community has grown to cover about 50 square miles. South of Hilton Head is the city of Savannah, which is about a 45-minute

TOP REASONS TO GO

Beachcombing: Hilton Head Island has 12 miles of beaches. You can swim, soak up the sun, or walk along the sand.

Beaufort: This small antebellum town offers large doses of heritage and culture; nearly everything you might want to see is within its downtown historic district.

Challenging Golf: Hilton Head's nickname is "Golf Island," and its many challenging courses have an international reputation.

Serving Up Tennis: Home to hundreds of tennis courts, Hilton Head is one of the nation's top tennis destinations.

Staying Put: This semitropical island has been a resort destination for decades, and it has all the desired amenities for visitors: a vast array of lodgings, an endless supply of restaurants, and excellent shopping.

drive from the island. North of Hilton Head is Beaufort, a cultural treasure and a graceful antebellum town. Beaufort is also about 45 minutes from Hilton Head.

Hilton Head Island. One of the Southeast coast's most popular tourist destinations, Hilton Head is known for its golf courses and tennis courts. It's a magnet for time-share owners and retirees. Bluffton is Hilton Head's quirky neighbor to the west. The old-town area is laden with history and charm.

Beaufort. This charming town just inland from Hilton Head is a destination in its own right, with a lively dining scene and cute bed-and-breakfasts.

Daufuskie Island. A scenic ferry ride from Hilton Head, Daufuskie is now much more developed than it was during the days when Pat Conroy wrote *The Water Is Wide,* but it's still a beautiful island to explore, even on a day trip. You can stay for a few days at a variety of fine rental properties, tool down shady dirt roads in a golf cart, and delight in the glorious, nearly deserted beaches.

8

PLANNING

WHEN TO GO

The high season follows typical beach-town cycles, with June through August and holidays year-round being the busiest and most costly. Mid-April, during the annual RBC Heritage Golf Tournament, is when rates tend to be highest. Thanks to the Lowcountry's mostly moderate year-round temperatures, tourists are ever-present. Spring is the best time to visit, when the weather is ideal for tennis and golf. Autumn is almost as active for the same reason.

WILL IT RAIN? **Don't be discouraged when you see a weather forecast during the summer months saying there's a 30% chance of rain for Hilton Head. It can be an absolutely gorgeous day and suddenly a storm will pop up late in the afternoon. That's because on hot sunny days, the hot air rises up into the atmosphere and mixes with the cool air, causing the atmosphere to become unstable, thereby creating thunderstorms. Not to worry, though: these storms move in and out fairly quickly.**

To get a good deal, it's imperative that you plan ahead. The choicest locations can be booked six months to a year in advance, but booking agencies can help you make room reservations and get good deals during the winter season, when the crowds fall off. Villa-rental companies often offer snowbird rates for monthly stays during the winter season. Parking is always free at the major hotels, but valet parking can cost from $17 to $25; the smaller properties have free parking, too, but no valet service.

PLANNING YOUR TIME

No matter where you stay, spend your first day relaxing on the beach or hitting the links. After that, you'll have time to visit some of the area's attractions, including the Coastal Discovery Museum or the Sea Pines Resort. You can also visit the Tanger outlet malls on U.S. 278 in Bluffton. Oldtown Bluffton is a quaint area with many locally owned shops and art galleries. If you have a few more days, visit Beaufort on a day trip or even spend the night there. This historic antebellum town is rich with history. Savannah is also a short drive away.

GETTING HERE AND AROUND

AIR TRAVEL

Most travelers use the Savannah/Hilton Head International Airport, less than an hour from Hilton Head, which is served by American Eagle, Delta, JetBlue, United, and US Airways. Hilton Head Island Airport is served by US Airways.

Air Contacts Hilton Head Island Airport ✉ *120 Beach City Rd., North end, Hilton Head* ☎ *843/255-2950* ⊕ *www.hiltonheadair port.com.* **Savannah/Hilton Head International Airport** ✉ *400*

Airways Ave., Northwest, Savannah, Georgia ☎ *912/964–0514* ⊕ *www.savannahairport.com.*

BOAT AND FERRY TRAVEL

Hilton Head is accessible via boat, with docking available at Harbour Town Yacht Basin, Skull Creek Marina, and Shelter Cove Harbor.

Boat Docking Information **Harbour Town Yacht Basin** ⊠ *Sea Pines, 149 Lighthouse Rd., South end, Hilton Head* ☎ *843/363–8335* ⊕ *www.seapines.com.* **Shelter Cove Marina** ⊠ *Shelter Cove, 1 Shelter Cove La., Mid-island, Hilton Head* ☎ *843/842–7001* ⊕ *www. palmettodunes.com.* **Skull Creek Marina** ⊠ *1 Waterway La., North end, Hilton Head* ☎ *843/681–8436* ⊕ *www.theskullcreekmarina.com.*

BUS TRAVEL

The Lowcountry Regional Transportation Authority, known as the Palmetto Breeze, has buses that leave Bluffton in the morning for Hilton Head, Beaufort, and some of the islands. The fare is $2, and exact change is required.

Bus Contacts **Lowcountry Regional Transportation Authority** ☎ *843/757–5782* ⊕ *www.palmettobreezetransit.com.*

CAR TRAVEL

Driving is the best way to get onto Hilton Head Island. Off Interstate 95, take Exit 8 onto U.S. 278 East, which leads you through Bluffton (where it's known as Fording Island Road) and then to Hilton Head. Once on Hilton Head, U.S. 278 forks: on the right is William Hilton Parkway, and on the left is the Cross Island Parkway (a toll road that costs $1.25 each way). If you take the Cross Island (as the locals call it) to the south side where Sea Pines and many other resorts are located, the trip will take about 10 to 15 minutes. If you take William Hilton Parkway the trip will take about 30 minutes. Be aware that at check-in and checkout times on Friday, Saturday, and Sunday, traffic on U.S. 278 can slow to a crawl. ■TIP→ **Be careful of putting the pedal to the metal, particularly on the Cross Island Parkway. It's patrolled regularly.**

Once on Hilton Head Island, signs are small and blend in with the trees and landscaping, and nighttime lighting is kept to a minimum. The lack of streetlights makes it difficult to find your way at night, so be sure to get good directions.

TAXI TRAVEL

There are several taxi services available on Hilton Head, including Hilton Head Taxi and Limousine, Yellow Cab HHI, and Diamond Transportation, which has SUVs and passenger vans available for pickup at Savannah/Hilton Head International Airport and Hilton Head Airport. Prices range from $20 to $120, depending on where you're headed.

Taxi Contacts **Diamond Transportation** ☎ *843/247–2156* ⊕ *hilton-headrides.com.* **Hilton Head Taxi and Limousine** ☎ *843/785–8294.* **Yellow Cab HHI** ☎ *843/686–6666* ⊕ *www.yellowcabhhi.com.*

TRAIN TRAVEL

Amtrak gets you as close as Savannah or Yemassee.

Train Contacts **Savannah Amtrak Station** ⊠ *2611 Seaboard Coastline Dr., Savannah, Georgia* ☎ *800/872–7245* ⊕ *www.amtrak.com.*

RESTAURANTS

The number of fine-dining restaurants on Hilton Head is extraordinary, given the size of the island. Because of the proximity to the ocean and the small farms on the mainland, most locally owned restaurants are still heavily influenced by the catch of the day and seasonal harvests. Most upscale restaurants open at 11 and don't close until 9 or 10, but some take a break between 2 and 4. Many advertise early-bird menus, and sometimes getting a table before 6 can be a challenge. During the height of the summer season, reservations are a good idea, though in the off-season you may need them only on weekends. There are several locally owned breakfast joints and plenty of great delis where you can pick up lunch or the fixings for a picnic. Smoking is prohibited in restaurants and bars in Bluffton, Beaufort, and on Hilton Head. Beaufort's restaurant scene has certainly evolved, with more trendy restaurants serving contemporary cuisine moving into the downtown area.

HOTELS

Hilton Head is known as one of the best vacation spots on the East Coast, and its hotels are a testimony to its reputation. The island is awash in regular hotels and resorts, not to mention beachfront or golf-course-view villas, cottages, and luxury private homes. You can expect the most modern conveniences and world-class service at the priciest places. Clean, updated rooms and friendly staff are everywhere, even at lower-cost hotels—this is the South, after all. Staying in cooler months, for extended periods of time, or commuting from nearby Bluffton can save money.

WHAT IT COSTS				
	$	$$	$$$	$$$$
Restaurants	under $15	$15–$19	$20–$24	over $24
Hotels	under $150	$150–$200	$201–$250	over $250

Restaurant prices are for a main course at dinner, excluding sales tax. Hotel prices are for two people in a standard double room in high season, excluding service charges and tax.

TOURS

Hilton Head's Adventure Cruises hosts dolphin-watching cruises, sport crabbing, and more. Several companies, including H20 Sports, Live Oac, Outside Hilton Head, and Low Country Nature Tours run dolphin-watching, shark-fishing, kayak, sunset, and delightful environmental trips. Low Country Nature Tours offers a family-friendly fireworks tour during the summer, as well as educational and fun bird-watching tours that children are sure to enjoy.

Gullah Heritage Trail Tours gives a wealth of history about slavery and the Union takeover of the island during the Civil War; tours leave from the Coastal Discovery Museum at Honey Horn Plantation. Tickets are $32.

There's a wide variety of tours available at Harbour Town Yacht Basin, including sunset cruises, fireworks, and dolphin tours. Pau Hana & Flying Circus Sailing Charters offers tours on a catamaran sailboat, and fireworks and sunset cruises. The captains provide an interactive, educational adventure, and the catamaran makes for smooth sailing.

Tour Contacts Adventure Cruises ⊠ *Shelter Cove Marina, 9 Harbourside La., Mid-Island, Hilton Head Island* ☎ *843/785–4558* ⊕ *www.cruisehiltonhead.com.* **Gullah Heritage Trail Tours** ⊠ *Coastal Discovery Museum, 70 Honey Horn Dr., North end, Hilton Head* ☎ *843/681–7066* ⊕ *www.gullaheritage.com.* **H2O Sports** ⊠ *Harbour Town Marina, 149 Lighthouse Rd., South End, Hilton Head Island* ☎ *843/671–4386, 877/290–4386* ⊕ *www.h2osports. com.* **Harbour Town Yacht Basin** ⊠ *Sea Pines, 149 Lighthouse Rd., South End, Hilton Head Island* ☎ *843/363–2628* ⊕ *harbourtownyachtbasin.com.* **Live Oac** ⊠ *Hilton Head Harbor, 43A Jenkins Rd., North End, Hilton Head Island* ☎ *843/384–4141* ⊕ *www.liveoac. com.* **Low Country Nature Tours** ⊠ *Shelter Cove Marina, 1 Shelter Cove La., Mid-Island, Hilton Head Island* ☎ *843/683–0187* ⊕ *www.*

lowcountrynaturetours.com. **Outside Hilton Head** ⊠ *Shelter Cove Marina, 1 Shelter Cove La., Mid-Island, Hilton Head Island* ☏ *843/686–6996* ⊕ *www.outsidehiltonhead.com.* **Pau Hana & Flying Circus Sailing Charters** ⊠ *Palmetto Bay Marina, 86 Helmsman Way, South End, Hilton Head Island* ☏ *843/686–2582* ⊕ *www. hiltonheadislandsailing.com.*

VISITOR INFORMATION

As you're driving into town, you can pick up brochures and maps at the Hilton Head Island-Bluffton Chamber of Commerce and Visitor and Convention Bureau.

Visitor Information **Hilton Head Island-Bluffton Chamber of Commerce and Visitor and Convention Bureau** ⊠ *1 Chamber of Commerce Dr., Mid-Island, Hilton Head Island* ☏ *843/785–3673* ⊕ *www.hiltonheadisland.org.*

HILTON HEAD ISLAND

Hilton Head Island is known far and wide as a vacation destination that prides itself on its top-notch golf courses and tennis programs, world-class resorts, and beautiful beaches. But the island is also part of the storied American South, steeped in a rich, colorful history. It has seen Native Americans and explorers, battles from the Revolutionary War to the Civil War, plantations and slaves, and development and environmentally focused growth.

More than 10,000 years ago, the island was inhabited by Paleo-Indians. From 8000 to 2000 BC, Woodland Indians lived on the island. A shell ring made from their discarded oyster shells and animal bones from that period can be found in the Sea Pines Nature Preserve.

The recorded history of the island goes back to the early 1500s, when Spanish explorers sailing coastal waters came upon the island and found Native American settlements. Over the next 200 years, the island was claimed at various times by the Spanish, the French, and the British. In 1663, Captain William Hilton claimed the island for the British crown (and named it for himself), and the island became home to indigo, rice, and cotton plantations.

During the Revolutionary War, the British harassed islanders and burned plantations. During the War of 1812, British troops again burned plantations, but the island recovered from both wars. During the Civil War, Union troops took Hilton Head in 1861 and freed the more than 1,000 slaves

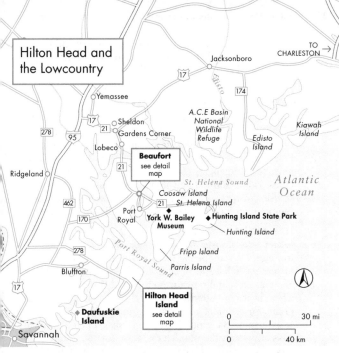

Beaufort
see detail
map

Hilton Head
Island
see detail
map

Hilton Head and
the Lowcountry

TO
CHARLESTON →

Jacksonboro

Yemassee

Sheldon
Gardens Corner

Lobeco

Ridgeland

A.C.E Basin
National
Wildlife
Refuge

Edisto
Island

Kiawah
Island

St. Helena Sound

*Atlantic
Ocean*

Coosaw Island
St. Helena Island

Port
Royal

◆ York W. Bailey
Museum

◆ Hunting Island State Park

Hunting Island

Port Royal Sound

Fripp Island

Parris Island

Bluffton

◆ Daufuskie
Island

Savannah

0   30 mi

0   40 km

on the island. Mitchelville, one of the first settlements for freed blacks, was created. There was no bridge to the island, so its freed slaves, called "Gullah," subsisted on agriculture and the seafood-laden waters.

Over the years, much of the plantation land was sold at auction. Then, in 1949, General Joseph Fraser purchased 17,000 acres, much of which would eventually become various communities, including Hilton Head Plantation, Palmetto Dunes, and Spanish Wells. The general bought another 1,200 acres, which his son, Charles, used to develop Sea Pines. The first bridge to the island was built in 1956, and modern-day Hilton Head was born.

What makes Hilton Head so special now? Charles Fraser and his business associates focused on development while preserving the environment. And that is what tourists will see today: an island that values its history and its natural beauty.

GETTING HERE AND AROUND

Hilton Head Island is 19 miles east of Interstate 95. Take Exit 8 off Interstate 95 and then U.S. 278 east, directly to the bridges. If you're heading to the southern end of the island, your best bet to save time and avoid traffic is the Cross Island Parkway toll road. The cost is $1.25 each way.

EXPLORING

Your impression of Hilton Head depends on which of the island's developments you make your temporary home. The oldest and best known of Hilton Head's developments, Sea Pines occupies 4,500 thickly wooded acres. It's not wilderness, however; among the trees are three golf courses, tennis clubs, riding stables, and shopping plazas. A free trolley shuttles visitors around the resort. Other well-known communities are Palmetto Dunes and Port Royal Plantation.

TOP ATTRACTIONS

★ Fodor's Choice **Coastal Discovery Museum.** This wonderful
FAMILY museum tells about the history of the Lowcountry. For instance, you'll learn about the early development of Hilton Head as an island resort from the Civil War to the 1930s. There is also a butterfly enclosure, various hands-on programs for children, guided walks, and much more. Take a walk around the grounds to see marshes, open fields, live oaks dripping with Spanish moss, as well as South Carolina's largest southern red cedar tree, which dates back to 1595. Admission is free, but lectures and tours on various subjects cost $10. Although the museum is just off the Cross Island Parkway, the peaceful grounds make it feel miles away. ⊠ *70 Honey Horn Dr., off Hwy. 278, North End* ☎ *843/689–6767* ⊕ *www.coastaldiscovery.org* ⊡ *Free* ⊗ *Mon.–Sat. 9–4:30.*

Old Town Bluffton. Tucked away from the resort areas, charming Old Town Bluffton has several historic homes and churches on oak-lined streets. At the end of Wharf Street in this artsy community is the Bluffton Oyster Company (63 Wharf Street), a place to buy fresh raw local shrimp, fish, and oysters. Grab some picnic fixings from the Downtown Deli (27 Mellichamp Drive) and head to the boat dock at the end of Pritchard Street for a meal with a view. Another incredibly beautiful spot for a picnic is the grounds of the Church of the Cross. ⊠ *May River Rd. and Calhoun St., Old Town, Bluffton* ⊕ *www.oldtownbluffton.com.*

Sea Pines Forest Preserve. Walking and biking trails take you past a stocked fishing pond, a waterfowl pond, and a 3,400-year-old Native American shell ring at this 605-acre public wilderness tract. Pick up the extensive activity guide at the Sea Pines Welcome Center to take advantage

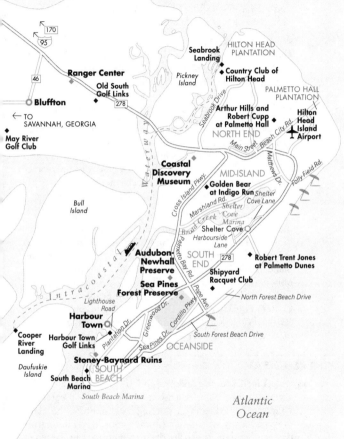

Hilton Head Island

Port Royal Sound

HILTON HEAD PLANTATION

Seabrook Landing

Pickney Island

Ranger Center

Old South Golf Links

Country Club of Hilton Head

PALMETTO HALL PLANTATION

Bluffton

← TO SAVANNAH, GEORGIA

Arthur Hills and Robert Cupp at Palmetto Hall

Hilton Head Island Airport

May River Golf Club

NORTH END

Main Street

Beach City Rd.

Matthews Dr.

Folly Field Rd.

Coastal Discovery Museum

MID-ISLAND

Golden Bear at Indigo Run

Cross Island Pkwy.

Marshland Rd.

Shelter Cove Lane

Bull Island

Shelter Cove Marina

Broad Creek

Shelter Cove

Harbourside Lane

Audubon-Newhall Preserve

SOUTH END

Robert Trent Jones at Palmetto Dunes

Sea Pines Forest Preserve

Shipyard Racquet Club

Palmetto Bay Rd.

Pope Ave.

North Forest Beach Drive

Lighthouse Road

Harbour Town

Plantation Dr.

Greenwood Dr.

Cordillo Pkwy.

South Forest Beach Drive

Cooper River Landing

Harbour Town Golf Links

Sea Pines Dr.

OCEANSIDE

Stoney-Baynard Ruins

Daufuskie Island

SOUTH BEACH

South Beach Marina

South Beach Marina

Atlantic Ocean

0   1/2 mi

0   1/2 km

of goings-on—moonlight hayrides, storytelling around campfires, and alligator- and bird-watching boat tours. The preserve is part of the grounds at Sea Pines Resort. Overlooking a small alke, the outdoor chapel has five wooden pews and a wooden lectern engraved with the Prayer of St. Francis. ✉ *Sea Pines Resort, 32 Greenwood Dr., South End* ☎ *843/363–4530, 866/561–8802* ⊕ *www.seapines.com* 🖃 *$5 per car* ☉ *Daily dawn–dusk.*

WORTH NOTING

Audubon-Newhall Preserve. There are hiking trails, a self-guided tour, and seasonal walks on this 50-acre preserve. Native plant life is tagged and identified in this pristine forest. ✉ *Palmetto Bay Rd., off the Cross Island Pkwy., South End* ☎ *843/842–9246* ⊕ *www.hiltonheadaudubon.org.*

Harbour Town. The closest thing the Sea Pines development has to a downtown is Harbour Town, a charming area centered on a circular marina that's filled with interesting shops and restaurants. Rising above it all is the landmark candy-cane-stripe Hilton Head Lighthouse, which you can climb to enjoy a view of Calibogue Sound. ✉ *Lighthouse Rd., South End.*

Stoney-Baynard Ruins. Check out the Stoney-Baynard Ruins, the remnants of a plantation home and slave quarters built in the 1700s by Captain John "Saucy Jack" Stoney. A cotton planter named William Edings Baynard bought the place in 1840. On the National Register of Historic Sites, only parts of the walls are still standing. The ruins are not easy to find, so ask for directions at the Sea Pines Welcome Center at the Greenwood Drive gate. ✉ *Plantation Dr., near Baynard Cove Rd., South End* ⊕ *www.exploreseapines.com/historical-sites.asp* 🖃 *Free* ☉ *Open 24 hrs.*

WHERE TO EAT

$$$ ✕ **Black Marlin Bayside Grill.** *Seafood.* If you want to dine with a view of the "blue," then head to this seafood eatery in Palmetto Bay Marina. Attracting local boaters, the place draws a steady stream of customers most days, but Saturday and Sunday brunch are the highlights for eggs Benedict and live entertainment. For lunch, the best bets include the fish tacos. The outdoor Hurricane Bar has a Key West vibe and hops during happy hour. There's an early dining menu from 4 to 5:30, and the kitchen cranks out entrées until 10 every night. ⑤ *Average main: $23* ✉ *Palmetto Bay Marina, 86 Helmsman Way, South End* ☎ *843/785–4950* ⊕ *www. blackmarlinhhi.com.*

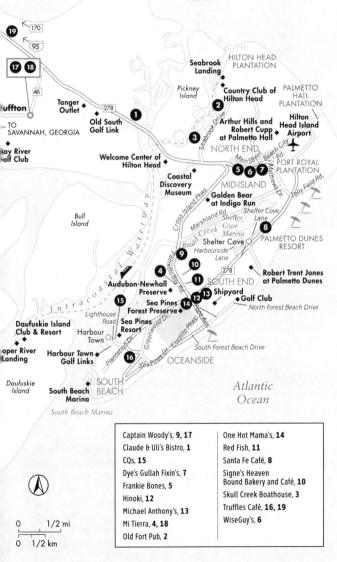

Where to Eat on Hilton Head Island

Port Royal Sound

HILTON HEAD PLANTATION

Seabrook Landing

Pickney Island

Country Club of Hilton Head **2**

PALMETTO HALL PLANTATION

Arthur Hills and Robert Cupp at Palmetto Hall **3**

Hilton Head Island Airport

NORTH END

5 **6** **7**

PORT ROYAL PLANTATION

Main Street

Matthews Dr.

Folly Field Rd.

Beach City Rd.

MID-ISLAND

Golden Bear at Indigo Run

Shelter Cove Lane

Shelter Cove Marina

8

PALMETTO DUNES RESORT

Shelter Cove Harbourside Lane

9

10

4

Audubon-Newhall Preserve

11

SOUTH END

Robert Trent Jones at Palmetto Dunes

Shipyard **12** **13**

Golf Club

North Forest Beach Drive

Sea Pines Forest Preserve

14

15

Lighthouse Road

Sea Pines Resort

South Forest Beach Drive

Harbour Town

Harbour Town Golf Links

16

OCEANSIDE

SOUTH BEACH

South Beach Marina

South Beach Marina

Daufuskie Island Club & Resort

oper River Landing

Daufuskie Island

Coastal Discovery Museum

Welcome Center of Hilton Head

Old South Golf Link **1**

Tanger Outlet

17 **18**

19

uffton

TO SAVANNAH, GEORGIA

ay River olf Club

Bull Island

Intracoastal Waterway

Atlantic Ocean

170

95

46

278

278

Seabrook Drive

Cross Island Pkwy.

Marshland Rd.

Broad Creek

Palmetto Bay Rd.

Greenwood Dr.

Plantation Dr.

Sea Pines Dr.

Cordillo Pkwy.

Restaurant List

Captain Woody's, **9, 17**	One Hot Mama's, **14**
Claude & Uli's Bistro, **1**	Red Fish, **11**
CQs, **15**	Santa Fe Café, **8**
Dye's Gullah Fixin's, **7**	Signe's Heaven Bound Bakery and Café, **10**
Frankie Bones, **5**	Skull Creek Boathouse, **3**
Hinoki, **12**	Truffles Café, **16, 19**
Michael Anthony's, **13**	WiseGuy's, **6**
Mi Tierra, **4, 18**	
Old Fort Pub, **2**	

0 — 1/2 mi

0 — 1/2 km

$$$ ✕ **Captain Woody's.** *Seafood.* If you're looking for a fun,
FAMILY casual, kid-friendly seafood restaurant, the reasonably
priced Captain Woody's is the place to go. Start with the
creamy and delicious crab bisque, a dozen oysters on the
half shell or the sampler platter, which includes crab legs,
shrimp, and oysters. The grouper sandwiches—the buffalo
grouper, grouper melt, and grouper Reuben—are staples
here. The restaurant has a second location in Bluffton. Ⓢ *Average main: $22* ⊠ *6 Target Rd., South End* ☎ *843/785–2400*
⊕ *www.captainwoodys.com* ⌖ *Reservations not accepted.*

★ **Fodor's**Choice ✕ **CQs.** *Eclectic.* If you've heard that all of Hilton
$$$$ Head's restaurants lack atmosphere and are tucked away
in shopping centers, then you need to experience CQs.
Its rustic ambience—heart-pine floors, sepia-tone photos,
and a lovely second-story dining room—coupled with its
stellar cuisine, personable staff, and feel-good spirit, put
most of the island's other eateries to shame. Start with the
mussels with lemon butter broth or the oven-roasted beets
with pecan-crusted goat cheese to start, and then the ahi
tuna for your main course. The staff can suggest just the
right wine from an impeccable list. In Harbour Town, the
restaurant will reimburse you for the gate pass fee. Ⓢ *Average main: $29* ⊠ *140 Lighthouse Rd., Harbour Town,
South End* ☎ *843/671–2779* ⊕ *www.cqsrestaurant.com*
⌖ *Reservations essential* ⊘ *No lunch.*

$$ ✕ **Dye's Gullah Fixin's.** *Southern.* It's often hard to find the
real thing, but this is true Gullah food: decadent, delicious,
and comforting. Owner Dye Scott-Rhodan uses recipes
handed down by generations of her Gullah family: fried
chicken, shrimp and grits, collard greens, and Lowcountry
boil (shrimp, smoked sausage, potatoes, corn, and sea-
sonings). Wash it down with the South's most popular
beverage, sweet tea. There is also a full bar, and a Sunday
buffet from noon to 3. Ⓢ *Average main: $19* ⊠ *840 William Hilton Pkwy., Mid-Island* ☎ *843/681–8106* ⊕ *www.
dyesgullahfixins.com* ⌖ *Reservations essential* ▤ *No credit
cards* ⊘ *No lunch Sat.*

$$$ ✕ **Frankie Bones.** *Italian.* This restaurant is dedicated to the
loving memory of Frank Sinatra, so you might assume that
its name is also one of the handles of "Ole Blue Eyes." You'd
be wrong, because Bones was a Chicago gangster before
Prohibition. This dining room appeals to an older crowd
that likes the traditional parmesanas and marsalas on the
early dining menu. But during happy hour, the bar and the
surrounding cocktail tables are populated with younger
patrons who order flat-bread pizzas and small plates of

Shrimp Boats Forever

Watching shrimp trawlers coming into their home port at sunset, with mighty nets raised and an entourage of hungry seagulls, is a cherished Lowcountry tradition. The shrimping industry has been an integral staple of the South Carolina economy for nearly a century. (Remember Bubba Gump?) It was booming in the 1980s. But alas, cheap, farm-raised shrimp from foreign markets and now the cost of diesel fuel are decimating the shrimpers' numbers.

The season for fresh-caught shrimp is May to December. Lowcountry residents support the freelance fishermen by buying only certified, local wild shrimp in restaurants and in area fish markets and supermarkets. Visitors can follow suit by patronizing local restaurants and markets that display the logo that reads "Certified Wild American Shrimp." Or you can simply ask before you eat.

pasta. Some dishes have innovative twists, including the 16-ounce rib eye with a sweetened coffee rub. Consider drinking your dessert, something Amaretto-based such as a Godfather or a Burnt Almond. ⑤ *Average main: $22* ✉ *1301 Main St., North end, Hilton Head* ☎ *843/682–4455* ⊕ *www. frankieboneshhi.com* ♿ *Reservations essential.*

★ **Fodor's**Choice ✕ **Hinoki.** *Japanese.* A peaceful oasis awaits you
$$$ at Hinoki, which has some of the best sushi on Hilton Head. As you make your way into the dining room, fishponds and Japanese flora flank the boardwalk. The interior has an intimate feel, with bamboo touches throughout. Try the Hilton Head roll, which is white fish tempura and avocado, or the Hinoki roll with asparagus and spicy fish roe topped with tuna and avocado. One of the specialties of the house is a to-die-for tuna sashimi salad with spicy mayo, cucumbers, onions, salmon roe, and crabmeat. There are more than 50 sushi and sashimi choices on the menu, along with udon noodle dishes and bento boxes. There's also an extensive sake menu. ⑤ *Average main: $23* ✉ *Orleans Plaza, 37 New Orleans Rd., South End* ☎ *843/785–9800* ⊕ *hinokihhi.com* ☉ *Closed Sun.*

MODERN TAKEOUT. When you just don't feel like going out for a bite, a local delivery service is here to help. Hiltonheaddelivers.com delivers restaurant food to homes, condos, and hotels from 5 to 9:45 pm seven days a week for a $5.50 delivery charge. A variety of restaurants take part, including One Hot Mama's, WiseGuys, and more. Visit ⊕ *hiltonheaddelivers.com* for more details.

★ Fodor'sChoice ✕**Michael Anthony's.** *Italian.* Owned by a tal-
$$$$ ented, charismatic Philadelphia family, this restaurant has
a convivial spirit, and its innovative pairings and plate pre-
sentations are au courant. You can expect fresh, top-quality
ingredients, simple yet elegant sauces, and waiters who
know and care about the food they serve. An added bonus:
The restaurant offers cooking demonstrations/classes and
wine tastings in the upstairs dining room, which has a Tus-
can farmhouse feel. ⑤ *Average main: $30* ✉ *Orleans Plaza,
37 New Orleans Rd., Suite L, South End* ☎ *843/785–6272*
⊕ *www.michael-anthonys.com* ⬧ *Reservations essential*
⊗ *Closed Sun. No lunch.*

COOKING CLASS. **Learn to prepare Italian cuisine in a hands-on
cooking class at Michael Anthony's. Classes include samples of
the dishes and wine. Demonstration classes, wine tastings, and
programs for visiting corporate groups are also available. There
is a high demand for these classes, so reserve your place as far
in advance as possible on Michael Anthony's website (⊕ www.
michael-anthonys.com).**

$ ✕**Mi Tierra.** *Mexican.* There's nothing fancy here, just great
Mexican food. The decor has a Southwestern feel, with tile
floors, colorful sombreros, and paintings of chili peppers
hanging on the walls. Start with a margarita and the chips
and salsa, and don't forget to order the guacamole and
bean dip as well. For your main course, try the *enchiladas
suizas,* tortillas filled with chicken and topped with green
tomatillo sauce, sour cream, and avocado. Another local
favorite is the *arroz con camarones,* butterfly shrimp sau-
téed with garlic butter and vegetables. The menu is extensive and includes a kid's section. There's a second location
in Bluffton. ⑤ *Average main: $14* ✉ *130 Arrow Rd., South
End* ☎ *843/342–3409* ⊕ *www.mitierrabluffton.com* ⊗ *No
lunch weekends.*

$$$$ ✕**Old Fort Pub.** *European.* Overlooking the sweeping marshlands of Skull Creek, this romantic restaurant has almost
panoramic views. It offers one of the island's best overall
dining experiences: the building is old enough to have some
personality, and the professional staffers diligently do their
duty. More important, the kitchen serves flavorful food,
including a great starter of roasted calamari with sundried
tomatoes and olives. Entrées like the bouillabaisse and
filet mignon with chanterelles hit the spot. The wine list is
extensive, and there's outdoor seating on a third-floor porch
for toasting the sunset. Sunday brunch is celebratory and

includes a mimosa. ⑤ *Average main: $33* ✉ *65 Skull Creek Dr., Hilton Head Plantation, North End* ☎ *843/681–2386* ⊕ *www.oldfortpub.com* ⊘ *No lunch.*

$$ ✕ **One Hot Mama's.** *Barbecue.* This heavenly barbecue joint
FAMILY is a Hilton Head institution because of its upbeat atmosphere, graffiti-strewn walls, and melt-in-the-mouth pulled pork and fall-off-the-bone ribs. But the place also offers some unusual choices: the wings, which have won multiple awards at Hilton Head's Rib Burnoff and Wing Fest, come with tasty sauces ranging from strawberry-jalapeño to teriyaki to the Holy Hula Hula with pineapple, ginger, and ghost peppers. The delectable rib sampler includes hot Asian, chocolate barbecue, and "Mama's Perfect 10." In addition to food that will wake up your taste buds, there are also 15 beers on tap, about a dozen flat-screen TVs, and an outdoor patio with a big brick fireplace for the cooler months. ⑤ *Average main: $17* ✉ *7A Greenwood Dr., South End* ☎ *843/682–6262* ⊕ *onehotmamas.com.*

★ **Fodor'sChoice** ✕ **Red Fish.** *American.* This seafood eatery's
$$$$ "naked" catch of the day—seafood grilled with olive oil, lime, and garlic—is a heart-healthy specialty that many diners say is the best thing on the menu. Caribbean and Cuban flavors permeate the rest of the menu in dishes such as Latin ribs and a Cajun shrimp-and-lobster burger. The restaurant's wine cellar is filled with some 1,000 bottles, and there's also a retail wine shop so you can take a bottle home. Although the commercial-strip location isn't inspired, the lively crowd, the soft candlelight, and the subdued artwork more than make up for it. ⑤ *Average main: $28* ✉ *8 Archer Rd., South End* ☎ *843/686–3388* ⊕ *www.redfishofhiltonhead.com* ⊘ *No lunch Sun.*

$$$$ ✕ **Santa Fe Cafe.** *Southwestern.* Walk through the doors of the Santa Fe Cafe and you're greeted by the sights, sounds, and aromas of New Mexico: Native American rugs, Mexican ballads, steer skulls and horns, and the pungent smells of chilies and mesquite on the grill. The restaurant is perhaps best experienced on a rainy, chilly night when the adobe fireplaces are cranked up. Go for the rush of spicy food chased with an icy Mexican *cerveza* (beer) or one of the island's best margaritas (order one up, with top-shelf tequila, and let the fiesta begin). This place is a party for the senses: after the fiery and artistic Painted Desert soup (a thick puree of red pepper and chilies in chicken stock), you can chill with the tortilla-crusted salmon. Forgo burritos and other Tex-Mex standards and opt for dishes like mesquite lamb with cranberry-chipotle sauce. There are also

8

several gluten-free dishes available. Plan on listening to *guitarra* music in the rooftop cantina Wednesday to Saturday night. ⑤ *Average main: $28* ⊠ *807 William Hilton Pkwy., Mid-Island* ☎ *843/785–3838* ⊕ *santafecafehiltonhead.com* ⌔ *Reservations essential* ⊘ *No lunch weekends.*

★ Fodor'sChoice ✕ **Signe's Heaven Bound Bakery & Café.** *American.* Every morning locals roll in for the deep-dish French toast, crispy polenta, and whole-wheat waffles. Since 1972, European-born Signe has been feeding islanders her delicious soups and quiches, curried chicken salad, and loaded hot and cold sandwiches. The beach bag ($12 for a cold sandwich, pasta or fresh fruit, chips, and cookie) is a great deal, especially because they also throw in a beverage. The melt-in-your-mouth cakes and the rave-worthy breads are amazing. ⑤ *Average main: $8* ⊠ *93 Arrow Rd., South End* ☎ *843/785–9118* ⊕ *www.signesbakery.com* ⊘ *Closed Sun. Dec.–Feb. No dinner.*

★ Fodor'sChoice ✕ **Skull Creek Boathouse.** *American.* Soak up the salty atmosphere in this pair of dining areas where almost every table has a view of the water. Outside is a third dining area and a bar called the Buoy Bar at Marker 13. Adirondack chairs invite you to sit back, relax, and catch the sunset. The Dive Bar features raw seafood served as sushi, ceviche, or carpaccio. Options for lunch include chilled seafood dishes, salads, sandwiches, po'boys, burgers, and hot dogs. For dinner there's a wide variety of seafood dishes that are perfect for sharing, or you can also bring in your freshly caught fish and the chef will prepare it however you like. You may have trouble deciding what to order, but you can take your time and enjoy the beautiful view. ⑤ *Average main: $17* ⊠ *397 Squire Pope Rd., North End* ☎ *843/681–3663* ⊕ *www.skullcreekboathouse.com.*

$$ ✕ **Truffles Cafe.** *American.* When a restaurant keeps its customers happy for decades, there's a reason. You won't find any of the namesake truffles on the menu; instead there's grilled salmon with a mango-barbecue glaze and barbecued baby-back ribs. The Oriental Napa salad with tuna is big enough to be a main course. If you're on a budget, choose a specialty like the Kobe burger with pimento cheese. Or, for a splurge, opt for the juicy, center-cut steaks. There's a second Hilton Head location on Pope Avenue, and a Bluffton branch that has a lovely outdoor seating area. ⑤ *Average main: $17* ⊠ *Sea Pines Center, 71 Lighthouse Rd., South End* ☎ *843/671–6136* ⊕ *www.trufflescafe.com* ⌔ *Reservations essential* ⊘ *Closed Sun. No lunch.*

$$$$ ✕**WiseGuys.** *Steakhouse.* The red-and-black decor is modern and sophisticated at this restaurant—it's a little art deco, a little contemporary. The food is a spin on the classics, starting with seared tuna sliders and an incredible beef tenderloin carpaccio topped with baby arugula and horseradish cream. The go-to entrée is definitely the charred rib-eye steak, which comes with a choice of butters that include brandied mushroom, fois gras, and truffle. The attentive waitstaff is well trained and can recommend what to sip from the extensive wine list. To-die-for desserts include the delightful crème brûlée flight and deep-fried bread pudding so good you may feel like you just died and went to heaven. There's also a variety of gluten-free dishes. $ *Average main: $30* ⊠ *1513 Main St., North End* ☎ *843/842–8866* ⊕ *wiseguyshhi.com* ⊗ *No lunch.*

BLUFFTON

$$$$ ✕**Claude & Uli's Bistro.** *European.* It's hard to go wrong with a chef who has cooked at Maxim's in Paris, the Connaught Hotel in London, and Ernie's in San Francisco. Chef Claude Melchiorri, who grew up in Normandy, France, and his wife, Uli, offer divine food at this atmospheric restaurant tucked away in a strip mall right before the bridges to Hilton Head. Candles and fresh flowers top the white linen–covered tables. Parisian art lines the walls; a large painting of dogs at a French bar adds a touch of humor. The French-European cuisine is simply irresistible. Before ordering appetizers and dinner, order the Soufflé Grand Marnier with chocolate sauce ahead for dessert, then start with the seafood crepe with white-wine sauce. For the entrée, try the veal Normandy with brandied mushroom cream sauce. All the seafood is fresh, and all the sauces are handmade. $ *Average main: $25* ⊠ *Moss Creek Village, 1533 Fording Island Rd., Bluffton* ☎ *843/837–3336* ⊕ *claudebistro.com* ⊗ *No lunch Sun.–Tues. No lunch in summer.*

WHERE TO STAY

$$$ ⌂**Beach House Hilton Head Island.** *Resort.* On one of the island's most popular stretches of sand, the Beach House Hilton Head Island is within walking distance of lots of shops and restaurants. **Pros:** the location cannot be beat; renovations have made this a very desirable destination; professional staff. **Cons:** in summer the number of kids raises the noise volume; small front desk can get backed up. $ *Rooms from: $249* ⊠ *1 S. Forest Beach Dr., South End* ☎ *843/785–5126* ⊕ *www.hihiltonhead.com* ⇄ *202 rooms* ⊗ *No meals.*

$$$$ ⚏ **Disney's Hilton Head Island Resort.** *Resort.* The typical cheery
FAMILY   colors and whimsical designs at Disney's Hilton Head Island
Resort create a look that's part Southern beach resort, part
Adirondack hideaway. **Pros:** family-friendly vibe; young
and friendly staffers; plenty of space to spread out. **Cons:**
it's a time-share property; expensive rates. ⑤ *Rooms from:
$375* ⊠ *22 Harbourside La., Mid-Island* ☎ *843/341–4100*
⊕ *www.disneybeachresorts.com/hilton-head-resort* ⤳ *102
villas, 21 deluxe studios* ⦿ *No meals.*

$$$ ⚏ **Hampton Inn on Hilton Head Island.** *Hotel.* Although it's
FAMILY   not on the beach, this attractive hotel is a good choice for
budget travelers. **Pros:** good customer service; moderate
prices; more amenities than you might expect. **Cons:** not on
a beach; parking lot views. ⑤ *Rooms from: $209* ⊠ *1 Dillon
Rd., Mid-Island* ☎ *843/681–7900* ⊕ *www.hamptoninn.com*
⤳ *95 rooms, 8 suites, 12 studios* ⦿ *Breakfast.*

$$$$ ⚏ **Hilton Head Marriott Resort & Spa.** *Hotel.* Private balconies
with views of the palm-shaded grounds are the best reason
to stay at this resort facing the Atlantic Ocean. **Pros:** steps
from the beach; lots of amenities; one of the best-run opera-
tions on the island. **Cons:** rooms could be larger; in summer
kids are everywhere. ⑤ *Rooms from: $339* ⊠ *1 Hotel Circle,
Palmetto Dunes, Mid-Island* ☎ *843/686–8400* ⊕ *www.mar-
riott.com/hotels/travel/hhhgr-hilton-head-marriott-resort-
and-spa* ⤳ *476 rooms, 36 suites* ⦿ *No meals.*

★ **Fodor'sChoice** ⚏ **The Inn at Harbour Town.** *Hotel.* The most
$$$$ buzzworthy of Hilton Head's properties, this European-
style boutique hotel has a proper staff clad in kilts that
pampers you with British service and a dose of Southern
charm. **Pros:** a service-oriented property; central location;
unique, one of the finest hotels on island; complimentary
parking. **Cons:** no water views; two-day minimum on most
weekends. ⑤ *Rooms from: $293* ⊠ *Sea Pines, 7 Lighthouse
La., South End* ☎ *843/785–3333* ⊕ *www.seapines.com* ⤳ *60
rooms* ⦿ *No meals.*

★ **Fodor'sChoice** ⚏ **The Inn at Palmetto Bluff.** *B&B/Inn.* About 15
$$$$ minutes from Hilton Head, the Lowcountry's most luxuri-
ous resort sits on 20,000 acres that have been transformed
into a perfect replica of a small island town, complete with
its own clapboard church. **Pros:** member of the Preferred
Small Hotels of the World; tennis/bocce/croquet complex
has an impressive retail shop; the river adds both ambience
and boat excursions. **Cons:** the mock Southern town is not
the real thing; not that close to the amenities of Hilton
Head. ⑤ *Rooms from: $556* ⊠ *1 Village Park Sq., Bluffton*

Where to Stay on Hilton Head Island

KEY

⚞ *Beach*

🚢 *Ferry*

Port Royal Sound

170

95

46

← TO SAVANNAH, GEORGIA

Bluffton ⓬

Old South Golf Link

278

Welcome Center of Hilton Head

Coastal Discovery Museum

Pickney Island

Seabrook Landing

Country Club of Hilton Head

HILTON HEAD PLANTATION

PALMETTO HALL PLANTATION

Arthur Hills and Robert Cupp at Palmetto Hall

NORTH END

Hilton Head Island Airport

Main Street

Seabrook Drive

Beach City Rd.

Matthews Dr.

PORT ROYAL PLANTATION

⓶ ⓷

Folly Field Rd.

ay River lf Club

Bull Island

Cross Island Pkwy.

Palmetto Bay Rd.

Golden Bear at Indigo Run

MID-ISLAND

Marshland Rd.

Shelter Cove Lane

Shelter Cove

Shelter Cove Marina

Harbourside Lane

⓸

Broad Creek

PALMETTO DUNES RESORT

⓹

Robert Trent Jones at Palmetto Dunes

⓺

Golf Club

Intracoastal

Waterway

SOUTH END

278

Audubon-Newhall Preserve

Sea Pines Forest Preserve

Sea Pines Resort

⓻ **Shipyard**

⓼

Pope Ave.

North Forest Beach Drive

Greenwood Dr.

Cordillo Pkwy.

ⓐ ⓽

Daufuskie Island Club & Resort

Cooper River Landing

Lighthouse Road

Harbour Town

Plantation Dr.

Harbour Town Golf Links

⓾

⓫ **The Inn at Harbour Town**

Sea Pines Dr.

South Forest Beach Drive

OCEANSIDE

Daufuskie Island

South Beach Marina

SOUTH BEACH

South Beach Marina

Atlantic Ocean

Beach House Hilton Head Island, **9**

Candlewood Suites, **1**

Disney's Hilton Head Island Resort, **4**

Hampton Inn on Hilton Head Island, **2**

Hilton Head Marriott Resort & Spa, **5**

The Inn at Harbour Town, **11**

The Inn at Palmetto Bluff, **12**

Omni Hilton Head Oceanfront Resort, **6**

Park Lane Hotel & Suites, **7**

The Sea Pines Resort, **10**

Sonesta Resort, **8**

Westin Hilton Head Island Resort & Spa, **3**

0	1/2 mi
0	1/2 km

How to Talk to Locals

Hilton Head is known as a place where people come to start a new life, or to happily live out their golden years. It is politically incorrect to immediately ask someone you just met, "Where did you come from?" or "What brought you here?" or "What did you do in your former life?" Residents are asked these questions all the time, and it gets old, especially if they moved here decades ago. Their reluctance to tell all does not mean that they necessarily have skeletons in their closets.

Now, conversely, they are allowed to ask *you* where you are from—not to mention how long you are staying—or they may be considered unwelcoming. But do let them tell you about themselves in time, or over a cocktail. You may learn that your golfing partner was the CEO of a big national corporation, or the guy next to you at the bar is a best-selling author, or the friendly fellow in line at the store is a billionaire entrepreneur who might even be a household name.

☎ *843/706–6500, 866/706–6565* ⊕ *www.palmettobluffresort.com* ⇱ *50 cottages* ❑ *No meals.*

$$$$ ▣ **Omni Hilton Head Oceanfront Resort.** *Resort.* At this beachfront hotel with a Caribbean sensibility, the spacious accommodations range from studios to two-bedroom suites. **Pros:** competes more with condos than hotels because of the size of its accommodations; lots of outdoor dining options. **Cons:** wedding parties can be noisy; cell phone service is spotty. ⑤ *Rooms from: $283* ✉ *23 Ocean La., Palmetto Dunes, Mid-Island* ☎ *843/842–8000* ⊕ *www.omnihiltonhead.com* ⇱ *303 studios, 20 suites* ❑ *No meals.*

$$ ▣ **Park Lane Hotel & Suites.** *Hotel.* The island's only all-suites property has a friendly feel, which is probably why many guests settle in for weeks. **Pros:** one of the island's most reasonably priced lodgings; parking and Wi-Fi are free; playground for the kids. **Cons:** doesn't have an upscale feel; more kids mean more noise, especially around the pool area. ⑤ *Rooms from: $159* ✉ *12 Park La., South End* ☎ *843/686–5700* ⊕ *www.hiltonheadparklanehotel.com* ⇱ *156 suites.*

$$$$ ▣ **Sonesta Resort Hilton Head Island.** *Resort.* Set in a luxuriant garden that always seems to be in full bloom, the Sonesta Resort is the centerpiece of Shipyard Plantation, which means you'll have access to all its various amenities, including golf and tennis. **Pros:** close to all the restaurants and nightlife in Coligny Plaza; spacious rooms; free parking.

Cons: Wi-Fi and cell phone service can be a problem; service is sometimes impersonal. ⑤ *Rooms from: $289* ⊠ *Shipyard Plantation, 130 Shipyard Dr., South End, Hilton Head Island* ☎ *843/842–2400, 800/334–1881* ⊕ *www.sonesta. com/hiltonheadisland* ⇌ *331 rooms, 9 suites* ⦿ *No meals.*

$$$$ ⚏ **Westin Hilton Head Island Resort & Spa.** *Resort.* A circular drive winds around a sculpture of long-legged marsh birds as you approach this beachfront resort, whose lush landscape lies on the island's quietest stretch of sand. **Pros:** great for destination weddings; the beach here is absolutely gorgeous; pampering spa. **Cons:** lots of groups in the off-season. ⑤ *Rooms from: $309* ⊠ *2 Grass Lawn Ave., Port Royal Plantation, North End* ☎ *800/933–3102, 843/681–4000* ⊕ *www.westinhiltonheadisland.com* ⇌ *416 rooms* ⦿ *No meals.*

BLUFFTON

$ ⚏ **Candlewood Suites.** *Hotel.* At this suites-only hotel, the guest rooms are comfortable and tastefully decorated in muted browns and beiges. **Pros:** location makes it convenient to Hilton Head, Beaufort, and Savannah. **Cons:** cell phone service is hit-or-miss; set back from road, it can be difficult to find. ⑤ *Rooms from: $129* ⊠ *5 Young Clyde Court, Bluffton* ☎ *843/705–9600* ⊕ *www.candlewoodsuites. com/blufftonsc* ⇌ *124 suites* ⦿ *No meals.*

PRIVATE VILLA RENTALS

Hilton Head has some 6,000 villas, condos, and private homes for rent, almost double the number of the island's hotel rooms. Villas and condos seem to work particularly well for families with children, especially if they want to avoid the extra costs of staying in a resort. Often these vacation homes cost less per diem than hotels of the same quality. Guests on a budget can further economize by cooking some of their own meals.

Villas and condos are primarily rented by the week, Saturday to Saturday. It pays to make sure you understand exactly what you're getting before making a deposit or signing a contract. For example, a property owner in the Hilton Head Beach & Tennis Club advertised that his villa sleeps six. That villa had one small bedroom, a foldout couch, and a hall closet with two very narrow bunk beds. That's a far cry from the three-bedroom villa you might have expected. ■ TIP➔ **Before calling a vacation rental company, make a list of the amenities you want.** Ask for pictures of each room and ask when the photos were taken. If you're looking for a beachfront property, ask exactly how far it is to the beach. Make sure to ask for a list of all fees, including those for parking, cleaning, pets, security deposits, and utility costs. Finally, get a written contract and a copy of the refund policy.

RENTAL AGENTS

Hilton Head Vacation Rentals. Representing more than 250 vacation rentals ranging in size from one to seven bedrooms, Hilton Head Vacation Rentals has villas, condos, and homes with oceanfront views. It offers various packages that include golf and other activities. Rentals are generally for three to seven days. ⊠ *578 William Hilton Pkwy.* ☎ *843/785–8687* ⊕ *www.hiltonheadvacation.com.*

Resort Rentals of Hilton Head Island. This company represents some 275 homes and villas, including many located inside the gated communities of Sea Pines, Palmetto Dunes, and Shipyard Plantation. Others are in North and South Forest Beach and the Folly Field area. Stays are generally Saturday to Saturday during the peak summer season; three- or four-night stays may be possible off-season. Most of the properties are privately owned, so decor and amenities can vary. ⊠ *32 Palmetto Bay Rd., Suite 1B, Mid-Island* ☎ *800/845–7017* ⊕ *www.hhivacations.com.*

Sea Pines Resort. The vast majority of the overnight guests at Sea Pines Resort rent one of the 500 suites, villas, and beach houses. One- and two-bedroom villas have a minimum stay of four nights. For stays of four or more nights, you must arrive on Saturday, Sunday, Monday, or Tuesday. Three- and four-bedrooms villas have a minimum stay of seven nights, and you've got to check in on Saturday. All houses have Internet access, and most have Wi-Fi. Housekeeping is usually an additional charge. ⊠ *32 Greenwood Dr., South End* ☎ *843/785–3333, 866/561–8802* ⊕ *www. seapines.com/vacation-rentals.*

NIGHTLIFE AND PERFORMING ARTS

NIGHTLIFE

Bars, like everything else on Hilton Head, are often in gate communities or shopping centers. Some are hangouts frequented by locals, and others get a good mix of both locals and visitors. There are a fair number of clubs, many of them restaurants that crank up the music after diners depart.

Big Bamboo. Decked out like a World War II–era officers' club, this South Pacific–themed bar and restaurant features live music most nights of the week. ⊠*Coligny Plaza, 1 N. Forest Beach Dr., South End* ☎*843/686–3443* ⊕*www. bigbamboocafe.com.*

Comedy Magic Cabaret. Several nights a week this lounge brings top-flight comedic talent to Hilton Head. Start off with dinner and drinks downstairs at the Kingfisher, which serves some of the best crab in town, then head upstairs for the comedy. Tickets are $18 to $22 per person. ■TIP→ **Book ahead, because the shows sell out fairly quickly.** ⊠*Shelter Cove, 18 Harbourside La., South End* ☎*843/681–7757* ⊕*www.comedymagiccabaret.com.*

Hilton Head Plaza. Dubbed the "Barmuda Triangle" by locals, the bars at this plaza include One Hot Mama's, Reilley's, the Hilton Head Brewing Company, the Lodge Martini, and Jump & Phil's Bar & Grill. It's the closest thing Hilton Head Island has to a raging club scene. ⊠*Hilton Head Plaza, Greenwood Dr., right before gate to Sea Pines, South End.*

★ **Fodor'sChoice The Jazz Corner.** The elegant supper-club atmosphere at this popular spot makes it a wonderful setting in which to enjoy an evening of jazz, swing, and blues. The owner, horn player Bob Masteller, sometimes takes the stage. There's a special martini menu, an extensive wine list, and a late-night menu. ■TIP→ **The club fills up quickly, so make reservations.** ⊠*The Village at Wexford, 1000 William Hilton Pkwy., Suite C-1, South End* ☎*843/842–8620* ⊕*www.thejazzcorner.com.*

★ **Fodor'sChoice The Salty Dog Cafe.** If there's one thing you
FAMILY shouldn't miss on Hilton Head Island, it's the iconic Salty Dog Cafe. It's the ideal place to escape, sit back, and enjoy the warm nights and ocean breezes in a tropical setting at the outdoor bar. There's live music (think Jimmy Buffett) seven nights a week during high season. Bring the family along for kid-friendly entertainment, including music, magic, and face painting at 7 pm throughout the summer. ⊠*South Beach Marina, 224 S. Sea Pines Dr., South End* ☎*843/671–5199* ⊕*www.saltydog.com.*

Santa Fe Cafe. A sophisticated spot for cocktails in the early evening, the Santa Fe Cafe is also a great place to lounge in front of the fireplace or sip top-shelf margaritas at the rooftop cantina. ⊠*807 William Hilton Pkwy., Mid-Island* ☎*843/785–3838* ⊕*www.santafehhi.com.*

8

Turtle's Poolside Beach Bar & Grill. With an open-air deck where you can enjoy the cool breezes, this popular spot offers live entertainment nightly. If you're hungry, the kitchen serves Lowcountry food with a Caribbean twist. ✉ *2 Grasslawn Ave., Westin Resort & Spa, North End* ☎ *843/681–4000.*

PERFORMING ARTS

★ **Fodor**$Choice **Arts Center of Coastal Carolina.** Locals love the exhibits at the Walter Greer Gallery and the theater productions at the Arts Center of Coastal Carolina. Programs for children are also popular. ✉ *14 Shelter Cove La., Mid-Island* ☎ *843/686–3945* ⊕ *www.artshhi.com.*

Hilton Head Island Gullah Celebration. This showcase of Gullah life through arts, music, and theater is held at a variety of sites throughout the Lowcountry in February. ☎ *843/255–7304* ⊕ *www.gullahcelebration.com.*

Hilton Head Symphony Orchestra. A selection of summer concerts—including the popular "Picnic and Pops"—are among the year-round performances by the symphony. Most events are at the First Presbyterian Church. ✉ *First Presbyterian Church, 540 William Hilton Pkwy., Mid-Island* ☎ *843/842–2055* ⊕ *www.hhso.org.*

FAMILY **Main Street Youth Theatre.** A variety of performances showcasing young local talent are presented by Main Street Youth Theatre. ✉ *25 New Orleans Rd., Mid-Island* ☎ *843/689–6246* ⊕ *www.msyt.org.*

SPORTS AND THE OUTDOORS

Hilton Head Island is a mecca for the sports enthusiast and for those who just want a relaxing walk or bike ride on the beach. There are 12 miles of beaches, 24 public golf courses, more than 50 miles of public bike paths, and more than 300 tennis courts. There's also tons of water sports, including kayaking and canoeing, parasailing, fishing, sailing, and much more.

BEACHES

A delightful stroll on the beach can end with an unpleasant surprise if you don't put your towels, shoes, and other earthly possessions way up on the sand. Tides here can fluctuate as much as 7 feet. Check the tide chart at your hotel.

Alder Lane Beach Park. A great place for solitude even during the busy summer season, this beach has hard-packed sand

Island Gators

The most famous photo of Hilton Head's brilliant developer, Charles Fraser, ran in the *Saturday Evening Post* in the late 1950s. It shows him dressed as a dandy, outfitted with a cane and straw hat, with an alligator on a leash.

These prehistoric creatures are indeed indigenous to this subtropical island. What you will learn if you visit the Coastal Discovery Museum, where the old photograph is blown up for an interpretive board on the island's early history, is that

someone else had the gator by the tail (not shown) so that it would not harm Fraser or the photographer.

Nowadays, in Sea Pines Center, there is a life-size, metal sculpture of an alligator that all the tourists, and especially their kids, climb on to have their pictures taken. And should you happen to see a live gator while exploring the island or playing a round of golf, please don't feed it. Although, if you have the courage, you might want to take a snapshot.

---

at low tide, making it great for walking. It's accessible from the Marriott Grand Ocean Resort. **Amenities:** lifeguards; showers; toilets. **Best for:** solitude; walking; swimming. ⊠ *Alder La., off South Forest Beach Rd, South End.*

BEACH RULES. Animals are not permitted on Hilton Head beaches between 10 and 5 from Memorial Day through Labor Day. Animals must be on leash. No alcohol, glass, littering, indecent exposure, unauthorized vehicles, fires and fireworks, shark fishing, removal of any live beach fauna, sleeping between midnight and 6 am, and kites not under manual control.

Burkes Beach. This beach is usually not crowded, mostly because it is a bit hard to find and there are no lifeguards on duty. **Amenities:** none. **Best for:** solitude, sunrise, swimming, windsurfing. ⊠ *60 Burkes Beach Rd., at William Hilton Pkwy., Mid-Island.*

FAMILY Fodor'sChoice **Coligny Beach.** The island's most popular beach is
★ a lot of fun, but during high season it can get very crowded. Accessible from the Beach House Hilton Head Island and several other hotels, it has choreographed fountains that delight little children, bench swings, and beach umbrellas and chaise longues for rent. If you have to go online, there's also Wi-Fi access. **Amenities:** lifeguards; food and drink; parking; showers; toilets. **Best for:** windsurfing; swimming.

✉ *1 Coligny Circle, at Pope Ave. and South Forest Beach Dr., South End.*

FAMILY **Driessen Beach.** A good destination for families, Driessen Beach is peppered with people flying kites, making it colorful and fun. There's a long boardwalk to the beach. **Amenities:** parking; lifeguards; toilets; showers. **Best for:** walking; sunrise; swimming. ✉ *43 Bradley Beach Rd., at William Hilton Pkwy., Mid-Island.*

SAND DOLLARS. Hilton Head Island's beaches hold many treasures, including starfish, sea sponges, and sand dollars. Note that it is strictly forbidden to pick up any live creatures on the beach, especially live sand dollars. How can you tell if they are alive? Live sand dollars are brown and fuzzy and will turn your fingers yellow and brown. You can take sand dollars home only if they're white. Soak them in a mixture of bleach and water to remove the scent once you get home.

Folly Field Beach Park. Next to Driessen Beach, Folly Field is a treat for families. It can get crowded in high season, but even so it's a wonderful spot for a day of sunbathing and swimming. The first beach cottages on Hilton Head Island were built here in the 1950s. **Amenities:** lifeguards; parking; toilets; outdoor showers. **Best for:** swimming; sunrise; walking. ✉ *55 Starfish Dr., off Folly Field Rd., North End.*

Mitchelville Beach Park. Not ideal for swimming because of the many sharp shells on the sand and in the water, Mitchelville Beach Park is a terrific spot for a walk or beachcombing. It is not on the Atlantic Ocean, but rather on Port Royal Sound. **Amenities:** parking; toilets. **Best for:** solitude; walking. ✉ *124 Mitchelville Rd., Hilton Head Plantation, North End.*

MAY RIVER SANDBAR. Known as the "Redneck Riviera," the May River Sandbar is pure party. Basically, the sandbar is just that: a small island of sand on the May River in Bluffton, which is the town that vacationers must go through on U.S. 278 to get to Hilton Head. The sandbar is accessible only by boat and only at low tide. Locals will plan their weekends around the time of low tide to head out to the sandbar. Boaters drop anchor and the party begins. Horseshoe and cornhole games are set up, picnic baskets unpacked, and cold drinks poured. To get there, go north by boat on Calibogue Sound and turn left west at the May River. The sandbar is at Red Marker 6.

BIKING

More than 50 miles of public paths crisscross Hilton Head Island, and pedaling is popular along the firmly packed beach. The island keeps adding more to the boardwalk network as visitors are using it and because it's such a safe alternative for kids. Bikes with wide tires are a must if you want to ride on the beach. They can save you a spill should you hit loose sand on the trails. Keep in mind when crossing streets that, in South Carolina, vehicles have the right-of-way. ■TIP➔For a map of trails, visit ⊕ www.hilton-headislandsc.gov.

Bicycles from beach cruisers to mountain bikes to tandem bikes can be rented either at bike stores or at most hotels and resorts. Many can be delivered to your hotel, along with helmets, baskets, locks, child carriers, and whatever else you might need.

Hilton Head Bicycle Company. You can rent bicycles, helmets and adult tricycles from the Hilton Head Bicycle Company. ✉ *112 Arrow Rd., South End* ☎ *843/686–6888, 800/995–4319* ⊕ *www.hiltonheadbicycle.com.*

Pedals Bicycles. Rent beach bikes for adults and children, kiddy karts, jogging strollers, and mountain bikes at Pedals. ✉ *71A Pope Ave., South End* ☎ *843/842–5522, 888/699–1039* ⊕ *www.pedalsbicycles.com.*

South Beach Cycles. Rent bikes, helmets, tandems, and adult tricycles at this spot in Sea Pines. ✉ *230 South Sea Pines Dr., Sea Pines, South End* ☎ *843/671–2453* ⊕ *www.south-beach-cycles.com.*

CANOEING AND KAYAKING

This is one of the most delightful ways to commune with nature on this commercial but physically beautiful island. Paddle through the creeks and estuaries and try to keep up with the dolphins.

Outside Hilton Head. Boats, canoes, kayaks, and paddleboards are available for rent. The company also offers nature tours and dolphin-watching excursions. ✉ *Shelter Cove Marina, 1 Shelter Cove La., Mid-Island* ☎ *843/686–6996, 800/686–6996* ⊕ *www.outsidehiltonhead.com.*

8

FISHING

Although anglers can fish in these waters year-round, in April things start to crank up and in May most boats are heavily booked. May is the season for cobia, especially in Port Royal Sound. In the Gulf Stream you can hook king mackerel, tuna, wahoo, and mahimahi. ■TIP→ **A fishing license is necessary if you are fishing from a beach, dock, or pier. They are $11 for 14 days.** Licenses aren't necessary on charter fishing boats because they already have their licenses.

Bay Runner Fishing Charters. With more than four decades of experience fishing these waters, Captain Miles Altman takes anglers out for trips lasting three to eight hours. Evening shark trips are offered May to August. ✉ *Shelter Cove Marina, 1 Shelter Cove La., Mid-Island* ☎ *843/290–6955* ⊕ *www.bayrunnerfishinghiltonhead.com.*

FAMILY **Capt. Hook Party Boat.** Deep-sea fishing tours are available on this large party boat, which sells concessions as well. The friendly crew teaches children how to bait hooks and reel in fish. ✉ *Shelter Cove Marina, 1 Shelter Cove La., Mid-Island* ☎ *843/785–1700* ⊕ *www.hiltonheadisland.com/captainhook.*

Fishin' Coach. Captain Dan Utley offers a variety of fishing tours on his 22-foot boat to catch redfish and other species year-round. ✉ *1640 Fording Island Rd., Mid-Island* ☎ *843/368–2126* ⊕ *www.fishincoach.com.*

Gullah Gal Sport Fishing. Fishing trips are available on a pair of 34-foot boats, the *Gullah Gal* and *True Grits.* ✉ *Shelter Cove Marina, 1 Shelter Cove La., Mid-Island* ☎ *843/842–7002* ⊕ *www.hiltonheadislandcharterfishing.com/.*

Integrity. The 38-foot charter boat *Integrity* offers offshore and near-shore fishing. ✉ *Harbour Town Yacht Basin, Mariners Way, Sea Pines, South End* ☎ *843/671–2704, 843/422–1221* ⊕ *www.integritycharterfishing.com.*

Palmetto Bay Charters. This company offers a wide variety of charters on various size boats. ✉ *Palmetto Bay Marina, 86 Helmsman Way, South End, Hilton Head Island* ☎ *843/785–7131* ⊕ *www.palmettobaymarinahhi.com.*

Palmetto Lagoon Charters. Captain Trent Malphrus takes groups for half- or full-day excursions to the region's placid saltwater lagoons. Redfish, bluefish, flounder, and black drum are some of the most common trophy fish. ✉ *Shelter Cove Marina, 1 Shelter Cove La., Mid-Island* ☎ *866/301–4634* ⊕ *www.palmettolagooncharters.com.*

GOLF

Hilton Head is nicknamed "Golf Island" for good reason: the island itself has 24 championship courses (public, semi-private, and private), and the outlying area has 16 more. Each offers its own packages, some of which are great deals. Almost all charge the highest green fees in the morning and lower fees as the day goes on. Lower rates can also be found in the hot summer months. It's essential to book tee times in advance, especially in the busy spring and fall months; resort guests and club members get first choices. Most courses can be described as casual-classy, so you will have to adhere to certain rules of the greens. ■TIP→ **The dress code on island golf courses does not permit blue jeans, gym shorts, or jogging shorts. Men's shirts must have collars.**

The Heritage PGA Tour Golf Tournament. The most internationally famed golf event in Hilton Head is the annual RBC Heritage PGA Tour Golf Tournament, held mid-April. There is a wide range of ticket packages available. Tickets are also available at the gate. ⊠ *Sea Pines Resort, 2 Lighthouse La., South End* ⊕ *www.rbcheritage.com.*

TEE OFF ON A BUDGET. Golfing on Hilton Head can be very expensive after you tally up the green fee, cart fee, rental clubs, gratuities, and so on. But there are ways to save money. There are several courses in Bluffton that are very popular with the locals, and some are cheaper to play than the courses on Hilton Head Island. Another way to save money is to play late in the day. At some courses, a round in the morning is more expensive than 18 holes in the late afternoon.

GOLF SCHOOLS

Golf Learning Center at Sea Pines Resort. The well-regarded golf academy offers hourly private lessons by PGA-trained professionals and one- to three-day clinics to help you perfect your game. ⊠ *Sea Pines, 100 North Sea Pines Dr., South End* ☎ *843/785–4540* ⊕ *www.golfacademy.net.*

Palmetto Dunes Golf Academy. There's something for golfers of all ages at this academy: instructional videos, daily clinics, and multiday schools. Lessons are offered for ages three and up, and there are special programs for women. Free demonstrations are held with Doug Weaver, former PGA Tour pro and director of instruction for the academy. Take advantage of the free swing evaluation and club-fitting.

8

✉ *Palmetto Dunes Oceanfront Resort, 7 Trent Jones La., Mid-Island* ☎ *843/785–1138* ⊕ *www.palmettodunes.com.*

The Island Golf School of Palmetto Hall Plantation. This is a great place to learn golf, perfect your swing, or improve your overall skills. It's administered by qualified and experienced professionals. ✉ *Palmetto Hall Plantation, 108 Fort Hollow Dr., North End* ☎ *843/342–2582* ⊕ *www. palmettohallgolf.com.*

GOLF COURSES

Arthur Hills and Robert Cupp at Palmetto Hall. There are two prestigious courses at Palmetto Hall Plantation: Arthur Hills and Robert Cupp. Arthur Hills is a player favorite, with its trademark undulating fairways punctuated with lagoons and lined with moss-draped oaks and towering pines. Robert Cupp is a very challenging course, but is great for the higher handicappers as well. ✉ *Palmetto Hall, 108 Fort Howell Dr., North End* ☎ *843/689–9205* ⊕ *www.palmettohallgolf.com* 🎫 *$145* ⬧ *Reservations essential* ⚑ *Arthur Hills: 18 holes, 6257 yds, par 72. Robert Cupp: 18 holes, 6025 yds, par 72.*

Country Club of Hilton Head. Although it's part of a country club, the course is open for public play. A well-kept secret, it's rarely too crowded. This 18-hole Rees Jones–designed course is a more casual environment than many of the other golf courses on Hilton Head. ✉ *Hilton Head Plantation, 70 Skull Creek Dr., North End* ☎ *843/681–4653, 866/835–0093* ⊕ *www.clubcorp.com/Clubs/Country-Club-of-Hilton-Head* 🎫 *$85–$105* ⚑ *18 holes, 6543 yds, par 72.*

Golden Bear Golf Club at Indigo Run. Located in the upscale Indigo Run community, Golden Bear Golf Club was designed by golf legend Jack Nicklaus. The course's natural woodlands setting offers easygoing rounds. It requires more thought than muscle, yet you will have to earn every par you make. Though fairways are generous, you may end up with a lagoon looming smack ahead of the green on the approach shot. And there are the fine points—the color GPS monitor on every cart and women-friendly tees. After an honest, traditional test of golf, most golfers finish up at the plush clubhouse with some food and drink at Just Jack's Grille. ✉ *Indigo Run, 100 Indigo Run Dr., North End* ☎ *843/689–2200* ⊕ *www.goldenbear-indigorun.com* 🎫 *$79–$99* ⚑ *18 holes, 6184 yds, par 72.*

★ Fodor's Choice **Harbour Town Golf Links.** Considered by many golfers to be one of those must-play-before-you-die courses, Harbour Town Golf Links is extremely well known because it has hosted the RBC Heritage Golf Tournament every spring for the last four decades. Designed by Pete Dye, the layout is reminiscent of Scottish courses of old. The Golf Academy at the Sea Pines Resort is ranked among the top 10 in the country. ⊠ *Sea Pines Resort, 11 Lighthouse La., South End* ☎ *843/842–1020, 800/732–7463* ⊕ *www. seapines.com/golf* ⊡ *$215–$272* ⚑ *Reservations essential* ⚑ *18 holes, 7001 yds, par 71.*

Robert Trent Jones at Palmetto Dunes. One of the island's most popular layouts, this course's beauty and character are accentuated by the 10th hole, a par 5 that offers a panoramic view of the ocean (one of only two on the entire island). It's among the most beautiful courses in the Southeast, with glittering lagoons punctuating 11 of the 18 holes. ⊠ *Palmetto Dunes, 7 Robert Trent Jones La., North End* ☎ *843/785–1138* ⊕ *www.palmettodunes.com* ⊡ *$55–$155* ⚑ *Reservations essential* ⚑ *18 holes, 6122 yds, par 72.*

BLUFFTON GOLF COURSES

There are several beautiful golf courses in Bluffton, which is just on the other side of the bridges to Hilton Head Island. These courses are very popular with locals and can often be cheaper to play than the courses on Hilton Head Island.

Crescent Pointe. An Arnold Palmer Signature Course, Crescent Pointe is fairly tough, with somewhat narrow fairways and rolling terrain. There are numerous sand traps, ponds, and lagoons, making for some demanding yet fun holes. Some of the par 3s are particularly challenging. The scenery is magnificent, with large live oaks, pine-tree stands, and rolling fairways. Additionally, several holes have spectacular marsh views. ⊠ *Crescent Pointe, 1 Crescent Pointe, Bluffton* ☎ *843/706–2600* ⊕ *www.crescentpointegolf.com* ⊡ *$70–$95* ⚑ *18 holes, 6773 yds, par 71.*

Eagle's Pointe. This Davis Love III–designed course—located in the Eagle's Pointe community in Bluffton—is one of the area's most playable. Eagle's Pointe attracts many women golfers because of its women-friendly tees, spacious fairways, and large greens. There are quite a few bunkers and lagoons throughout the course, which winds through a natural woodlands setting that attracts an abundance of wildlife. ⊠ *Eagle's Pointe, 1 Eagle's Pointe Dr., Bluffton*

☎ *843/757–5900* ⊕ *www.eaglespointegolf.com* ✉ *$52* ⚑ *18 holes, 6126 yds, par 72.*

Island West Golf Club. Fuzzy Zoeller and golf course designer Clyde Johnston designed this stunningly beautiful course set amid the natural surroundings at Island West. There are majestic live oaks, plenty of wildlife, and expansive marsh views on several holes. Golfers of all skill levels can find success on this succession of undulating fairways. There are several holes where the fairways are rather generous, while others can be demanding. This is a fun and challenging course for golfers of all handicaps. ✉ *Island West, 40 Island West Dr., Bluffton* ☎ *843/689–6660* ⊕ *www.islandwestgolf. net* ✉ *$35–$45* ⚑ *18 holes, 6208 yds, par 72.*

The May River Golf Club. An 18-hole Jack Nicklaus course, this has several holes along the banks of the scenic May River and will challenge all skill levels. The greens are Champion Bermuda grass and the fairways are covered by Paspalum, the latest eco-friendly turf. Caddy service is always required. No carts are allowed earlier than 9 am to encourage walking. One caveat: The staff can sometimes be unresponsive. ✉ *Palmetto Bluff, 476 Mount Pelia Rd., Bluffton* ☎ *843/706–6500* ⊕ *www.palmettobluffresort.com/ golf* ✉ *$175–$260* ⚓ *Reservations essential* ⚑ *18 holes, 7171 yds, par 72.*

Old South Golf Links. There are many scenic holes overlooking marshes and the intracoastal waterway at this Clyde Johnson–designed course. It's a public course, but that hasn't stopped it from winning awards. It's reasonably priced, and reservations are recommended. ✉ *50 Buckingham Plantation Dr., Bluffton* ☎ *843/785–5353* ⊕ *www.oldsouthgolf. com* ✉ *$65–$95* ⚑ *18 holes, 6772 yds, par 72.*

PARASAILING

For those looking for a bird's-eye view of Hilton Head, it doesn't get better than parasailing. Newcomers will get a lesson in safety before taking off. Parasailers are then strapped into a harness, and as the boat takes off, the parasailer is lifted about 500 feet into the sky.

Bay Parasail. You can glide 500 feet in the air over Palmetto Bay Marina and Broad Creek on a trip with Palmetto Bay Parasail. ✉ *Palmetto Bay Marina, 86 Helmsman Way, South End* ☎ *843/686–2200* ⊕ *www.parasailhiltonhead.com.*

H20 Sports. You can soar above Hilton Head and check out the views up to 25 miles in all directions with this popular

Fun for Kids

Hilton Head Island is a really fun place for little ones. Check out these kid-friendly sites.

Adventure Cove. With two miniature 18-hole golf courses and a large arcade, Adventure Cove is sure to please the kids. ⊠ *18 Folly Field Rd., Mid-Island* ☎ *843/842-9990* ⊕ *www.adventurecove.com.*

Black Dagger Pirate Ship. The kids get to put on pirate gear, learn how to talk like a pirate, and set sail to search for underwater treasure. The ship sails from Harbour Town. ⊠ *Mariners Way, Sea Pines Resort, South End* ☎ *843/363-7000* ⊕ *www.piratesofhiltonhead.com.*

Island Playground. Near the bridges to Hilton Head, the Island Playground has giant inflatable slides, a fairy-tale castle, toddler exploration area, and snack counter. ⊠ *1538 Fording Island Rd., Bluffton* ☎ *843/837-8383* ⊕ *www.islandplayground.com.*

Lawton Stables. Riding lessons, pony rides, horseback excursions through the Sea Pines Forest Preserve are offered at Lawton Stables. The animal farm includes goats, sheep, and pigs. ⊠ *190 Greenwood Dr., Sea Pines Resort, South End* ☎ *843/671-2586* ⊕ *www.lawtonstableshhi.com.*

Pirate's Island. Two miniature golf courses are set amid tumbling waterfalls in the tropical-themed Pirate's Island. ⊠ *8 Marina Side Dr., Mid-Island* ☎ *843/686-4001* ⊕ *www.piratesislandgolf.com.*

Fodor'sChoice★ The Sandbox, An Interactive Children's Museum. A hands-on place for the youngest members of your family, this museum includes a cockpit where kids can put on a pilot's uniform and pretend to fly the friendly skies. In the Builders of Tomorrow exhibit, children dress up like construction workers and move materials to the building site, raise walls, and maneuver equipment. There's also a Learner's Loft where kids play with a puppet theater, puzzles, games, and toys ⊠ *18A Pope Ave., South End* ☎ *843/842-7645* ⊕ *www.thesandbox.org.*

Station 300. Two dozen state-of-the-art bowling lanes, an arcade, and a restaurant make Station 300 a very welcome addition to the Bluffton area. ⊠ *25 Innovation Dr., Bluffton* ☎ *843/815-2695* ⊕ *station-300bluffton.com.*

8

company located in Sea Pines. ⊠ *149 Lighthouse Rd., Sea Pines, South End* ☎ *843/671-4386, 877/290-4386* ⊕ *www.h2osports.com.*

TENNIS

There are more than 300 courts on Hilton Head. Tennis comes in at a close second as the island's premier sport after golf. It is recognized as one of the nation's best tennis destinations. Hilton Head has a large international organization of coaches. ■TIP➔ **Spring and fall are the peak seasons for cooler play, with numerous tennis packages available at the resorts and through the schools.**

★ Fodor'sChoice **Palmetto Dunes Tennis Center.** Ranked among the best in the world, this facility at the Palmetto Dunes Oceanfront Resort has 25 clay and 2 hard courts (a total of six are lighted for night play). There are lessons geared to players of every skill level given by enthusiastic staffers. Daily round-robin tournaments add to the festive atmosphere. ✉*Palmetto Dunes Oceanfront Resort, 6 Trent Jones La., Mid-Island* ☎*843/785–1152* ⊕*www.palmettodunes.com.*

Port Royal Racquet Club. The occasional magnolia tree dots the grounds of the Port Royal Racquet Club, which has 10 clay and 4 hard courts. The professional staff, stadium seating, and frequent tournaments are why it is ranked among the best in the world. ✉*Port Royal Plantation, 15 Wimbledon Court, Mid-Island* ☎*843/686–8803* ⊕*www.portroyalgolfclub.com.*

Sea Pines Racquet Club. The highly rated club has 23 clay courts, as well as instructional programs and a pro shop. There are special deals for guests of Sea Pines. ✉*5 Lighthouse La., Sea Pines Resort, South End* ☎*843/363–4495* ⊕*www.seapines.com.*

Shipyard Racquet Club. Play on 4 hard courts, 3 indoor courts, and 13 clay courts at this club in Shipyard Plantation. ✉*116 Shipyard Dr., Shipyard Plantation, South End* ☎*843/686–8804* ⊕*www.vandermeertennis.com.*

Van der Meer Tennis Center. Recognized for its tennis instruction for players of all ages and skill levels, this highly rated club has 17 hard courts, 4 of which are covered and lighted for night play. ✉*19 DeAllyon Ave., Shipyard Plantation, South End* ☎*843/785–8388* ⊕*www.vandermeertennis.com.*

ZIP LINE TOURS

ZipLine Hilton Head. Take a thrilling tour of Hilton Head on a zip line over ponds and marshes and past towering oaks and pines. This company offers eight zip lines, two suspended sky bridges, and a dual-cable racing zip line. Guests are harnessed and helmeted, and must be at least

10 years old and weigh between 80 and 250 pounds. ✉ *33 Broad Creek Marina Way, Mid-Island* ☎ *843/682–6000* ⊕ *ziplinehiltonhead.com.*

SHOPPING

Hilton Head is a great destination for those who love shopping, starting with the Tanger outlet malls. Although they're officially in Bluffton, visitors drive by the outlets on U.S. 278 to get to Hilton Head Island. Tanger Outlet I has been completely renovated and reopened with many high-end stores, including Saks OFF 5th, DKNY, Michael Kors, and more.

ART GALLERIES

Walter Greer Gallery. Part of the Arts Center of Coastal Carolina, this modern gallery showcases local artists. ✉ *Arts Center of Coastal Carolina, 14 Shelter Cove La., Mid-Island* ☎ *843/681–5060* ⊕ *www.artleaguehhi.org.*

★ **Fodor$Choice Images by Ben Ham.** The extraordinary photography of Ben Ham focuses on Lowcountry landscapes. ✉ *90 Capital Dr., Suite 104, Mid-Island* ☎ *843/842–4163* ⊕ *www.benhamimages.com.*

Morris & Whiteside Galleries. Original art by contemporary artists can be found at this upscale gallery. ✉ *220 Cordillo Pkwy., Mid-Island* ☎ *843/842–4433* ⊕ *www.morris-whiteside.com.*

GIFTS

Markel's. The very helpful and friendly staff at Markel's is known for wrapping gifts with giant bows. You'll find unique Lowcountry gifts, including hand-painted wineglasses and beer mugs, lawn ornaments, baby gifts, greeting cards, and more. ✉ *1008 Fording Island Rd., Bluffton* ☎ *843/815–9500.*

Pretty Papers. Fine stationery and gifts are available at Pretty Papers. ✉ *The Village at Wexford, 100 William Hilton Pkwy., Suite E7, Mid-Island* ☎ *843/341–5116* ⊕ *www.prettypapershhi.com.*

Salty Dog T-Shirt Factory. You can't leave Hilton Head without a Salty Dog T-shirt, so hit this factory store for the best deals. The iconic T-shirts are hard to resist, and there are lots of choices for kids and adults in various colors and styles. ✉ *69 Arrow Rd., South End* ☎ *843/842–6331* ⊕ *www.saltydog.com.*

8

FAMILY **The Storybook Shoppe.** Charming, whimsical, and sweet describe this children's bookstore. It has a darling area for little ones to read as well as educational toys for infants to teens. ✉ *41A Calhoun St., Bluffton* ☎ *843/757–2600* ⊕ *www.thestorybookshoppe.com.*

Top of the Lighthouse Shop. The Hilton Head Lighthouse is the island's iconic symbol, and this shop celebrates the red-and-white-striped landmark. ✉ *149 Lighthouse Rd., Sea Pines, South End* ☎ *866/305–9814* ⊕ *www.harbourtownlighthouse.com/shop.*

JEWELRY

Forsythe Jewelers. This is the island's leading jewelry store, offering pieces by famous designers. ✉ *71 Lighthouse Rd., Sea Pines, South End* ☎ *843/671–7070* ⊕ *www.forsythejewelers.biz.*

Goldsmith Shop. Classic jewelry, much of it with island themes, is on sale at the Goldsmith Shop. ✉ *3 Lagoon Rd., South End* ☎ *843/785–2538* ⊕ *www.thegoldsmithshop.com.*

MALLS AND SHOPPING CENTERS

Coligny Plaza. Things are always humming at this shopping center, which is within walking distance of the most popular beach on Hilton Head. Coligny Plaza has more than 60 shops and restaurants, including unique clothing boutiques, souvenir shops, and the expansive Piggly Wiggly grocery store. There are also bike rentals and free family entertainment throughout summer. ✉ *Coligny Circle, 1 North Forest Beach Dr., South End* ☎ *843/842–6050.*

Harbour Town. Distinguished by a candy-striped lighthouse, Harbour Town wraps around a marina and has plenty of shops selling colorful T-shirts, casual resort wear, and beach-themed souvenirs. ✉ *Sea Pines, 32 Greenwood Dr., South End* ☎ *866/561–8802* ⊕ *www.seapines.com/resort_activities/harbour_town.*

Shops at Sea Pines Center. Clothing for men and women, the best local crafts, and fine antiques are the draw at this outdoor shopping center. You can even get a massage at the on-site day spa. ✉ *71 Lighthouse Rd., South End* ☎ *843/363–6800* ⊕ *www.theshopsatseapinescenter.com.*

South Beach Marina. Looking like a New England fishing village, South Beach Marina is the place for beach-friendly fashions. ✉ *232 South Sea Pines Dr., South End* ☎ *843/671–6498.*

KID STUFF. Free outdoor children's concerts are held at Harbour Town in Sea Pines and Shelter Cove Harbor throughout the summer months. Guitarist Gregg Russell has been playing for children under Harbour Town's mighty Liberty Oak tree for decades. He begins strumming nightly at 8 in the summer, except on Saturday. It's also tradition for kids to get their pictures taken at the statue of Neptune at Harbour Town. At Shelter Cove, longtime island favorite Shannon Tanner performs a fun, family show at 6:30 pm and 8 pm weekdays from Memorial Day through Labor Day.

Old Town Bluffton. A charming area, Old Town features local artist galleries, antiques, and restaurants. ⊠ *Downtown Bluffton, May River Rd. and Calhoun St., Old Town, Bluffton* ☎ *843/706–4500* ⊕ *www.oldtownbluffton.com.*

★ Fodor'sChoice **Tanger Outlets.** There are two halves to this popular shopping center: Tanger Outlet I has more than 40 upscale stores, as well as popular eateries like Olive Garden, Panera Bread, and Longhorn Steakhouse. Tanger Outlet II has Abercrombie & Fitch, Banana Republic, the Gap, and Nike, along with 60 others stores. There are also several children's stores, including Gymboree, Carter's, and Baby Gap. Dine at Food Network star Robert Irvine's restaurant, Nosh. ⊠ *1414 Fording Island Rd., Bluffton* ☎ *843/837–5410, 866/665–8679* ⊕ *www.tangeroutlet. com/hiltonhead.*

The Village at Wexford. Upscale shops, including Lilly Pulitzer and Le Cookery, as well as several fine-dining restaurants can be found in this shopping area. There are also some unique gift shops and luxe clothing stores. ⊠ *1000 William Hilton Parkway, Hilton Head* ☎ *843/686–3090* ⊕ *www. villageatwexford.com.*

SPAS

Spa visits have become a recognized activity on the island, and for some people they are as popular as golf and tennis. In fact, spas have become one of the top leisure-time destinations, particularly for golf "widows." And this popularity extends to the men as well; previously spa-shy guys have come around, enticed by couples massage, deep-tissue sports massage, and even the pleasures of the manicure and pedicure.

There are East Indian–influenced therapies, hot-stone massage, Hungarian organic facials—the treatments span the

8

globe. Do your research, go online, and call or stop by the various spas and ask the locals their favorites. The quality of therapists island-wide is noteworthy for their training, certifications, and expertise.

Auberge Spa at Palmetto Bluff. Dubbed the "celebrity spa" by locals, this two-story facility is the ultimate pamper palace. The names of the treatments, which often have a Southern accent, are almost as creative as the treatments themselves. There are Amazing Grace and High Cotton body therapies, sensual soaks and couples massage, special treatments for gentlemen and golfers, and the soothing Belles and Brides package. Nonguests are welcome. ✉ *Palmetto Bluff, 1 Village Park Sq., Bluffton* 🕾 *843/706–6500* ⊕ *www.palmettobluffresort.com/spa.*

Faces. This place has been pampering loyal clients for more than three decades, thanks to body therapists, stylists, and cosmetologists who really know their stuff. Choose from the line of fine cosmetics, enjoy a manicure and pedicure, or have a professional do your evening makeup for that special occasion. ✉ *The Village at Wexford, 1000 William Hilton Pkwy., South End* 🕾 *843/785–3075* ⊕ *www.facesdayspa.com.*

★ **Fodor's Choice Heavenly Spa by Westin.** This is the quintessential spa experience on Hilton Head. Known internationally for its innovative treatments, the beautifully renovated Heavenly Spa incorporates local traditions. Prior to a treatment, clients are told to put their worries in a basket woven from local sweetgrass; de-stressing is a major component of the therapies here. The relaxation room with its teas and healthy snacks and the adjacent retail area with products like sweetgrass scents are heavenly, too. In-room spa services are available, as are romance packages. ✉ *Westin Resort Hilton Head Island, 2 Grasslawn Ave., Port Royal Plantation, North End* 🕾 *843/681–4000* ⊕ *www.westinhiltonheadisland.com.*

Spa Soleil. A wide variety of massages and other treatments are offered at Spa Soleil. The tantalizing teas and snacks make your time here a soothing, therapeutic experience. This is an amazing island treasure. ✉ *Hilton Head Marriott Resort & Spa, 1 Hotel Circle, Palmetto Dunes, Mid-Island* 🕾 *843/686–8420* ⊕ *www.csspagroup.com.*

BEAUFORT

38 miles north of Hilton Head via U.S. 278 and Rte. 170;
70 miles southwest of Charleston via U.S. 17 and U.S. 21.

Charming homes and churches grace this old town on Port
Royal Island. Come here on a day trip from Hilton Head,
Savannah, or Charleston, or to spend a quiet weekend at a
B&B while you shop and stroll through the historic district.
Beaufort continues to gain recognition as an art town and
supports a large number of galleries for its diminutive size.
Visitors are drawn equally to the town's artsy scene and to
the area's water-sports possibilities. The annual Beaufort
Water Festival, which takes place over 10 days in July,
is the premier event. For a calendar of Beaufort's annual
events, check out ⊕ *www.beaufortsc.org.*

More and more transplants have decided to spend the rest
of their lives here, drawn to Beaufort's small-town charms,
and the area is burgeoning. A truly Southern town, its picturesque backdrops have lured filmmakers here to shoot
The Big Chill, The Prince of Tides, and *The Great Santini,*
the last two being Hollywood adaptations of best-selling
books by author Pat Conroy. Conroy has waxed poetic
about the Lowcountry and calls the Beaufort area home.

To support Beaufort's growing status as a tourist destina-
tion, it has doubled the number of hotels in recent years.
Military events like the frequent graduations (traditionally
Wednesday and Thursday) at the marine base on Parris
Island tie up rooms.

GETTING HERE AND AROUND
Beaufort is 25 miles east of Interstate 95, on U.S. 21. The
only way to get here is by private car or Greyhound bus.

ESSENTIALS
Well-maintained public restrooms are available at the Beaufort Visitors Center. You can't miss this former arsenal; a
crenellated, fortlike structure, it is now beautifully restored
and painted ocher.

The Beaufort County Black Chamber of Commerce
(⊕ *www.bcbcc.org*) puts out an African American visitor's
guide, which takes in the surrounding Lowcountry. The
Beaufort Visitors Center gives out copies.

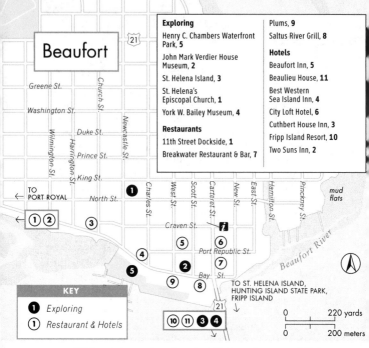

Beaufort

Exploring

Henry C. Chambers Waterfront Park, **5**

John Mark Verdier House Museum, **2**

St. Helena Island, **3**

St. Helena's Episcopal Church, **1**

York W. Bailey Museum, **4**

Restaurants

11th Street Dockside, **1**

Breakwater Restaurant & Bar, **7**

Plums, **9**

Saltus River Grill, **8**

Hotels

Beaufort Inn, **5**

Beaulieu House, **11**

Best Western Sea Island Inn, **4**

City Loft Hotel, **6**

Cuthbert House Inn, **3**

Fripp Island Resort, **10**

Two Suns Inn, **2**

KEY

❶ *Exploring*

① *Restaurant & Hotels*

Visitor Information **Beaufort Visitors Center** ✉ *713 Craven St.* ☎ *843/525–8500* ⊕ *www.beaufortsc.org.* **Regional Beaufort Chamber of Commerce** ✉ *1106 Carteret St.* ☎ *843/525–8500* ⊕ *www.beaufortchamber.org.*

EXPLORING

TOP ATTRACTIONS

★ **Fodor'sChoice** **Henry C. Chambers Waterfront Park.** Off Bay Street, this park is a great place to survey the scene. Trendy restaurants and bars overlook these seven beautifully landscaped acres along the Beaufort River. At night everyone strolls along the river walk. ✉ *1006 Bay St.* ☎ *843/525–7000* ⊕ *www.cityofbeaufort.org.*

Johnson Creek Tavern. There are times when you just want a cold one accompanied by some raw oysters. Head to Johnson Creek Tavern and sit outside to take advantage of the marsh views. Or opt for a seat in the sporty bar, where every surface is covered with dollar bills. You may even feel compelled to add one of your own—ask for the staple gun and try to find an empty spot for your George Washington.

✉ *2141 Sea Island Pkwy., Harbor Island* ☎ *843/838–4166* ⊕ *www.johnsoncreektavern.com.*

St. Helena Island. About 9 miles southeast of Beaufort, St. Helena Island is a stronghold of the Gullah culture. Several African American–owned businesses in its tightknit community of Frogmore make this quite the tourist magnet. ✉ *Rte. 21, St. Helena Island* ⊕ *www.beaufortsc.org/area/st.-helena-island.*

FAMILY **York W. Bailey Museum.** The museum at the Penn Center has displays on the heritage of Sea Island African Americans; it also has pleasant grounds shaded by live oaks. Dating from 1862, the Penn Center was the first school for the newly emancipated slaves. These islands are where Gullah, a musical language that combines English and African languages, developed. This museum and the surrounding community of St. Helena Island are a major stop for anyone interested in the Gullah history and culture of the Lowcountry. ✉ *30 Penn Center Circle W, St. Helena Island* ☎ *843/838–2432* ⊕ *www.penncenter.com* ✍ *$5* ⊙ *Mon.–Sat. 9–4.*

Barefoot Farm. Check out this farm stand for perfect watermelons, rhubarb, and strawberry jam. ✉ *939 Sea Island Pkwy., St. Helena Island* ☎ *843/838–7421.*

WORTH NOTING

John Mark Verdier House Museum. Built in the Federal style, this 1804 house has been restored and furnished as it would have been prior to a visit by Marquis de Lafayette in 1825. It was the headquarters for Union forces during the Civil War. ✉ *801 Bay St., Downtown Historic District* ☎ *843/379–6335* ⊕ *historicbeaufort.org* ✍ *$10* ⊙ *Mon.–Sat. 10–4.*

St. Helena's Episcopal Church. The 1724 church was turned into a hospital during the Civil War, and gravestones were brought inside to serve as operating tables. While on church grounds stroll the peaceful cemetery and read the fascinating inscriptions. ✉ *505 Church St.* ☎ *843/522–1712* ⊕ *www.sthelenas1712.org* ⊙ *Mon.–Wed. and Fri. 10–4, Thurs. 1–4, Sat. 10–1.*

8

WHERE TO EAT

$$$ ✕ **11th Street Dockside.** *Seafood.* Start with the fried green tomatoes or jalapeno-stuffed shrimp at this friendly eatery, then succumb to the succulent fried oysters, shrimp, and fish. More healthful options are also available, including a steamed seafood hot pot filled with crab legs, oysters, mussels, and shrimp. Everything is served in a classic wharfside environment, where you can eat on a screened porch with water views from nearly every table. $ *Average main: $21* ✉ *1699 11th St. W, 6 miles southwest of Beaufort, Port Royal* ☎ *843/524–7433* ⊕ *www.11thstreetdockside.com* ⚷ *Reservations not accepted* ⊘ *No lunch.*

$$$$ ✕ **Breakwater Restaurant & Bar.** *Eclectic.* This downtown restaurant offers small tasting plates such as tuna tartare and fried shrimp, but if you prefer not to share there are main dishes like lamb meat loaf and filet mignon with a truffle demi-glace. The presentation is as contemporary as the decor. There's also an impressive and affordable wine list. $ *Average main: $25* ✉ *203 Carteret St., Downtown Historic District* ☎ *843/379–0052* ⊕ *www.breakwatersc. com* ⊘ *Closed Sun. No lunch.*

$$$ ✕ **Plums.** *American.* This hip restaurant began its life in 1986 in a homey frame house with plum-color awnings shading the front porch. The namesake awnings are still around, but the dining room has been expanded to make it a more contemporary space. An oyster bar that looks out to Bay Street, Plums still uses old family recipes for its soups, crab-cake sandwiches, and curried chicken salad. At lunch you can chow down on inventive burgers, po'boys, and wraps. Dinner is more sophisticated with creative pairings and artistic presentations, particularly with the pasta and seafood dishes. There's live music Tuesday through Saturday evening. $ *Average main: $22* ✉ *904 Bay St., Downtown Historic District* ☎ *843/525–1946* ⊕ *www. plumsrestaurant.com.*

★ **Fodor's**Choice ✕ **Saltus River Grill.** *American.* The hippest eat-
$$$$ ery in Beaufort, Saltus River Grill wins over diners with its sailing motifs, breezy patio, and modern Southern menu. The bar opens at 4 pm, as does the raw bar with its tempting array of oysters and sushi spacials. Take in the sunset from the outdoor seating area overlooking the riverfront park. A flawless dinner might start off with the signature crab bisque, then segue to the seared sea scallops with green pea and pancetta risotto. The wine list is admirable, and desserts change nightly. $ *Average main: $30* ✉ *802 Bay St., Downtown Historic District* ☎ *843/379–3474* ⊕ *www.saltusrivergrill.com* ⚷ *Reservations essential* ⊘ *No lunch.*

CLOSE UP

Writer Pat Conroy on Beaufort

Many fans of best-selling author Pat Conroy consider Beaufort *his* town because of his autobiographical novel *The Great Santini*, which was set here. He, too, considers it home base: "We moved to Beaufort when I was 15. We had moved 23 times. (My father was in the Marines.) I told my mother, 'I need a home.' Her wise reply was: 'Well, maybe it will be Beaufort.' And so it has been. I have stuck to this poor town like an old barnacle. I moved away, but I came running back in 1993."

A number of Hollywood films have been shot here, not just Conroy's. "The beautiful white house on the Point was called the 'Big Santini House' until the next movie was shot and now it is known as 'The Big Chill House.' If a third movie was made there, it would have a new name.

"One of the great glories of Beaufort is found on St. Helena Island," he says. "You get on Martin Luther King Jr. Boulevard and take a right at the Red Piano Too Art Gallery to the Penn Center. Before making the right turn, on the left, in what was the Bishop family's general store, is Gullah Grub, one of the few restaurants that serve legitimate Gullah food."

He continues: "At the end of St. Helena, toward the beach, take Seaside Road. You will be in the midst of the Gullah culture. You end up driving down a dirt road and then an extraordinary avenue of oaks that leads to the Coffin Point Plantation, which was the house where Sally Field raised Forrest Gump as a boy."

8

WHERE TO STAY

Even though accommodations in Beaufort have increased in number, prime lodgings can fill up fast, so do call ahead.

$$ ☒ **Beaufort Inn.** *B&B/Inn.* This 1890s Victorian inn charms you with its handsome gables and wraparound verandas. **Pros:** in the heart of the historic district; beautifully landscaped space; light afternoon refreshments are complimentary. **Cons:** atmosphere in the main building may feel too dated for those seeking a more contemporary hotel; no water views. ⑤ *Rooms from: $165* ☒ *809 Port Republic St., Downtown Historic District* ☎ *843/379–4667* ⊕ *www. beaufortinn.com* ⌨ *7 rooms, 7 suites, 8 cottages, 1 apartment, 1 house* ⑩ *Breakfast.*

$$$ ☒ **Beaulieu House.** *B&B/Inn.* From the French for "beautiful place," Beaulieu House is the only waterfront bed-and-breakfast in Beaufort—it's a quiet, relaxing inn with airy rooms decorated in Caribbean colors. **Pros:** great views; scrumptious gourmet hot breakfast; short drive to Beaufort historic district. **Cons:** thin walls; hot water can be a problem; a bit off the beaten path. ⑤ *Rooms from: $205* ✉ *3 Sheffield Ct.* ☎ *843/770–0303* ⊕ *beaulieuhouse.com* ↻ *4 rooms, 1 suite* ❍❘ *Breakfast.*

$$ ⌶ **Best Western Sea Island Inn.** *Hotel.* This well-maintained motel in the heart of the Historic District puts you within walking distance of many shops and restaurants. **Pros:** only swimming pool in downtown Beaufort; directly across from marina and an easy walk to art galleries and restaurants; breakfast included. **Cons:** air-conditioning is loud in some rooms, breakfast room can be noisy. ⑤ *Rooms from: $153* ✉ *1015 Bay St.* ☎ *843/522–2090, 800/528–1234* ⊕ *www. sea-island-inn.com* ↻ *43 rooms* ❍❘ *Breakfast.*

$$ ⌶ **City Loft Hotel.** *Hotel.* This 1960s-era motel was cleverly transformed by its hip, young owners to reflect their high-tech, minimalist style. **Pros:** stylish decor; use of the adjacent gym; very accommodating staff. **Cons:** the sliding Asian screen that separates the bathroom doesn't offer full privacy; no lobby or public spaces. ⑤ *Rooms from: $179* ✉ *301 Carteret St., Downtown Historic District* ☎ *843/379–5638* ⊕ *www.citylofthotel.com* ↻ *22 rooms, 1 suite.*

$$ ⌶ **Cuthbert House Inn.** *B&B/Inn.* Named after the original Scottish owners, who made their money in cotton and indigo, this 1790 home is filled with 18th- and 19th-century heirlooms and retains the original Federal fireplaces and crown and rope molding. **Pros:** owners are accommodating; complimentary wine and hors d'oeuvres service; great walk-about location. **Cons:** some furnishings are a bit busy; some artificial flower arrangements; stairs creak. ⑤ *Rooms from: $200* ✉ *1203 Bay St., Downtown Historic District* ☎ *843/521–1315* ⊕ *www.cuthberthouseinn.com* ↻ *7 rooms, 3 suites* ❍❘ *Breakfast.*

FRIPP ISLAND

$$$ ⌶ **Fripp Island Resort.** *Resort.* On the island made famous in
FAMILY *Prince of Tides,* with 3½ miles of broad, white beach and unspoiled scenery, this resort has long been known as one of the more affordable and casual on the island. **Pros:** fun for all ages; the beach bar has great frozen drinks and live music. **Cons:** far from Beaufort; some dated decor; could use another restaurant with contemporary cuisine. ⑤ *Rooms from: $201* ✉ *1 Tarpon Blvd., 19 miles south of Beaufort, Fripp Island* ☎ *843/838–1558, 888/741–8974* ⊕ *www.fripp islandresort.com* ↻ *210 units* ❍❘ *No meals.*

The World of Gullah

In the Lowcountry, Gullah refers to several things: a language, a people, and a culture. Gullah (the word itself is believed to be derived from *Angola*), an English-based dialect rooted in African languages, is the unique language, more than 300 years old, of the African Americans of the Sea Islands of South Carolina and Georgia. Most locally born African Americans of the area can understand, if not speak, Gullah.

Descended from thousands of slaves who were imported by planters in the Carolinas during the 18th century, the Gullah people have maintained not only their dialect but also their heritage. Much of Gullah culture traces back to the African rice-coast culture and survives today in the art forms and skills, including sweetgrass basket making, of Sea Islanders. During the colonial period, when rice was king, Africans from the West African rice kingdoms drew high premiums as slaves. Those with basket-making skills were extremely valuable because baskets were needed for agricultural and household use. Made by hand, sweetgrass baskets are intricate coils of marsh grass with a sweet, hay-like aroma.

Nowhere is Gullah culture more evident than in the foods of the region. Rice appears at nearly every meal—Africans taught planters how to grow rice and how to cook and serve it as well. Lowcountry dishes use okra, peanuts, *benne* (a word of African origin for sesame seeds), field peas, and hot peppers. Gullah food reflects the bounty of the islands: shrimp, crabs, oysters, fish, and such vegetables as greens, tomatoes, and corn. Many dishes are prepared in one pot, a method similar to the stewpot cooking of West Africa.

On St. Helena Island, near Beaufort, Penn Center is the unofficial Gullah headquarters, preserving the culture and developing opportunities for Gullahs. In 1852 the first school for freed slaves was established at Penn Center. You can delve into the culture further at the York W. Bailey Museum.

On St. Helena, many Gullahs still go shrimping with hand-tied nets, harvest oysters, and grow their own vegetables. Nearby on Daufuskie Island, as well as on Edisto, Wadmalaw, and John's islands near Charleston, you can find Gullah communities. A famous Gullah proverb says, *If oonuh ent kno weh oonuh dah gwine, oonuh should kno weh oonuh come f'um.* Translation: If you don't know where you're going, you should know where you've come from.

8

Writer Pat Conroy on Fripp Island

"What has Fripp Island meant to me?" Pat Conroy, one of the Lowcountry's famous writers, answered: "The year was 1964. I was living in Beaufort. And when the bridge to Fripp Island was built, I was a senior in high school. My English teacher *and* my chemistry teacher moonlighted as the island's first security guards. It was a pristine island; there were no houses on it yet, and it was as beautiful as any desert island. "In 1978, my mother moved over there, and all our summers were spent on the island. It was to be her last home. That sealed the island in our family's history. In 1989, I bought a house there, both because it is a private island and thus good for a writer, but also so that our family—my brothers and sisters—could always have a home on Fripp to come to."

PRIVATE VILLAS ON FRIPP ISLAND

There are more than 200 private villas for rent on Fripp Island (but no hotels). Fripp Island Golf & Beach Resort (⊕ *www.frippislandresort.com*) offers a range of rental options, including homes, villas, and golf cottages, many with oceanfront or golf views.

NIGHTLIFE AND PERFORMING ARTS

Emily's. This fun hangout is populated with locals who graze on tapas while eyeing one of the four wide-screen TVs. The piano sits idle until a random patron sits down and impresses the crowd. The bar is full of local characters. ⊠ *906 Port Republic St., Downtown Historic District* ☎ *843/522–1866* ⊕ *www.emilysrestaurantandtapasbar.com.*

Luther's. A late-night waterfront hangout, Luther's is casual and fun, with a young crowd watching the big-screen TVs or dancing to live rock music bands on Thursday, Friday, and Saturday nights. Luther's also has a terrific late-night menu. The decor features exposed brick, pine paneling, and old-fashioned posters on the walls. ⊠ *910 Bay St., Downtown Historic District* ☎ *843/521–1888* ⊕ *www.luthersrareandwelldone.com.*

SPORTS AND THE OUTDOORS

BEACHES

Hunting Island State Park. This secluded park 18 miles southeast of Beaufort has 4 miles of public beaches—some dramatically eroding. The light sand beach decorated with driftwood and the subtropical vegetation is breathtaking. The state park was founded in 1938 to preserve and promote the area's natural wonders, and it harbors 5,000 acres of rare maritime forests. You can kayak in the tranquil lagoon; stroll the 1,300-foot-long fishing pier (among the longest on the East Coast); and go fishing or crabbing. For sweeping views, climb the 167 steps of the 1859 **Hunting Island Lighthouse.** Bikers and hikers can enjoy 8 miles of trails. The nature center has exhibits, an aquarium, and lots of turtles; there is a resident alligator in the pond. **Amenities:** none. **Best for:** solitude; sunrise; swimming; walking. ⊠ *2555 Sea Island Pkwy., off St. Helena Island, Hunting Island* ☎ *843/838–2011* ⊕ *www.southcarolinaparks.com* 🖃 *$5* ⊗ *Park: Apr.–Oct., daily 6 am–9 pm; Nov.–Mar., daily 6–6. Lighthouse daily 10–4:45.*

BIKING

Beaufort looks different from two wheels. In town, traffic is moderate, and you can cruise along the waterfront and through the historic district. However, if you ride on the sidewalks or after dark without a headlight and a rear red reflector, you run the risk of a city fine of nearly $150. If you stopped for happy hour and come out as the light is fading, walk your bike back "home." Some inns lend or rent out bikes to guests, but alas, they may not be in great shape and usually were not the best even when new.

Lowcountry Bicycles. If you want a decent set of wheels, contact Lowcountry Bicycles. Bikes are $8 an hour or $25 a day. ⊠ *102 Sea Island Pkwy.* ☎ *843/524–9585* ⊕ *www. lowcountrybicycles.com.*

BOATING

Beaufort is where the Ashepoo, Combahee, and Edisto rivers form the A.C.E. Basin, a vast wilderness of marshes and tidal estuaries loaded with history. For sea kayaking, tourists meet at the designated launching areas for fully guided, two-hour tours.

Barefoot Bubba's. Less than 1 mile from Hunting Island, Barefoot Bubba's rents bikes and kayaks and will deliver them to the park or anywhere in the area. ⊠ *2135 Sea*

Sea Monkeys

There is a colony of monkeys living on Morgan Island, a little isle near Fripp Island. If you are in a boat cruising or on a fishing charter and think you might be seeing monkeys running on the beach, you are not hallucinating from sun exposure. The state of South Carolina leases one of these tiny islands to raise monkeys, both those that are used for medical research and also rare golden rhesus monkeys sold as exotic pets. This deserted island and the subtropical climate and vegetation have proved ideal for their breeding. But you can't land on the island or feed the monkeys, so bring binoculars or a long-lens camera.

Island Pkwy., St. Helena ☎ *843/838–9222* ⊕ *barefootbubbasurfshop.com.*

Beaufort Kayak Tours. Owner-operators Kim and David Gundler of Beaufort Kayak Tours are degreed naturalists and certified historical guides. The large cockpits in the kayaks make for easy accessibility, and the tours go with the tides, not against them, so paddling isn't strenuous. The tours, which cost $50 per person, meet at various public landings throughout Beaufort County. ☎ *843/525–0810* ⊕ *www.beaufortkayaktours.com.*

GOLF

Most golf courses are about a 10- to 20-minute scenic drive from Beaufort.

Dataw Island. This upscale island community is home to Tom Fazio's Cotton Dike golf Course, with spectacular marsh views, and Arthur Hill's Morgan River Golf Course, with ponds, marshes, and wide-open fairways. The lovely 14th hole of the latter overlooks the river. To play you must be accompanied by a member or belong to another private club. ✉ *100 Dataw Club Rd., 6 miles east of Beaufort, Dataw Island* ☎ *843/838–8250* ⊕ *www.dataw.org* ✏ *$69–$120* ⚑ *Cotton Dike: 18 holes, 6787 yds, par 72. Morgan River: 18 holes, 6657 yds, par 72.*

Fripp Island Golf & Beach Resort. This resort has a pair of championship courses. Ocean Creek Golf Course, designed by Davis Love, has sweeping views of saltwater marshes. Designed by George Cobb, Ocean Point Golf Links runs alongside the ocean the entire way. This is a wildlife refuge, so you'll see plenty of animals, particularly the graceful marsh deer. In fact, the wildlife and ocean views may make it difficult for you to keep your eyes on the ball. To play, nonguests must belong to a private golf club. ⊠ *2119 Sea Island Pkwy., Fripp Island* ☏ *843/838–3535, 843/838–1576* ⊕ *www.frippislandresort.com* ⊜ *$75–$99* ⅄ *Ocean Creek: 18 holes, 6643 yds, par 71. Ocean Point: 18 holes, 6556 yds, par 72.*

Sanctuary Golf Club at Cat Island. This is a semiprivate club, so members get priority. Its scenic course is considered tight with plenty of water hazards. ⊠ *Cat Island, 8 Waveland Ave.* ☏ *843/524–0300* ⊕ *www.sanctuarygolfcatisland.com* ⊜ *$40–$80* ⅄ *18 holes, 6673 yds, par 71.*

SHOPPING

ART GALLERIES

Longo Gallery. The colorful designs of Suzanne and Eric Longo decorate the Longo Gallery. Suzanne creates ceramic sculpture—couples dancing and mothers with children are among her favorite motifs. Eric's whimsical paintings often feature fish. ⊠ *103 Charles St., Downtown Historic District* ☏ *843/522–8933.*

★ **Fodor's Choice** **Red Piano Too Gallery.** More than 150 Lowcountry artists are represented at the Red Piano Too Gallery, considered one of the area's best (if not the best) art spaces. It carries folk art, books, fine art, and much more. Much of the art at the gallery represents the Gullah culture. ⊠ *870 Sea Island Pkwy., St. Helena* ☏ *843/838–2241* ⊕ *redpianotoo.com.*

Rhett Gallery. The Rhett Gallery sells Lowcountry art by four generations of the Rhett family, including remarkable wood carvings. There are also antique maps, books, Civil War memorabilia, and Audubon prints. ⊠ *901 Bay St., Downtown Historic District* ☏ *843/524–3339* ⊕ *rhett-gallery.com.*

8

DAUFUSKIE ISLAND

13 miles (approximately 45 minutes) from Hilton Head via ferry.

From Hilton Head you can take a 45-minute ferry ride to nearby Daufuskie Island, the setting for Pat Conroy's novel *The Water Is Wide,* which was made into the movie *Conrack.* The boat ride may very well be one of the highlights of your vacation. The Lowcountry beauty unfolds before you, as pristine and unspoiled as you can imagine. The island is in the Atlantic, nestled between Hilton Head and Savannah. Many visitors do come just for the day, to play golf and have lunch or dinner; kids might enjoy biking or horseback riding. On weekends, the tiki hut at Freeport Marina whirrs out frozen concoctions as a vocalist sings or a band plays blues and rock and roll. The famous Jack Nicklaus signature golf course at Melrose on the Beach is one of the highlights of Daufuskie Island. For tee times, call ☏ *843/422–6963.* The golf club has an arrangement with Harbourtown Adventures for charter ferry service for golfers (⊕ *www.melroseonthebeach.com*). The island also has acres of unspoiled beauty. On a bike, in a golf cart, on horseback, you can easily explore the island. You will find remnants of churches, homes, and schools—some reminders of antebellum times. Guided tours include such sights as an 18th-century cemetery, former slave quarters, a "praise house," an 1886 African Baptist church, the schoolhouse where Pat Conroy taught, and the Haig Point Lighthouse. There are a number of small, artsy shops like the Iron Fish Gallery.

GETTING HERE AND AROUND

The only way to get to Daufuskie is by boat, as it is a bridgeless island. The public ferry departs from Broad Creek Marina on Hilton Head Island several times a day. On arrival to Daufuskie you can rent a golf cart (not a car) or bicycle or take a tour. Golf carts are the best way to get around the island. Enjoy Daufuskie (enjoydaufuskie.com) offers golf cart rentals to tourists when they come to visit. If you are coming to Daufuskie Island for a multiday stay with luggage and/or groceries, and perhaps a dog, be absolutely certain that you allow a full hour to park and check in for the ferry, particularly on a busy summer weekend. Whether you are staying on island or just day-tripping, the ferry costs $34 round-trip. Usually the first two pieces of luggage are free, and then it is $10 apiece.

TOURS

Freeport Marina, where the public ferry disembarks on Daufuskie Island, includes the Freeport General Store, a restaurant, overnight cabins, and more. A two-hour bus tour of the island by local historians will become a true travel memory. The ferry returns to Hilton Head Island on Tuesday night in time to watch the fireworks at Shelter Cove at sundown.

Live Oac, based on Hilton Head, is an owner-operated company that offers Lowcountry water adventures such as nature tours, fishing excursions, and dolphin cruises. On its first-class hurricane-deck boats you are sheltered from sun and rain; tours, usually private charters, are limited to six people. Captains are interpretive naturalist educators and U.S. Coast Guard licensed.

Take a narrated horse-drawn carriage tour of historic Beaufort with Southurn Rose Buggy Tours and learn about the city's fascinating history and its antebellum and Victorian architecture.

Tour Contacts Daufuskie Island Adventures ✉ *421 Squire Pope Rd., Hilton Head* ☎ *843/384–4354* ⊕ *www.daufuskiediscovery. com.* **Live Oac** ✉ *43 Jenkins Rd., North End, Hilton Head Island* ☎ *888/254–8362* ⊕ *www.liveoac.com.* **Southurn Rose Buggy Tours** ✉ *1002 Bay St., Downtown Historic District, Beaufort* ☎ *843/524–2900* ⊕ *www.southurnrose.com.*

WHERE TO EAT

$$ ✕**Old Daufuskie Crab Company Restaurant.** *Seafood.* Everyone calls this restaurant the Freeport Marina because of its location. A cold beer may be in order at the colorful bar that plays reggae and rock tunes, especially after a warm-water boat ride. This outpost, with its rough-hewn tables facing the water, serves up surprisingly good fare. The specialties are deviled crab and chicken salad on buttery grilled rolls. Many also enjoy the Lowcountry buffet with its pulled pork and sides like butter beans and potato salad. Dinner entrées include shrimp, rib eyes, and the catch of the day. ⑤ *Average main: $17* ✉ *Freeport Marina, 1 Cooper River Landing Rd.* ☎ *843/342-8687* ⊕ *www.enjoydaufuskie. com/#!restaurant/cesh* ⊙ *Closed Mon.*

WHERE TO STAY

$$$$ ⛱ **Sandy Lane Villa.** *Rental.* A luxurious, oceanfront low-rise condominium complex, the twin Sandy Lane Villa buildings look out to the simple boardwalk that leads directly to a nearly deserted beach. **Pros:** spacious and private; unobstructed ocean views. **Cons:** not a homey beach cottage; 20 minutes from Freeport Marina. ⑤ *Rooms from: $400* ✉ *Sandy Lane Resort, 2302 Sandy La.* ☎ *843/785–8021* ⊕ *www.daufuskievacation.com* ↩ *3 rooms* ⦿ *No meals.*

SPORTS AND THE OUTDOORS

FAMILY **Seagrass Stables at Melrose on the Beach.** There are trail rides, hayrides, and romantic drives in a 200-year-old surrey at Seagrass Stables. It also offers an equestrian center. ✉ *47 Ave. of the Oaks* ☎ *843/341–2894* ⊕ *www.melroseonthe beach.com/.*

TRAVEL SMART
SAVANNAH

GETTING HERE AND AROUND

▌ AIR TRAVEL

Savannah/Hilton Head International Airport caters to both destinations, though it is an almost half-hour drive from either. For transportation into the cities, taxis circle outside the baggage claim area, and some of the larger hotels offer shuttles. ■TIP➡ **If the flights into Savannah/Hilton Head International Airport aren't convenient, consider the international airports in Jacksonville and Charlotte. The drive time to Savannah is just shy of two hours.** Jacksonville has the added bonus of low-cost carriers like Southwest, and JetBlue services several destinations out of Charleston. Sometimes the price difference can almost cover that of the car rental. Additionally, approaching Savannah from the south gives you an opportunity to stop at Jekyll Island and other treasures of southeastern Georgia. From the north, visit scenic Beaufort or Bluffton.

Airlines and Airports

Airline and Airport Links.com. This comprehensive airline and aiport database is helpful to those traveling by plane. ⊕ *www.airlineand airportlinks.com.*

Airline-Security Issues

Transportation Security Administration ⊕ *www.tsa.gov.*

AIRPORTS

Savannah/Hilton Head International Airport (SAV) is 11 miles west of downtown. The airport is only 20 minutes by car from the Historic District and around 40 minutes from Hilton Head Island. Another option is the tiny Hilton Head Island Airport.

Airport Information Hilton Head Island Airport ⊠ *120 Beach City Rd., North end, Hilton Head, South Carolina* ☎ *843/255–2950* ⊕ *www. hiltonheadairport.com.* **Savannah/ Hilton Head International Airport** ⊠ *400 Airways Ave., Northwest* ☎ *912/964–0514* ⊕ *www.savanna-hairport.com.*

GROUND TRANSPORTATION

There are no airport shuttles other than those operated by hotels, so visitors not renting a car must taxi to their lodging accommodations. The going rate for the approximately 11-mile trip to the Historic District is $30. Savannah Limousine Service offers executive sedans starting at around $100 per hour, and can also arrange vans for groups to the Historic District starting around $25 per person. Another option for transporting groups into Savannah, Old Savannah Tours has larger vehicles that can be chartered.

Airport Transfers Old Savannah Tours ☎ *912/234–8128* ⊕ *www.old-savannahtours.com.* **Savannah Limousine Service** ☎ *912/897–5466* ⊕ *www.limosavannah.com.*

FLIGHTS

Savannah is serviced by American, Delta, JetBlue, United, and US Airways.

▎ BOAT AND FERRY TRAVEL

Located on the Savannah River, the Port of Savannah is the busiest port between New Orleans and New York. Savannah Belles Ferry provides regular service from the City Hall dock in the Historic District to the Westin Savannah Harbor Golf Resort & Spa at the International Convention Center, on Hutchinson Island. Ferries are part of the citywide transit system and run daily 7 am to midnight with departures every 15 to 20 minutes. The complimentary crossing takes two minutes.

Contacts Savannah Belles Ferry ⊠ City Hall Dock, River St., Historic District ☎ 912/447–4029 ⊕ www.catchacat.org.

▎ BUS TRAVEL

Savannah is a coastal stop for Greyhound. The newly renovated station is conveniently located on the western edge of the Historic District.

Contacts Greyhound ⊠ 610 W. Oglethorpe Ave., Historic District ☎ 912/232–2135 ⊕ www.greyhound.com.

▎ CAR TRAVEL

Interstate 95 slices north–south along the Eastern Seaboard, intersecting 10 miles west of town with east–west Interstate 16, which dead-ends in downtown Savannah. U.S. 17, the Coastal Highway, also runs north–south through town. U.S. 80 is another east–west route through Savannah.

Unless you have plans to explore beyond the Historic District, Savannah is one destination where smart city planning and abundant public transportation render a rental car unnecessary. If you'll be centrally located during your visit, choose from the plentiful buses, taxis, pedicabs (up to two persons can be pedaled in a cart attached to a bicyclist), horse carriages, trolley tours (some of which allow on-and-off privileges), free ferries, and rental bikes, scooters, and Segway rentals. This is a walking city, so bring a pair of comfortable shoes.

GASOLINE

In general, gas prices in Savannah hover around the national average. Gas stations are not difficult to find; there are several on Martin Luther King Jr. Boulevard and 37th Street, the thoroughfares that access Interstate 16 to route back to Interstate 95 and the airport.

PARKING

Downtown parking can be a challenge; there are often more options in nearby residential neighborhoods. Tourists may purchase one- and two-day parking passes for $7 and $12 from the Savannah Visitors Center, the Parking Services Department, and some hotels and inns (several properties give you this pass for free if you're staying with them). Rates vary at local parking garages, but in a City of Savannah–owned lot you should expect to pay at least $1 to $2 per hour during business hours on weekdays, a $2 flat rate in the evenings, and a flat rate of $5 to $10 on weekends. Special-events parking can double the rates. Metered-parking costs per hour vary depending on location, from 25¢ up to $1. You don't have to feed meters after 6 pm or on weekends. Most downtown hotels have paid parking, and some B&Bs and inns have their own parking lots or advise guests on how to park on the street. Few restaurants have parking.

RENTAL CARS

Major rental agencies can be found in town and at the airport, and many provide pickup and delivery service. Almost all car-rental offices are closed on Sunday.

RENTAL CAR INSURANCE

When renting a car, is the added insurance a necessary expense? No one—including us—has a simple answer. If you own a car, your personal auto insurance may cover a rental to some degree; always read your policy's fine print. If you don't have auto insurance, then seriously consider buying the collision- or loss-damage waiver (CDW or LDW) from the car-rental company, which eliminates your liability for damage to the car. Some credit cards offer CDW coverage, but it's usually supplemental to your own insurance and rarely covers SUVs, minivans, luxury models, and the like.

If your coverage is secondary, you may still be liable for loss-of-use costs from the car-rental company. But no credit-card insurance is valid unless you use that card for *all* transactions, from making a reservation to paying the final bill. It's sometimes cheaper to buy insurance as part of your general travel insurance policy.

ROADSIDE EMERGENCIES

Discuss with the car-rental agency what to do in the case of an emergency, as this sometimes differs from company to company. Make sure you understand what your insurance covers and what it doesn't, and it's a good rule of thumb to let someone at your hotel know where you are heading and when you plan to return. Keep emergency numbers (car-rental agency and your accommodation) with you, just in case.

ROAD CONDITIONS

Roads in Savannah are a mixed bag. Certain streets in the Historic District are brick or cobblestone, which makes for a bumpy ride. In other areas—particularly in the Midtown and Southside neighborhoods—roads are paved and in good condition. Traffic can be tricky in the Historic District, with one-way streets and large numbers of pedestrians, cyclists, and other vehicles; you may encounter slow-moving trolleys and horse-drawn carriages, but please don't honk at the horses. There's heavy truck traffic on Interstate 95, where the speed limit is 70 mph. Interstate 16 gets backed up for about an hour around rush hour.

PUBLIC TRANSPORTATION

Chatham Area Transit (CAT) operates buses in Savannah and Chatham County Monday through Saturday from just before 6 am to just shy of midnight, Sunday from 7 am to 9 pm. (Some lines stop running earlier or may not run on Sunday.) A free shuttle runs a loop throughout the Historic District. The Riverfront Trolley—a refurbished 1930s streetcar—runs the length of River Street Wednesday to Sunday.

Contacts **Chatham Area Transit** (*CAT*). ☎ 912/233–5767 ⊕ www.catchacat.org.

TAXI TRAVEL

AAA Adam Cab is a locally owned and operated, dependable 24-hour taxi service. Calling ahead for reservations could yield a flat rate. Yellow Cab Company is another reliable ride. Both companies charge $1.92 per mile. MC Transportation is a taxi and shuttle service that operates 24 hours a day and will take you anywhere, anytime.

You can hail these cabs on the street if they do not have riders or assignments. Most cab services offer flat rates to and from the airport, usually in the range of $30, plus $5 for each additional person.

Savannah Pedicab is a people-peddled vehicle that costs $45 per hour. They operate from 11 am to midnight (2 am on weekends).

Cruiser-style bikes are available for $20 per day, and can be delivered to your inn.

Contacts **AAA Adam Cab** ☎ 912/927–7466. **MC Transportation** ☎ 912/786–9191. **Savannah Pedicab** ☎ 912/232–7900 ⊕ www.savannahpedicab.com. **Yellow Cab** ☎ 912/236–1133, 912/604–9845 ⊕ www.yellowcabofsavannah.com.

TRAIN TRAVEL

Amtrak runs its Silver Service/Palmetto route down the East Coast from New York to Miami, stopping in Savannah. The station is about 6 miles from downtown.

Contacts **Savannah Amtrak Station** ✉ 2611 Seaboard Coastline Dr. ☎ 800/872–7245 ⊕ www.amtrak.com.

ESSENTIALS

▌ COMMUNICATIONS

INTERNET

Many hotels and inns offer complimentary Internet access. If you're out and about, your best bet for free Wi-Fi is probably a corner coffee shop. The Live Oak Public Library also offers free Internet access on a first-come, first-served basis at several of its branches.

PHONES

The area code in Savannah is 912. There are fewer than a half dozen pay phones in the greater downtown area.

▌ EMERGENCIES

St. Joseph's/Candler Hospital and Memorial Health University Medical Center are the area hospitals with 24-hour emergency rooms.

Hospitals **Memorial Health University Medical Center** ✉ *4700 Waters Ave., Midtown* ☎ *912/350–8000* ⊕ *www.memorialhealth.com.* **St. Joseph's/Candler Hospital** ✉ *11705 Mercy Blvd., Southside* ☎ *912/819–6000* ⊕ *www.sjchs.org.*

Late-Night Pharmacy **CVS Pharmacy** ✉ *Medical Arts Shopping Center, 4725 Waters Ave., Midtown* ☎ *912/355–7111* ⊕ *www.cvs.com/ pharmacy.*

▌ HOURS OF OPERATION

Most businesses operate on a 9-to-5 basis, although some offices open at 8:30. Boutiques and shops that are geared to tourists usually open daily at 10 and close around 6, including Sunday.

▌ MAIL

There is a post office in the Historic District on the corner of Barnard and State streets, as well as Federal Express and UPS outlets within a couple of blocks.

Mailing and Shipping **FedEx** ✉ *5 W. Broughton St., Historic District* ☎ *912/443–1901* ⊕ *www.fedex. com.* **UPS Store** ✉ *22 W. Bryan St., Historic District* ☎ *912/233–7807* ⊕ *www.theupsstorelocal.com.* **U.S. Post Office** ✉ *118 Barnard St., Historic District* ☎ *912/232–2952, 800/275–8777* ⊕ *www.usps.com.*

▌ MONEY

Bank of America, Wells Fargo, BB&T, and other major financial outlets have branches in Savannah; most operate normal office hours weekdays, with half days on Saturday.

ATMs are numerous, especially on River Street, around Johnson Square, and in City Market.

Reporting Lost Cards **American Express** ☎ *800/992-3404* ⊕ *www.americanexpress.com.* **MasterCard** ☎ *800/627-8372* ⊕ *www.mastercard.com.* **Visa** ☎ *800/847-2911* ⊕ *www.visa.com.*

▌ SAFETY

Savannah officials are serious about your safety, and you'll notice both police cars and security patrol cars throughout the downtown area. The streets are safe for pedestrians during the day, but at night you should exercise reasonable caution, especially in poorly lit areas along the perimeter of the Historic District. Avoid walking alone downtown after 10 pm. Always lock your car and remove valuables that are visible through the windows. Utilize your hotel's safe for your cash and valuables. Keep handy phone numbers for taxi companies.

▌ TAXES

The sales tax is 7%; hotel room tax is 13%.

▌ TIPPING

Tip as you would in any other U.S. city; waiters in restaurants expect to receive 10% to 20% (the larger amount in more upscale establishments); 15% is still the norm here. Tip hotel maids about $1 or $2 per day.

▌ TOURS

Savannah boasts tours aplenty and offers comfortable prospects of the city's history, landmarks, and landscapes.

BOAT TOURS

Savannah Riverboat Cruises has daily departures from docks on River Street. The causeway is mainly commercial, with many deserted warehouses, so it's not a terribly scenic ride, but it is narrated, has a bar, plays Jimmy Buffet, and is a relaxing trip on the river. The one-hour ride costs $21.95 per person, and departure times change seasonally. The Gospel Dinner Cruise has a Southern buffet and a choir to entertain and goes for $44.95.

Contacts **Savannah Riverboat Cruises** ✉ *9 E. River St.* ☎ *800/786-6404* ⊕ *www.savannahriverboat.com.*

BUS AND TROLLEY TOURS

Operating out of City Market, Carriage Tours of Savannah travels the Historic District at a 19th-century clip-clop pace, with coachmen spinning tales and telling ghost stories along the way. A romantic evening tour in a private carriage costs $85 per couple. Regular tours start at a modest $15 per person.

Savannah's rich African American history can be experienced via the daily departing Freedom Trail Tour. This comprehensive black-history tour visits significant landmarks like the First African Baptist Church, the Ralph Mark Gilbert Civil Rights Museum, and the slave burial grounds at Laurel Grove Cemetery.

Historic Savannah Carriage Tours specializes in private tours aboard a picturesque European carriage. The romantic Moonlight and Roses Tour includes a dozen roses and a stop at a local martini bar. Private tours cost $95 for two people. Tours open to the public are a little easier on the wallet: $20 per person. Either tour includes a horse-drawn amble through Savannah's historic streets.

Old Savannah Tours is the city's award-winning company with years of experience and the widest variety of tours. Popular options include the historic hop-on, hop-off trolley tour, the 90-minute Historic Overview, and the ghost tour that includes dinner at Pirates' House. Prices start at $27 per person.

Old Town Trolley Tours has narrated 90-minute tours traversing the Historic District. Trolleys stop at 16 designated stops every 30 minutes daily from 9 to 5 (August to March) or 9 to 6 (April to July). You can hop on and off as you please. The cost is $31, with discounts for purchasing ahead online.

Savannah Movie Tours circuits locations of many Hollywood films shot in the area, with running commentary offering an inside scoop. This same company offers the popular Foody Tours, as well as the Martini Tour, Shopping Tour, and Scary Ghost Tour.

Hearse Ghost Tours may be like nothing you've ever experienced before. For 15 years these hearses did the job they were intended for; when they were retired, their roofs were removed to make space for eight live bodies cruising around the haunted sites in the Historic District. Count on macabre guides for irreverently funny narration throughout the tour.

Contacts **Carriage Tours of Savannah** ☎ *912/236–6756* ⊕ *www.carriagetoursofsavannah. com.* **Freedom Trail Tours** ☎ *912/232–7477.* **Hearse Ghost Tours** ✉ *412 E. Duffy St., Historic District* ☎ *912/695–1578* ⊕ *www. hearseghosttours.com.* **Historic Savannah Carriage Tours** ☎ *912/443–9333* ⊕ *www.savannah carriage.com.* **Old Savannah Tours** ☎ *800/517–9007* ⊕ *www.old savannahtours.com.* **Old Town Trolley Tours** ☎ *912/233–0083 Local, 888/910–8687 Toll-free* ⊕ *www. trolleytours.com/savannah.* **Savannah Movie Tours** ☎ *912/303–7155* ⊕ *www.savannahmovietours.com.*

SPECIAL-INTEREST TOURS

Personalized Tours of Savannah is a small company offering upscale and intimate tours of the city, with customized themes covering movies filmed in Savannah, the city's amazing architecture, and a highly recommended Jewish-heritage tour. The friendly owner is a longtime Savannah resident, and tours are peppered with plenty of insider knowledge.

Contacts **Personalized Tours of Savannah** ☎ *912/234–0014* ⊕ *www.savannahsites.com.*

WALKING TOURS

A Ghost Talk Ghost Walk tour should send chills down your spine during an easygoing 1-mile jaunt through the old colonial city. Tours, lasting 1½ hours, leave from the middle of Reynolds Square, at the John Wesley Memorial at 7:30 pm and 9:30 pm, weather permitting. The cost is $10 per person.

Savannah Tours by Foot's Creepy Crawl Haunted Pub Tour is a great option for anyone who loves a good ghost story and a visit to local watering holes. Believers say there are so many ghosts in Savannah they're actually divided into subcategories. These charismatic guides specialize in tavern ghosts, and they'll regale you with tales of secret subbasements, possessed gum-ball machines, and animated water faucets. Tours traditionally depart from the Six Pence Pub at 8 pm. Because this is a cocktail tour, children are not permitted. Routes can vary, so call for departure times and locations; the tour costs $20 and lasts for 2½ hours.

Sixth Sense Savannah was created by Shannon Scott, who leverages his knowledge of lesser-known Savannah ghost stories into one of the spookiest tours in town. Get an insider's perspective of Savannah's poltergeists. Prices start at $25.

Savannah Fun Tours is a unique way to explore the city at your own pace, with a "to-go cup" if you like. The company offers a self-guided scavenger hunt. Solve the puzzle, see the city, and collect a prize at the end.

Contacts A Ghost Talk Ghost Walk Tour ☎ 912/233–3896 ⊕ www.ghosttalkghostwalk.com. **Savannah Fun Tours** ☎ 912/604–3425 ⊕ www.savannahfuntour.com. **Savannah Tours by Foot** ☎ 912/238–3843 ⊕ www.savannahtours.com. **Sixth Sense Savannah** ☎ 866/666–3323 ⊕ www.sixthsensesavannah.com.

▌ TRIP INSURANCE

Comprehensive travel policies typically cover trip cancellation and interruption, letting you cancel or cut short your trip due to personal emergency, illness, or, in some cases, acts of terrorism at your destination. Such policies also cover evacuation and medical care. Some also cover trip delays as a result of bad weather or mechanical problems, as well as lost or delayed baggage. Another type of coverage to look for is financial default—that is, when your trip is disrupted because a tour operator, airline, or cruise line goes out of business. Generally you must buy this when you book your trip or shortly thereafter, and it's only available to you if your operator isn't on a list of excluded companies.

Expect comprehensive travel insurance policies to cost about 4% to 8% of the total price of your trip (it's more like 8% to 12% if you're over age 70). Always read the fine print of your policy to make sure that you are covered for the risks that are of most concern to you. Compare several policies to make sure you're getting the best price and range of coverage available.

■TIP➔ You can save a bundle on trips to warm-weather destinations by traveling in the rainy season, but there's a chance that a severe storm will disrupt your plans. The solution? Look for hotels that let you rebook if a storm strikes.

Comprehensive Travel Insurers
Allianz Travel Insurance
☎ 866/884-3556 ⊕ www.allianz travelinsurance.com. **AIG Travel Guard** ☎ 800/826-4919 ⊕ www. travelguard.com. **CSA Travel Protection** ☎ 877/243-4125 ⊕ www. csatravelprotection.com. **HTH Worldwide** ☎ 888/243-2358 ⊕ www.hthtravelinsurance.com. **Travelex Insurance** ☎ 800/228-9792 ⊕ www.travelexinsurance. com. **Travel Insured International** ☎ 800/243-3174 ⊕ www.travel insured.com.

Insurance Comparison Sites
Insure My Trip ☎ 800/487-4722 ⊕ www.insuremytrip.com. **Square-Mouth.com** ☎ 800/240-0369 ⊕ www.squaremouth.com.

▌ VISITOR INFORMATION

The Savannah Visitor Information Center is easily accessed from all major thoroughfares and is open daily weekdays 8:30 to 5. The center has a useful audiovisual overview of the city and a staff of knowledgeable trip counselors.

For detailed information about Tybee Island, drop by the island's visitor center, just off Highway 80. It's open daily 9 to 5:30.

Contacts **Savannah Visitor Information Center** ✉ 301 Martin Luther King Jr. Blvd., Historic District ☎ 912/944-0455 ⊕ www.visit savannah.com. **Tybee Island Visitor Information Center** ✉ 802 1st St., Tybee Island ☎ 877/344-3361 ⊕ www.visittybee.com. **Savannah/ Hilton Head International Airport** ✉ 400 Airways Ave. ☎ 912/964-0514 ⊕ www.savannahairport.com. **Alamo** ☎ 888/826-6893 ⊕ www. alamo.com.

INDEX

A

A-J's ✕, *42*
Adventure Cove, *157*
African-American history sites, *34, 35, 36, 165, 183*
Air travel
Hilton Head, 126–127
Savannah, 14, 178–179
Al Salaam Deli ✕, *64*
Alex Raskin Antiques, *113*
Alligators, *149*
Andaz Savannah ⊞, *73*
Andrew Low House, *23*
Angel's BBQ ✕, *48, 67*
Antiques, *19, 111, 112–113*
Aquarium, *41*
Art galleries
Beaufort, 173
Hilton Head Island, 159
Savannah, 29, 33–34, 111, 113–114, 122
Arts Center of Coastal Carolina, *148*
ATMs, *182*
Audubon-Newhall Preserve, *134*
Azalea Inn & Gardens ⊞, *73*

B

B&D Burgers ✕, *48–49*
B. Matthews Eatery ✕, *52*
B. Tillman ✕, *65*
Back in the Day Bakery ✕, *64*
Ballastone Inn ⊞, *73–74*
Banks, *182–183*
Barefoot Farm, *165*
Bars, *88–91, 94, 147–148, 170*
Baseball, *100, 101*
Beach House Hilton Head Island ⊞, *141*

Beach Institute African-American Cultural Center, *34*
Beaches, *100–102, 148–151, 171*
Beaufort, *125, 163–173*
dining, 165–166
exploring, 164–165
lodging, 167–168, 170
nightlife & the arts, 170
shopping, 173
sports & the outdoors, 171–173
transportation, 163
visitors informtion, 164
Beaufort Inn ⊞, *167*
Beaulieu House ⊞, *167–168*
Bed & Breakfast Inn ⊞, *74*
Bella's Italian Café ✕, *64–65*
Best Western Sea Island Inn ⊞, *168*
Bier Haus ✕, *52*
Biking, *101, 102–103, 151, 171*
Black Dagger Pirate Ship, *157*
Black Marlin Bayside Grill ✕, *134*
BlueBelle Boutique (shop), *121–122*
Bluffton, *132, 141, 145*
Boat and ferry travel
Daufuskie Island, 174
Hilton Head, 127
Savannah, 179
Boat tours, *175, 183*
Boating and kayaking, *104–106, 151, 171–172*
Bohemian The ⊞, *74*
Bonaventure Cemetery, *38*
Book shops, *114–115*
Breakwater Restaurant & Bar ✕, *166*
Brice The ⊞, *74*

Brighter Day ✕, *52–53*
Broughton Street, *19, 110–111*
Bus and trolley tours, *183–184*
Bus travel
Savannah, 179
Business hours, *46, 182*

C

Candlewood Suites ⊞, *145*
Canoeing & kayaking, *104–105, 151, 171–172*
Captain Mike's Dolphin Tours, *104*
Captain Woody's ✕, *136*
Car rental, *14, 180*
Car travel
Hilton Head, 127
Savannah, 14, 179–180
Carriage tours, *175, 184*
Cathedral of St. John the Baptist, *34–35*
Catherine Ward House Inn ⊞, *74–75*
Cemeteries, *26, 38*
Cha Bella ✕, *53*
Children
Hilton Head, 132, 136, 139, 142, 148, 149–150, 152, 157, 160, 161, 165, 168, 176
Savannah, 20, 26, 27, 29, 32–33, 34, 37, 41, 42, 43, 48–49, 54, 61, 63, 65, 66, 68, 81, 82, 86, 94, 95, 96–97, 100, 104, 105–106, 117
Chippewa Square, *18, 23*
Christ Episcopal Church, *35*
Churches, *34–35, 36–37, 165*
Circa 1875 ✕, *53, 88*
City Hall (Savannah), *35*

City Loft Hotel 🖭 , *168*
City Market, *19, 26, 111*
Civil War sites, *41, 42*
Claude & Uli's Bistro
   ✕ , *141*
Climate, *16*
Clothing, *111, 115–116,
   121–122*
Club at Savannah Har-
   bor, *The, 107*
Coastal Discovery
   Museum, *132*
Coastal Georgia Botani-
   cal Gardens, *39*
Coffee Fox, *The, 92*
Coffeehouses, *92*
Coligny Beach,
   149–150
Collins Quarter ✕ , *54*
Colonial Park Ceme-
   tery, *26*
Communications, *182*
Conroy, *Pat, 167, 170*
Cooking school, *53,
   138*
Cotton Sail 🖭 , *78*
CQs ✕ , *136*
Crab Shack ✕ , *68*
Credit cards, *10, 182*
Crosswinds Golf Club,
   107
Cruises, *129–130, 175,
   183*
Crystal Beer Parlor
   ✕ , *54*
Cuthbert House Inn 🖭 ,
   168

D
Daufuskie Island, *125,
   174–176*
Deposito's ✕ , *65*
Dept. 7 East ✕ , *54*
Design District, *19,
   111–112*
Dining, *10.* ⇨ See also
   Restaurants
Beaufort, 165–166
best bets, 49
Daufuskie Island, 175
*Hilton Head, 128, 134,
   136–141*

price categories, 47, 129
*Savannah, 27, 34, 42,
   45–70*
Tybee Island, 68, 70
Dinner cruises, *129–130*
Disney's Hilton Head
   Island Resort 🖭 , *142*
Dresser Palmer House
   🖭 , *78*
Dye's Gullah Fixin's
   ✕ , *136*

E
E. Shaver Booksell-
   ers, *115*
East Bay Inn 🖭 , *78*
Ebenezer, *39*
11th Street Dockside ✕ ,
   165–166
Eliza Thompson House
   🖭 , *78*
Elizabeth on 37th ✕ ,
   54–55
Ellis Square, *18, 26*
Emergencies, *180, 182*
Etiquette, *144*

F
Factors Walk, *26, 112*
Fannie's on the Beach
   ✕ , *68*
Festivals and special
   events, *16, 94–97, 148*
Fire Street Food ✕ , *55*
First African Baptist
   Church, *35*
Fishing, *104–106, 152*
Flannery O'Conner
   Childhood Home,
   35–36
Florence, *The* ✕ , *55*
Flying Monk Noodle
   Bar, *The* ✕ , *57*
Foley House Inn 🖭 ,
   78–79
Foodstuffs, *116–118,
   122*
Football, *106*
Form (shop), *116*
Forsyth Park, *27*

Fort Pulaski National
   Monument, *41*
45 Bistro ✕ , *48*
Foxy Loxy (coffeehouse),
   92
Frankie Bones ✕ ,
   136–137
Fripp Island Resort 🖭 ,
   168

G
Garibaldi's ✕ , *57*
Gasoline, *179*
Gastonian 🖭 , *78–80*
Georgia State Railroad
   Museum, *27*
Ghost tours, *184*
Gifts
Hilton Head, 159–161
Savannah, 111, 118
Girl Scout National Cen-
   ter, *29–30*
Glow MedSpa & Beauty
   Boutique, *120*
Golf
Beaufort, 172–173
Hilton Head, 153–156
Savannah, 101, 106–107
Green-Meldrim
   House, *36*
Green Palm Inn 🖭 , *80*
Green Truck Pub ✕ ,
   18, 66
Gryphon Tea Room
   ✕ , *57*
Gullah, *169*
Gutstein Gallery, *114*

H
Hamilton-Turner Inn 🖭 ,
   80–81
Hampton Inn & Suites
   🖭 , *81*
Hampton Inn-Historic
   District 🖭 , *81*
Hampton Inn on Hilton
   Head Island 🖭 , *142*
Handbag shops, *120*
Harbour Town, *134*
Harbour Town Golf
   Links, *155*

Haunted lodgings, *80*
Heavenly Spa by Westin, *162*
Henry C. Chambers Waterfront Park, *164*
Hilton Head & the Low Country, *123–176*
Beaufort, 125, 163–173
dining, 128
Daufuskie Island, 125, 174–176
Hilton Head Island, 125, 130–162
lodging, 128
price categories, 129
tours, 129–130
transportation, 126–128
visitor information, 130
when to go, 125–126
Hilton Head Island, *125, 130–162*
dining, 134, 136–141
lodging, 141–146
nightlife & the arts, 146–148
shopping, 159–161
sightseeing, 132, 134
sports & the outdoors, 148–159
transportation, 131–132
Hilton Head Marriott Resort & Spa ⌸, *142*
Hilton Savannah Desoto ⌸, *81*
Hinoki ✕, *137*
Historic district, *12, 23–38, 47–64*
Historic district tours, *184*
Holiday Inn Express Historic District ⌸, *81*
Home décor, *111, 118–119*
Homes, *historic*
Beaufort, 165
Savannah, 23, 28–29, 30–31, 35–36
Horseback riding, *157, 176*
Huey's Southern Café ✕, *57–58*
Hunting Island Lighthouse, *171*

Hunting Island State Park, *171*
Hyatt Regency Savannah ⌸, *82*

I

Images by Ben Ham (gallery), *159*
Inn at Ellis Square ⌸, *82*
Inn at Harbour Town ⌸, *142*
Inn at Palmetto Bluff ⌸, *142, 144*
Insurance, *180, 185–186*
Internet, *182*
Isaiah Davenport House, *28–29*
Island Playground, *157*
Isle of Hope, *41*
Itinerary ideas, *17*

J

Jazz Corner (club), *147*
Jepson Cafe ✕, *58*
Jepson Center for the Arts, *29*
Jet-skiing, *106*
Jewelry, *120, 160*
John Mark Verdier House Museum, *165*
Johnny Harris ✕, *66, 67*
Johnny Mercer Theater, *97*
Johnson Creek Tavern ✕, *164–165*
Johnson Square, *29*
Juliette Gordon Low Birthplace/Girls Scout National Center, *29–30*

K

Kayak Cafe ✕, *66*
Kehoe House ⌸, *82*
Kiteboarding, *108*
Kobo Gallery, *114*

L

Lady & Sons, The ✕, *58*
Lafayette, *Marquis de, 30*

Lafayette Square, *18, 30*
Lawton Stables, *157*
Leather goods shops, *120*
Leoci's Trattoria ✕, *18, 59*
Leopold's ✕, *27*
Lighthouse Inn ⌸, *86*
Lighthouses, *43, 171*
Local 11ten ✕, *59*
Lodging, *10*
Beaufort, 167–168, 170
best bets, 75
Daufuskie Island, 176
Hilton Head, 128, 141–142, 144–145
price categories, 73, 129
Savannah, 72–85
Tybee Island, 85–86
Low, Andrew, *23*
Low, Juliette Gordon, *29–30*
Lucas Theater, *97*
Lulu's Chocolate Bar ✕, *90*

M

Madison Square, *30, 112*
Mail, *182*
Mansion on Forsyth Park ⌸, *82*
Marshall House ⌸, *82–83*
May River Sandbar, *150–151*
Mercer, *Johnny, 28, 97*
Mercer Williams House, *30*
Mermaid Cottages ⌸, *86*
Mi Terra ✕, *138*
Michael Anthony's ✕, *138*
Mighty Eighth Air Force Heritage Museum, *41–42*
Money, *15, 182–183*
Monkeys, *172*
Monterey Square, *18–19, 36*
Movie tours, *184*

Mrs. Wilkes Dining Room ✕ , *59–60*
Museums
Beaufort, 165
Hilton Head, 132, 157
Savannah, 27, 29, 30, 31, 32–34, 36, 41–42, 43
Music clubs, *93, 147–148, 170*

N
Nightclubs, *88–91*
Nightlife and the arts
Beaufort, 170
Hilton Head, 146–148
Savannah, 87–98
Noble Fare ✕ , *60*
North Beach, *100–101*

O
Oatland Island Wildlife Center, *42*
O'Connor, *Flannery, 28*
Old Daufuskie Crab Company Restaurant ✕ , *175*
Old Fort Jackson, *42*
Old Fort Pub ✕ , *138–139*
Old Towne Bluffton, *132*
Olde Harbour Inn 🖭 , *83*
Olde Pink House ✕ , *18, 30–31, 60*
Omni Hilton Head Oceanfront Resort 🖭 , *144*
One Hot Mama's ✕ , *139*
Owens-Thomas House and Museum, *31*

P
Pacci's Kitchen + Bar ✕ , *60–61*
Paddleboarding, *108*
Palmetto Dunes Tennis Center, *158*
Parasailing, *156–157*
Paris Market & Brocante, The (shop), *119*

Park Lane Hotel & Suites 🖭 , *144*
Parking, *179–180*
Parks, *27, 34, 164*
Patton, *Antwan "Big Boi", 28*
Pierpont, *James L., 28*
Pin Point Heritage Museum, *42–43*
Pirates House ✕ , *61*
Pirate's Island, *156*
Plantations, *134*
Planters Inn 🖭 , *83*
Planters Tavern, *90–91*
Plums ✕ , *166*
Preserves, *42, 132, 134*
President's Quarters 🖭 , *83*
Price categories, *10, 47, 73*
Public Kitchen and Bar ✕ , *61*
Public transportation, *181*

R
Ralph Mark Gilbert Civil Rights Museum, *36*
Red Fish ✕ , *139*
Red Piano Gallery, *173*
Rental agents, *146*
Reservations, *15*
Residence Inn 🖭 , *83*
Restaurants
American, 47, 48, 52–53, 54, 57, 58, 61–62, 70, 139, 140, 166
Asian Fusion, 57
bakery, 64
barbeque, 48, 49, 56, 67, 139
brunch, 49
burger, 48–49, 66
café, 54, 147
Caribbean, 67
Creole, 57–58
eclectic, 52, 60, 62, 136, 166
European, 138–139, 141
French, 47, 53
German, 52
Greek, 68

Italian, 59, 60–61, 64–65, 136–137, 138
Japanese, 62–63, 137
Lowcountry, 56
Mexican, 138
Middle Eastern, 64
modern American, 48, 59, 70
Modern Asian, 55
Modern Italian, 55, 57
pizza, 63
seafood, 56, 65, 68, 134, 136, 165–166, 175
South African, 63–64
southern, 54–55, 58, 59–60, 61, 63, 65, 66, 136
southwestern, 139–140
steakhouse, 141
vegetarian, 66
Revolutionary War sites, *26, 29, 30, 34, 36, 41*
Reynolds Square, *32*
River Street, *19*
River Street Inn 🖭 , *84*
Riverfront Plaza, *112*
Rocks on the Roof (bar), *91*
Roller derby, *108*
Roots Up Gallery, *114*
Rousakis Plaza, *32*

S
Safety, *183*
St. Helena Island, *165*
St. Helena's Episcopal Church, *165*
St. John's Episcopal Church, *36–37*
St. Patrick's Day Parade, *96*
Saltus River Grill ✕ , *166*
Salty Dog Cafe, *147*
Sand box, An Interactive Children's Museum, *157*
Sand dollars, *150*
Sandy Lane Villa 🖭 , *176*
Santa Fe Café ✕ , *139–140*

Sapphire Grill ✕, 61–62
Satchel (shop), 120
Savannah Bee Company, 18, 117
Savannah Book Festival, 94–95
Savannah Canoe and Kayak, 105
Savannah Children's Museum, 32
Savannah College of Art and Design (SCAD), 33
Savannah Craft Brew Festival, 95
Savannah Film Festival, 95
Savannah Folk Music Festival, 95
Savannah History Museum, 32–33
Savannah Jazz Festival, 95
Savannah Marriot Riverfront ☲, 84
Savannah Music Festival, 95–96
Savannah Squeeze ✕, 66
Savannah Theatre, 98
SCAD Museum of Art, 33
Scarborough, William, 31
Sea Pines Forest Preserve, 132, 134
Sea Pines Resort ☲, 146
700 Drayton Restaurant ✕, 48
17th Street Inn ☲, 86
Ships of the Sea Maritime Museum, 31, 33
Shoe shops, 120
Shopping
Beaufort, 173
Hilton Head, 159–161
Savannah, 19, 109–122
ShopSCAD (shop), 118
Shrimp boats, 137

Sidewalk Arts Festival, 96
Signe's Heaven Bound Bakery & Café ✕, 140
Skull Creek Boathouse ✕, 140
SoHo South Cafe ✕, 62
Sonesta Resort Hilton Head Island ☲, 144–145
South End beach, 101–102
Spanish moss, 39
Spas, 120–121, 122, 161–162
Sports and the outdoors
Beaufort, 171–173
Daufuskie Island, 176
Hilton Head, 148–159
Savannah, 99–108
Springhill Suites ☲, 84
Station 300, 157
Stoney-Baynard Ruins, 134
Suites on Lafayette ☲, 84
Sundae Cafe ✕, 70
Sushi Zen ✕, 62–63
Symbols, 10
Synagogues, 30

T

Tanger Outlets, 161
Taxes, 183
Taxi travel
Hilton Head, 128
Savannah, 181
Telephones, 182
Telfair Museum of Art, 33–34
Telfair Square, 19
Temple Mickve Israel, 38
Tennis, 125, 158
Theaters, 97, 98, 148
39 Rue de Jean ✕, 47
Thunderbird Inn ☲, 84–85
Tipping, 183
Toucan Café ✕, 67
Tours
Daufuskie Island, 175

Hilton Head, 129–130, 158–159
Savannah, 183–185
Train travel
Hilton Head, 128
Savannah, 14, 181
Transportation
Daufuskie Island, 174
Hilton Head, 126–128
Savannah, 14, 178–179
Tricentennial Park and Battlefield, 34
Trolley tours, 183–184
Truffles Café ✕, 140
Trustees Theater, 98
22 Square Restaurant & Bar ✕, 47
24e (shop), 118–119
Tybee Island, 12, 43–44
dining, 68, 70
lodging, 85–86
Tybee Island Fish Camp ✕, 70
Tybee Island Lighthouse and Museum, 43
Tybee Island Marine Science Center, 43
Tybee Island Pier and Pavilion, 102
Tybee Island Pirate Festival, 96–97
Tybee Island Social Club ✕, 70
Tybee Vacation Rentals ☲, 85

U

University of Georgia Aquarium, 41

V

Venues, 97–98
Vic's on the River ✕, 63
Villa rentals, 145–146, 170
Vinnie VanGoGo's ✕, 63
VIP Dining Club Card, 52
Visitor information, 14, 130, 164, 186

W

Walking tours, *185*
Watersports, *101, 108*
Waving Girl Statue, *38*
Weather, *16, 126*
Web sites, *186*
Wesley, John, *28*
Westin Hilton Head Island Resort & Spa 🏨, *145*
Westin Savannah Harbor Golf Resort & Spa 🏨, *85*
When to go, *16, 125–126*
Wiley's Championship BBQ ✕, *67*
WiseGuys ✕, *141*
World War II exhibits, *41–42*
Wormsloe, *44*
Wright Square, *38*

Y

Yia Yia's Kitchen ✕, *68*
York W. Bailey Museum, *165*

Z

Zeigler House Inn 🏨, *85*
Zip line tours, *158–159*
Zunzi's ✕, *63–64*

PHOTO CREDITS

Cover: David Davis / age fotostock [Description: Taliaferro gravesite in the Bonaventure Cemetery in Savannah Georgia]. 1,(c) Dndavis | Dreamstime.com. 2, Jeff Greenberg / age fotostock. 3 (top), David Davis / age fotostock. 3 (bottom), Ferne Arfin / Alamy. 4, Savannah Music Festival. 5 (top), Danita Delimont / Alamy. 5 (bottom), ZUMA Wire Service / Alamy. 6 (top), Richard Cummins / age fotostock. 6 (bottom), Andy Palmer /Alamy. 7, Katherinedavisgothel | Dreamstime.com. 8 (top left), Cindy Roberts/savannahphotos.com. 8 (top right), River North Photography/iStock Photo. 8 (bottom), Scott Anderson / Alamy. 11, Jesse Kunerth / Shutterstock. 21, Lane V. Erickson / Shutterstock. 45, dbimages / Alamy. 71, Courtesy of The Kessler Collection. 87, Courtesy of Savannah Music Festival/Ayano Hisa. 99, Steve Nudson / Alamy. 109, Ralph Daniel Photography, Inc. 123, LeeAnn White / Shutterstock. Spine: PhilAugustavo/iStockphoto.

About Our Writers: All photos are courtesy of the writers except for the following: Summer Teal Simpson, courtesy of Alicja Colon.

NOTES

NOTES

NOTES

NOTES

NOTES

Fodor's InFocus SAVANNAH

Publisher: Amanda D'Acierno, *Senior Vice President*

Editorial: Arabella Bowen, *Editor in Chief*; Linda Cabasin, *Editorial Director*

Design: Tina Malaney, *Associate Art Director*; Chie Ushio, *Senior Designer*; Ann McBride, *Production Designer*

Photography: Jennifer Arnow, *Associate Director of Photography*; Jennifer Romains, *Researchers*

Production: Linda Schmidt, *Managing Editor*; Evangelos Vasilakis, *Associate Managing Editor*; Angela L. McLean, *Senior Production Manager*

Maps: Rebecca Baer, *Senior Map Editor*; Mark Stroud, Moon Street Cartography, *Cartographers*

Sales: Jacqueline Lebow, *Sales Director*

Marketing & Publicity: Heather Dalton, *Marketing Director*; Katherine Punia, *Publicity Director*

Business & Operations: Susan Livingston, *Vice President, Strategic Business Planning*; Sue Daulton, *Vice President, Operations*

Fodors.com: Megan Bell, *Executive Director, Revenue & Business Development*; Yasmin Marinaro, *Senior Director, Marketing & Partnerships*

Editorial Contributors: Sally Mahan, Summer Teal Simpson

Editor: Mark Sullivan

Production Editor: Carrie Parker

4th Edition

ISBN 978-1-101-87811-8

ISSN 1943-0116

SPECIAL SALES

This book is available at special discounts for bulk purchases for sales promotions or premiums. For more information, e-mail specialmarkets@penguinrandomhouse.com

PRINTED IN THE UNITED STATES OF AMERICA

10 9 8 7 6 5 4 3 2 1

ABOUT OUR WRITERS

Sally Mahan is originally from Detroit. She fell in love with the Lowcountry several years ago when she moved to Savannah to work at *The Savannah Morning News*. She left the Lowcountry to work as an editor in Key West, and then went back to Michigan to work at *The Detroit Free Press*. However, her heart remained in the Lowcountry. In 2004 she settled in her adopted home-town of Bluffton, SC, just minutes from Hilton Head Island. She updated the Hilton Head chapter for this edition.

A product of the Deep South, **Summer Teal Simpson** began her writing career after a happenstance move to Savannah, Georgia, led her to follow her passion and pursue a livelihood in writing and journalism. She is highly food (and wine) motivated, dive certified, and collects vintage Eva Zeisel, deer antlers, and local contemporary art. She is a contributor to *Savannah Magazine*, *South Magazine*, and *Connect Savannah*, as well as local blogs. She updated the Experience, Exploring, Where to Eat, Where to Stay, Nightlife, Sports and the Outdoors, Shopping, and Travel Smart chapters for this book.

EUGENE FODOR

Hungarian-born Eugene Fodor (1905–91) began his travel career as an interpreter on a French cruise ship. The experience inspired him to write *On the Continent* (1936), the first guidebook to receive annual updates and discuss a country's way of life as well as its sights. Fodor later joined the U.S. Army and worked for the OSS in World War II. After the war, he kept up his intelligence work while expanding his guidebook series. During the Cold War, many guides were written by fellow agents who understood the value of insider information. Today's guides continue Fodor's legacy by providing travelers with timely coverage, insider tips, and cultural context.